Creating New
Superstars

Creating New Superstars

A Guide to Businesses that Soar above the Sea of Normality

Ennio Fatuzzo
Carol L. Fatuzzo

ISBN-13: 978-1537040653
ISBN-10: 1537040650

PREFACE

Why have a few, extraordinary, Fortune 500 companies grown **exponentially** in revenues (annual growth rates of more than 30%) for at least the last 10 years, compared to a median Fortune 500 company that has grown at a mediocre 3.9% per year over the same period of time? Is the emergence of these giant "Superstars" a new phenomenon; and if so, why? What would it take for existing, healthy companies to achieve similar extreme growth, or at least significantly improve their performance? How can entrepreneurs maximize their chances for creating new Superstars? How can those seeking exceptional careers or investments identify high growth areas? On what types of companies should they focus?

Intrigued, we began a quest to answer these questions and others about extreme growth and highly successful, large businesses. Only later, did we consider writing a book. But why would we write one more business book? The answer is we believe we have uncovered important and exciting new information that can provide insight and direction to ambitious business leaders (both existing and potential). We also feel that our perspectives from the real world of business are a practical complement to advice from the often theoretical world of academia.

Thus we decided to turn the answers to our questions

into a book, but what kind of a book? Yes, we wanted it to be a guide for achieving extreme business growth. But is that a book about business creativity and brilliant leadership, or is it one about identifying and building on fast-developing technology super-platforms (what we call "Launching Pads")?

As we followed the evolution of our identified Superstars, it became clear: both are essential. For example, if the goal is starting a new business, the question of which type of business is obvious. But the answer can be elusive because a "flash of insight" or a "life-changing scientific discovery" or a "disruptive technology" is needed for the creation of a highly successful one. Without that innovation, nothing "big" happens. And that isn't all. The desire for exceptional results also becomes a question of what kind of leadership is needed to achieve "extreme" success in today's rapidly-changing, chaotic world.

So, while our book addresses exceptional leadership and the needed revolution in business management, it is just as much about the power of new technology and science. In our fast-paced, technology-rich environment, it is impossible to ignore these forces that are shaping the future for business and for humanity. Successful new businesses and new technologies have become irreversibly intertwined. Because of this, we first focus on the technology Launching Pads that have created or enabled the current Superstars and may still create others. But what comes next? To provide new entrepreneurs, job seekers, and even investors with a head start, we explore several rapidly-advancing areas of science and technology that we predict will be the breeding grounds for future Superstars.

Summing it all up, with its focus on how to identify and/or create highly successful new businesses capable of extreme growth, our book is aimed at job-seekers and investors seeking exceptional opportunities, and at entrepreneurial "free spirits" who are ambitious enough to want to make a **big** difference, who are willing to take risks, **and** who are open to embracing new and unconventional concepts and technologies to achieve "far better than average" results.

ABOUT THE AUTHORS

 Dr. Ennio Fatuzzo and Dr. Carol L. Fatuzzo are husband and wife, both of whom have held leadership positions in multi-national corporations and founded and now run successful consulting businesses. They began their professional careers as scientists, then became corporate leaders, and now are business entrepreneurs.

The Fatuzzos' diverse business experiences have caused them to become passionate about the need for management changes in today's business world, and their own successes in business and consulting have convinced them of the need for new leadership approaches. Thus their current efforts are focused on sharing their insights through a series of books and articles. Their next endeavor is a book about future "Launching Pads." This is a follow-on to *Creating New Superstars*.

Drawing on their business experiences and interactions with academia, the Fatuzzos have co-authored and/or published several books (available from amazon.com), including: *Survival in the Sea of Economic Chaos (Perspectives on Leadership Actions for Businesses in Crisis)* and *Dynamic Business*

Planning Basics (An Adaptable Planning Process for Disruptive Times).

Information about these books and the Fatuzzos' other publications can be found on their Amazon author's pages and on their joint Web site: <u>fatuzzobooks.com</u>. In addition, their social media efforts to share their opinions and other useful leadership information include a blog (fatuzzobooksblog.com) and a Facebook business page (<u>facebook.com/fatuzzobooks</u>).

For brief biographies of the Fatuzzos, see the "Authors' Biographies" section at the end of the book. Additional information may be found on their respective companies' Web sites: <u>efmainc.com</u> and <u>nhbvinc.com</u>.

ACKNOWLEDGEMENTS

We are deeply indebted to DR. GREGORY M. VERCELLOTTI, MD, professor of Medicine, University of Minnesota Medical School, Minneapolis, MN, for an enormous amount of good advice and leads in the choice of the subjects covered under the heading of "Future Launching Pads," and for his reviews of early drafts of the manuscript. His advice and mentorship, especially in areas related to the newest developments in medicine and medical research have been invaluable.

We wish to thank DR.PROFESSOR MAHMOOD A. ZAIDI, PhD, Distinguished International Emeritus Professor, Professor Emeritus of Human Resources & Founding Director of International Programs (Now Carlson Global Institute), Carlson School of Management University of Minnesota, for early conversations advocating a more extensive use of science in management to improve the business results of corporations. We are thankful for his encouragement to pursue these ideas as a part of this book.

We are also grateful to DR. ELIZABETH R. SMITH, EdD, visiting professor of Journalism, Pepperdine University, Malibu, CA, for reading the entire manuscript and providing extremely useful and insightful comments regarding the content and layout of this book for publication, along with suggestions for improving its appeal and impact.

We wish to thank our son, DR. MARCO FATUZZO, PhD, professor and chair, Department of Physics, Xavier University, Cincinnati, OH, for his assistance in analyzing the numerical data and for finding the best way to present them in graphic form.

Ennio and Carol Fatuzzo

CONTENTS

PART III: WHY SUPERSTARS ONLY NOW?

PART IV: A LEADER'S PATH TO SUPERSTARS

PART V: FUTURE LAUNCHING PADS

KEY FINDINGS

INTRODUCTION

It is no longer business as usual. There is a new phenomenon emerging that we call "Superstar" companies. These are the few, extraordinary, publicly-traded, Fortune 500 companies that have managed to sustain **exponential** growth over time, even as they became giants. What companies are these, what exactly have they achieved, and how?

Creating New Superstars: A Guide to Businesses that Soar above the Sea of Normality is a book about starting and/or identifying new businesses with the potential of becoming Superstars. More specifically it is a book about how the intersection of explosively advancing technology super-platforms (what we call technology "Launching Pads") and today's revolutionary "Agents of Change" has created an environment where Superstars can exist. The book specifically identifies and explores these key forces and others necessary for creating new companies capable of extreme growth. And the book shows how this information can be useful not only for creating Superstars but also for substantially improving the performance of existing companies.

We begin by looking at today's Superstars. In **Part I** these companies are identified: a first wave, perhaps approaching maturity, based on the intersection of

Microelectronics and the Internet (Amazon and Apple) and a second, more embryonic wave of Biotechnology-based companies (Genentech, Amgen, and Gilead Sciences). Brief histories of these companies are provided against the backdrop of two other successful Fortune 500 companies that we call "Enablers" (Microsoft and Intel) to show how the Superstars are different. In addition, we highlight two companies likely to become Superstars in the near term (Facebook and Alphabet/Google) and three private companies (Uber, Airbnb, and Moderna Therapeutics) that may have the potential to become Superstars in the longer term. In subsequent parts of the book we focus on what we consider to be the key differences between Superstars and other successful companies to provide insights (and guidelines) into the requirements for the creation of new Superstars. Based on this information, we suggest a path forward for those aspiring to be "star builders" or to dramatically improve the performance of their existing businesses.

Of course this path to extreme success involves strong and unconventional leadership, as we highlight in **Part II**. But it all depends on a spark of creativity, or "Act of Creation" as we call it. And in the case of our Superstars, this includes business creativity, not just technical creativity or artistic creativity. In order to clarify what we mean, we provide several examples to explain the concept. Then the question becomes, "How can such an Act of Creation lead to the development of explosive new businesses?" As we show, our Superstars were all started in the United States where funding is generally more available than in the rest of the world; and they were first to develop and commercialize new-to-the-world products that addressed new global, end-user markets in unique ways.

But business creativity focused on large and untapped markets isn't enough. It is essential that a business be built on the right technology base to become a Superstar. More specifically, for a company to evolve into a Superstar it must be **based on** or **enabled by** an **explosively developing technology**. Thus, we begin Part II by identifying and exploring the three explosively developing technology areas (Microelectronics, the Internet, and Biogenetics) that have given rise to today's Superstar companies. We call such broad-based, exponentially advancing technologies "Launching Pads." And, as we show, these specific Launching Pads still have the potential to give rise to more Superstars.

However, before going further, it's important to take a step back and consider the questions: Is the phenomenon of Superstar companies really all that new? If so, why didn't they exist in the past? What has changed? To answer these questions, in **Part III** we first explore the evolution of business in the relatively recent past through the use of examples (Ford Motor Company, McDonald's, RCA, and FedEx). We then focus on what we call "Agents of Change." These are the new societal forces that only recently have created a dramatically different business environment where Superstars can develop

Then, in **Part IV** we explore the questions: Why are there so few Superstars today, and what is a path for leaders toward more Superstars? To answer these questions we start with some insights from the past based on the rise and fall of RCA. We then examine the way large companies today are often managed. We do this by focusing on common business practices in some of the current Fortune 500 companies. Specifically, we use fictional scenarios to show how these practices create roadblocks for potential Superstars. Areas addressed include obtaining support (including financing) for new business ideas and risk management.

We also show that many existing "normal" companies do not fully utilize all of the new, science-based management tools available today. We believe adoption of these tools could lead to improved business performance in general and fewer road blocks for budding Superstars. Therefore we describe the ones we believe are most useful. In addition, we identify and explore emerging business practices that we believe can lead to new levels of performance for existing companies and perhaps even new Superstars in the near term.

Up to this point we have mostly dealt with the present. In **Part V** the focus is on the future. First we take a look at the not-too-distant future and explore explosive new technology developments that we believe could become new Launching Pads for new Superstars. These include advances in Biogenetics (CRISPR, cloning, and stem cell research), Nanotechnology (with a focus on Nanomedicine), and Human Brain Research. We then present some "further out" ideas for areas of science that someday could develop into future Launching Pads. Bottom line, this look at future science and technology is where the book has been heading. It is the beginning of creating the next generation of Superstars and can provide a head start for those entrepreneurs who recognize their potential.

In the last section (**Key Findings)**, we bring together key insights about creating Superstars that are discussed throughout the book and present them as "fundamental requirements." We then summarize the needed new directions for business leaders that revolve around science-based approaches. And finally, we comment on our predictions for new technology Launching Pads and address the dangers they present for the future..

On a final note, we have made two key assumptions about the evolution of business that provide the foundation for this book:

1. In general, different areas of knowledge and technology evolve at different rates, but

progress made in a rapidly changing area can often be applied to a slower developing one.

2. Today, business practices in most companies are developing **very slowly** compared to other areas of knowledge such as Microelectronics or Nanotechnology. Thus these practices in general, and business management more specifically, are not benefiting from advances in these other faster moving areas—a situation that needs to be corrected soon to prevent a further "fracture" between business management and the scientific foundations of the industrialized world.

Therefore our book has the objective not only of describing what is occurring (or not occurring) in the business arena against the backdrop of other areas of knowledge, but also of outlining for ambitious business leaders and entrepreneurs a direction to take for bringing business practices more in line with the faster developing technology areas, both in the short term and in the longer term. In the end, we believe this will result in dramatically improved performance for "normal" companies as well as removing roadblocks and opening the doors for creating new Superstars.

INTRODUCING THE "SUPERSTARS"

PART I

One

WHAT IS A
SUPERSTAR?

Big. Fast growing. Profitable. Innovative. World changing. There are many criteria used for separating "good" companies from "great" or "special" ones. For example, Fortune magazine, in the September 1, 2015 issue had a list of the 100 fastest growing companies. Their criteria for inclusion in that list include a market capitalization of at least $250 million and an annualized growth in revenue of at least 15% annually over a period of three years.

Yes, Fortune's fast-growing list includes many very good companies. However there are a few (very few) extraordinary, large companies (also on the Fortune 500 list) that have profitably and consistently grown in sales at rates of more than 30% per year for at least the past 10 years. These are what we call "Superstar" companies.

However, our definition of Superstars is more specific and quantitative than this. We define "Superstars" as those publicly traded companies that have reached the Fortune 500 list **and** from that point on have grown **exponentially in sales**[1] for at least a decade (including the most recent decade) while remaining profitable. This level of performance can be compared to a median Fortune 500 company that has grown at only 3.9% in the last year.[2]

Of course smaller companies, particularly startups, often have exceptionally high growth—for a while. But just consider how incredibly difficult it is for a large company to sustain not just high growth but exponential growth. These rare few are truly today's Superstars of the business world. But what about tomorrow? What can we learn from today's Superstars about the creation of future Superstars? This is the focus of our book.

In Chapter 2, as background, we identify and provide brief descriptions of current Superstars, including charts of financial data that justify their inclusion in this elite group. We start with the two most highly visible and publicized Superstars (Amazon and Apple)—ones we consider to be the "first wave." These are two companies that took advantage of the explosive advances in microelectronics and the Internet. Then we consider in somewhat more detail the "second wave" of Superstars—three biotechnology-based companies that are quite different in some respects from those of the "first wave" and certainly less well-known (Amgen, Genentech, and Gilead Sciences). We do not devote the same space to each company, but rather dedicate more space to those that we feel can teach the most about creating extreme growth. And our descriptions are not presented as case studies. Instead, we highlight different aspects of each Superstar's history that we believe offer insights as to why that company has performed so well.

In later parts of the book, as we described in the Introduction, we use the information about today's Superstars to identify several basic requirements for creating new Superstars, including what we call technology "Launching Pads" and the "Act of Creation." And we explore commonalities among today's Superstars that are likely to contribute to the creation of more such giants in the future such as strong and unconventional leadership and market focus.

But today's Superstars are not the whole story. There are other exceptional companies that are worth considering when thinking about future Superstars. This is what Chapter 3 is all about. First there are the companies that are exceptional, but not quite Superstars. These are companies that are either too "young" to fit our definition of Superstars but appear to be on the path to becoming future Superstars or companies with extreme growth that isn't quite exponential. We identify and briefly describe two of these "Potential Superstars." While there are a number of such companies to choose from, we have focused on the two we believe can provide new insights for the ambitious entrepreneur.

But companies do not become Superstars or even Potential Superstars in isolation. It often takes what we call the "Enablers." These are the "supplier" companies that have made the growth of the Superstars possible with the innovative and advanced components and technology that they invent and provide. Through their symbiotic relationship with the Superstars, these Enablers also have prospered, become giants, and achieved and sustained high growth. It's just not exponential growth. Thus Enablers are also exceptional companies, and we have selected two (Microsoft and Intel) for a more detailed look.

Finally, we take a brief look at a three examples of private companies that we believe are worth watching. It is harder to get quantitative data on these companies, but they are clearly high potential and exceptional in their own arenas. It is companies like these that have the possibility of becoming future Superstars. However a key question is whether or not they are capable of re-inventing themselves again and again to create a sequence of highly innovative new products and services—as our current Superstars did.

Two

TODAY'S
SUPERSTARS

And now for today's Superstars. Following are brief histories of five companies that today meet our definition of Superstars from Chapter 1. As a reminder, Superstars are large, Fortune 500 companies with not just high growth, but with **exponential** growth sustained over at least a decade. The five companies on which we focus are all exceptional, but have achieved Superstar performance in two waves related to different technology advances. So this is how we have chosen to group them.

We give more in-depth detail on the lesser-known Superstars of the second technology wave and on those companies that we believe provide insights into creating new Superstars as well as significantly improving the performance of existing companies. Although we don't provide a specific "recipe for success," we highlight common factors among these Superstars and, later in the book, use this information to suggest guidelines for those wanting to start new, high-growth businesses. (Note: The financial information for the Superstars was obtained from their respective Annual Reports and "Fortune 500.")

Before starting, there is one caution to keep in mind:

Nothing is forever. At some point today's Superstars may explode and burn out like supernovas. Or, more likely, their growth will slow; and they too will become median Fortune 500 companies. But they will be replaced by new Superstars.

THE FIRST WAVE: ARISING FROM THE INTERSECTION OF MICROELECTRONICS AND THE INTERNET

Amazon.com, Inc.[3]: An online Retail Giant

Amazon was the brainchild of Jeffrey "Jeff" Bezos. Bezos graduated from Princeton University *summa cum laude* in 1986, and worked in computer science for several companies over the next few years. Although he was successful, he left this relatively safe environment and made a big jump into the unknown when he founded a company based on **Internet use**. Clearly a risk-taker, he had created this company in his mind, in a spark of creativity, during a long car drive from New York to Seattle, in 1994. By the time he arrived at his destination, he had written a business plan for this new company and soon thereafter Amazon.com became a reality.

Amazon.com started as an online bookstore, but Bezos changed its business definition, again and again. The company expanded by selling DVDs, CDs, video and MP3 downloads; then added software, video games, electronics, apparel, furniture, food, toys, and jewelry; and the list goes on. Today, Amazon produces consumer electronics such as Amazon Kindle e-book readers, Fire tablets, Fire TV and Fire Phone; sells products like USB cables under its in-house brand; and even is a provider of cloud computing services as well as original content video streaming. Amazon also has changed its business model numerous times. Amazon fulfillment and free 2-day shipping with Amazon Prime are just two examples. Bottom line, Amazon.com has become the largest e-retailer in the world by repeatedly re-inventing itself and expanding the online retail business into completely new areas.

Interestingly, Bezos has been described as a micromanager. Specifically, he is an executive who wants to know about everything from contract minutiae to how he is quoted in Amazon press releases. This is definitely opposite to what most business "gurus" teach about delegation. However, in the case of Amazon, micromanaging by Bezos appears to be a winning strategy.

Now, the financial results? After all, that is how we have defined Superstars. In the first 10 years from inception, Amazon.com grew from zero to $6.9 billion in revenues, quickly reaching the list of Fortune 500 companies. Since then, for more than 10 years its revenues have grown rapidly and at an increasing rate. In **Figure 1** below we have plotted revenues versus years on a linear graph. The curve, with its "hockey-stick" shape indicates that the increase is indeed exponential. Thus Amazon.com has become and is today a Superstar.

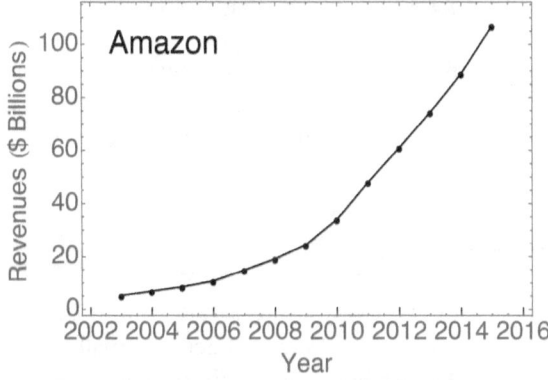

Figure 1. Amazon revenues on a linear graph

However, there are clouds on the horizon. The extremely fast growth of the company has been associated with a great volatility in profits (see **Figure 2** below). As this figure shows, annual profits peaked in 2010 at $1.1 billion, and have dropped substantially ever since. However, by the middle of 2015 Amazon unexpectedly achieved high profits for the previous quarter. This increased its valuation enough to give the company a market capitalization of $263.2 billion, surpassing the giant Walmart, which had a market capitalization of $232.7 billion at that time.

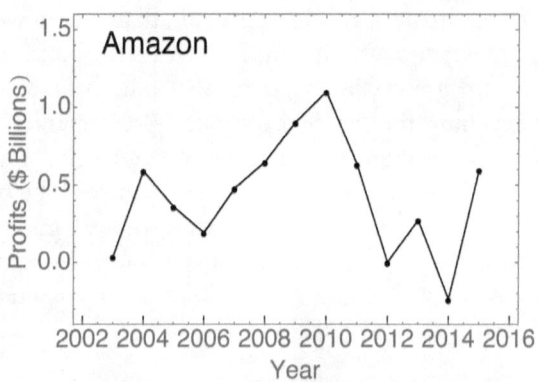

Figure 2. Amazon profits on a linear graph.

Although the human resources aspect of the Superstars generally is beyond the scope of this book, we would be remiss if we did not mention Amazon's experiments in how far it can "push" white-collar workers to get them to achieve its ever-expanding ambitions, as reported by the New York Times.[4] In the article, one former Amazon human resources director was quoted as saying: "The Company's winners dream up innovations that they roll out to a quarter-billion customers and accrue small fortunes in soaring stock. Losers leave or are fired in an annual culling of the staff—purposeful Darwinism."

Another uncommon practice that the article describes is the way team meetings are conducted. They are a far cry from consensus meetings and are instead based on the company belief that conflict brings about innovation. "We always want to arrive at the right answer," Tony Galbato, vice president for Human Resources, was quoted as saying in The New York Times article. And he continued: "It would certainly be much easier and socially cohesive to just compromise and not debate, but that may lead to the wrong decision." Unconventional attitudes. Nontraditional approaches. As our other examples show, these are part of being a Superstar.

Apple, Inc.[5]: A Global New Product Powerhouse

Apple is a Superstar whose tortuous path to greatness provides several alternative perspectives on extreme success. For example, from one perspective, a significant part of Apple's success can be attributed to its innovative marketing. From another perspective, innovative, disruptive, and frequently updated product lines can be considered the key contributor. And of course there was Steve Jobs, a dynamic and controversial leader with his own vision for Apple's future who left an indelible mark on the company. So, we begin. However since numerous books and articles have been written about Apple and Steve Jobs, we focus on only selected parts of the company's history.

Many have argued that Apple is the most successful company of today. From minuscule origins to one of the top companies on the Fortune 500 list in fewer than 40 years can be described as unprecedented performance. And this performance includes accumulating an unprecedented amount of cash. How did this happen?

The familiar story is that Apple, Inc. started in a garage, although Steve Wozniak, one of the founders, later said this was an exaggeration. Whatever the true story, the company started with minimal resources. The founders, Steve Jobs and Steve Wozniak, both college dropouts, formed the now famous company in 1976, a few years after they met and became friends. In the beginning, Apple was a computer design and manufacturing company that introduced its first product, the Apple I, in the same year it was founded. The Apple I was essentially a do-it-yourself kit and was not very successful, being purchased mostly by computer enthusiasts. The product that launched Apple, Inc. as a serious computer contender was the Apple II.

Simply explained, the Apple II was a fully assembled personal computer with an integrated keyboard and video display. This concept was so attractive that many people began to pre-order this computer, providing full payments in advance, even before it had a release date. It seems that Apple had been able to create a market "buzz" and a craving for something more when it came out with the Apple I. In other words, while the Apple I model did not sell much, it had created new customer expectations and started the "legend" of Apple, Inc., a legend that helped marketing all future products. Apple had created a new "philosophy of marketing" and the type of "buzz" associated with it persists today, before the launch of every new Apple product. And it is remarkable that the Apple I and the Apple II were not preceded by any market research. It was only after the Apple II was released and the sales skyrocketed, that the company gained a good understanding of the marketplace.

In late 1980, riding on the success of the Apple II and the newly introduced Apple III, the company launched its IPO, generating more capital than any other company before it, except for the Ford Motor Company. And by 1983, Apple entered the Fortune 500 list, after only five years of existence. This made it the fastest growing company in history at that point in time and qualified it as one of our Potential Superstars.

But Steve Jobs was ousted from his company in 1985, in hindsight a grave mistake. One should not fire the genius behind a company's success. Then, during most of the 1990s, as a result of Jobs' absence and poor company management, Apple endured decreasing sales and market share.

In 1997, in a major strategy shift, Apple scrapped its own internally developed operating system and acquired NeXT Software, the company that Steve Jobs had founded when he left Apple. And Jobs returned to Apple along with his new company, and in 2000 he became the CEO. Soon after he regained power, Jobs created a new corporate focus on easy-to-understand products and simple design. He also changed the company business definition, expanding it to include innovative and "disruptive" consumer electronic products beyond computers. The well-known, new-to-the-world successes that turned the company around are many, including:

- the iPod (and the iTunes Music Store), which transformed Apple and the entire music industry
- the iPhone, an explosive and continuing success that converted the world to smartphones
- the iPad, another new-to-the world product with skyrocketing sales

But Apple isn't just about iProducts. It's important to remember that Apple also is a computer company. As we have described, success started under Jobs with the Apple II/III computers, and in 1984 the first Macintosh was introduced, revolutionizing personal computing at that time. In spite of this, after Jobs left Apple, its personal computer business declined. It wasn't until the iMac and MacBook lines were introduced (1998 and 2006, respectively) that Apple's computer business was once again revitalized and became a cash generator.

Sales of these product lines were good from the beginning, partly because of Apple's usual excellent marketing that created expectations in advance of the market introduction, but also because these products appealed to the younger generation due to their sleek appearance, considerable ease of use, and their outstanding portability (MacBooks). These same features are why many people are completely loyal to these products today, even though the prices are often higher than comparable PC's.

However, Apple's extreme success more recently under Steve Jobs isn't just due to its products. Marketing and customer service have played a big role. The Apple Store, a physical retail site, is a powerful marketing tool that helps sell many Apple products. At these stores people can try out all of the Apple products, receiving help from very knowledgeable sales people. These so-called "Geniuses," who are experts in the field and in Apple products, are placed in each store to explain the simple to the most complex features to prospective customers. In addition, the Apple store gives people the opportunity to interact in person with technical service personnel and ask questions, have problems solved, and actually have their product fixed if needed. Apple Stores and their unique environment are just one of the unique ways that the company has been on the leading edge of innovation in business, including marketing. This "tool" has proven itself to be an excellent way to gain market share in a new, high-tech product area.

And now for a look at the financials. **Figure 3** (on the next page) shows the revenue growth of Apple by year, plotted in the same way as was done for the previous Superstar (Amazon). It is very interesting to note that there was a first period of time, under Steve Jobs, revenues did start to grow exponentially. But then Steve Jobs was ousted (1985) and sales first "flattened out" and then leveled off completely.

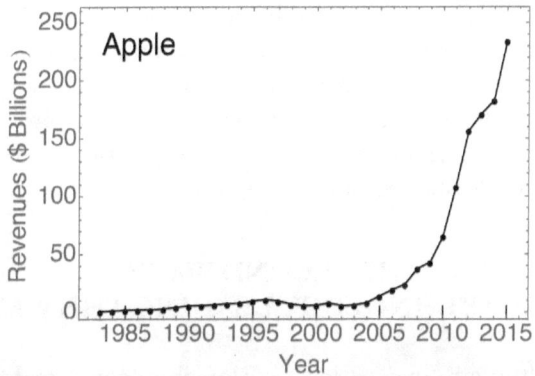

Figure 3. Apple revenues on a linear graph

Figure 4 (below) shows similar behavior for profits. Then, as both figures show, not very many years after Jobs returned to lead the company, sales again started to grow exponentially, and profits followed suit. This extreme growth has continued long enough for us to call the Apple of today a Superstar.

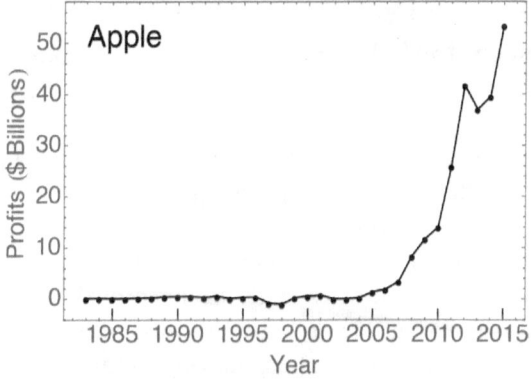

Figure 4. Apple profits on a linear graph.

It bears repeating that, on his return, Jobs rapidly reinvented and invigorated Apple by first changing both its business definition and its business model, and then by following through with the commercialization of innovative and disruptive products. In this way Steve Jobs was able to turn a dying Superstar into a star among Superstars. The question now is can Apple, under Tim Cook's leadership continue along this path?

THE SECOND WAVE: BIOTECHNOLOGY LEADING THE WAY

Although we discuss Biotechnology (and more specifically Medical Biotechnology or Biogenetics) in some detail in Chapter 4, the technology is not as familiar to most as Microelectronics and the Internet. Therefore we start this section with a simple definition. Medical Biotechnology (Biogenetics) can be defined as the science of using living cells and cell materials to produce pharmaceutical and diagnostic products that help treat and prevent human disease. And this is exactly what our next three Superstars do.

Genentech, Inc.[6]: The First Biotechnology-based Superstar

Genentech is a Superstar which is described in **more detail** than the "first wave" giants, partly because its history is not as well-known as that of Amazon and Apple and partly because of the new technical field that it pioneered. In addition, Genentech's path to becoming a Superstar differs somewhat from the others, and highlights noteworthy new issues. Thus, although Genentech took a little longer than the others to become a Superstar, we forgive it that extra time.

In 1976 Genentech (short for genetic engineering

technology), the first company based on genetic engineering, was founded by the biochemist Herbert Boyer and the venture capitalist Robert Swanson. It is interesting to note that this is the same year that Apple began. A year later Genentech was the first to produce a human protein (somatostatin) in a microorganism (E.coli bacteria). Then in 1978 Genentech announced a major breakthrough—the cloning of the human insulin gene. The year 1980 was a landmark year in two ways. First, the U.S. Supreme Court ruled that genetically altered "life" (such as what Genentech had created) could be patented.[7] Then, also in 1980, Genentech tendered an IPO, raising significant working capital. In 1982, Genentech's now patented insulin, branded Humulin, was approved by the Food and Drug Administration and licensed to Eli Lilly for sale, providing Genentech with needed capital but no sales of its own. But it was the world's first drug made by recombinant DNA. The business of biotechnology exploded with Genentech leading the way.

But let us start at the beginning. In the early 1970s, the biochemist Herbert Boyer and the geneticist Stanley Cohen pioneered a new scientific field called recombinant DNA technology, often called gene splicing. Who were Herbert Boyer and Stanley Cohen?

Herbert W. Boyer, born in 1936, received his Ph.D. from the University of Pittsburgh, was a Postdoctoral Fellow at Yale, and then a professor at the University of California, San Francisco—until he left to become part of Genentech. **Stanley N. Cohen**, born in 1935, received his Ph.D. from the University of Michigan, and joined the faculty at Stanford University in 1968.

As can be seen, Boyer and Cohen were neither college dropouts nor rebels. In fact, both had chosen the field of academic research as their career path. Further, they both chose to focus on the developing areas of biotechnology. But here the two careers diverged somewhat.

Cohen was studying plasmids, tiny rings of DNA in the cytoplasm (the cell substance between the cell membrane and the nucleus of **bacterial** cells that reproduce outside the main chromosome). He was using plasmids to transport genes and DNA fragments into bacteria; while others in Stanford University's biochemistry department were using viruses as transport vehicles. Stanford researchers at the time were at the forefront of developing techniques for joining DNA molecules from different sources, and in 1972, Paul Berg succeeded in making the first recombinant DNA molecules in a test tube. However, neither Berg nor any other member of the Stanford biochemistry faculty or anyone elsewhere had created a method for cloning DNA, and the various biochemical approaches developed for recombining DNA were technically complicated, requiring a battery of enzymes and skills beyond the ability of most labs at the time.

Boyer, on the other hand, was studying "restriction enzymes" (any of a group of enzymes that catalyze the cleavage of DNA molecules at specific sites). The important point to note here is that restriction enzymes can be used for gene splicing (the process by which the DNA of an organism is cut and a gene, perhaps from another organism, is inserted). Boyer's enzymes, with their natural ability to create "sticky ends" in just one step, offered a substantial leap in the ease and efficiency of splicing together DNA pieces to form recombinant molecules.

It can be seen that Cohen's and Boyer's studies were very complementary, although they had been carried out without each other's knowledge. In simplified, even if less rigorously accurate words, Cohen's studies led to the creation of useful compounds, while Boyer's work led to a process for the manufacture of these compounds, capable of being scaled-up to industrial production.

The two finally got together at a conference in Hawaii in 1972 where both were giving papers. A luncheon discussion in a sandwich bar allowed them to explain their studies to each other, aided by drawings on paper napkins. They immediately decided that they had to collaborate, and agreed to assign one of Cohen's research assistants the task of liaising between them. In March 1973, through their joint work, they proved that DNA could not only be recombined, but also cloned. Boyer wrote: "The [DNA] bands were lined up and you could just look at them and you knew... [that DNA recombination and cloning] had been successful...I was just ecstatic."[8]

However, getting two scientists together and having them make a major breakthrough is a far cry from having a company able to commercialize their ideas. Additionally, the two scientists had almost opposite personalities— Cohen was very reserved and unemotional while Boyer was gregarious, casual and temperamental.

The first step toward creating a company was taken when their respective Universities (Stanford University and the University of California, San Francisco) convinced them that it was necessary to file patents on their discoveries, especially since the press had already gotten hold of their story.

Boyer believed the first application of their inventions could be the production of insulin with higher yields than were then possible. He approached a large pharmaceutical company with this prospect but was turned down. Boyer then had a fleeting thought about starting a new company, but by his own admission, he had no idea how to do this. And at this point, enter Bob Swanson, the person who is regarded as instrumental, together of course with the scientists who did the research, in launching the Biogenetics revolution.

Robert A. Swanson was born in 1947, and received a B.S. in Chemistry from MIT. However, after serving as a summer employee in a large chemical company, he decided that a corporate technical career was not what he wanted.

He applied and was accepted in MIT's Sloan School of Management. While there he found his calling. He took a course in entrepreneurship and fell in love with that subject. When he graduated in 1970, he first joined Citicorp. Then in 1974 he left Citicorp to join a new "high-tech" venture capital partnership, Kleiner and Perkins, and moved to the San Francisco Bay area to explore new opportunities originating in that growing hotbed of entrepreneurship.

As a part of his new responsibilities, he went to a meeting on various possible business opportunities for a company, Cetus Corporation, which had just hired Stanley Cohen as a scientific advisor. Among the many other opportunities, Cohen gave a presentation on cloning and genetic engineering. Nobody in the meeting appeared to be interested, with the exception of Swanson who was fascinated by its prospects. Surprisingly, Kleiner and Perkins were easily convinced by Swanson regarding the potential business opportunities for recombinant DNA and Swanson tried very hard to convince Cetus to pursue this opportunity, but to no avail. Not only did Cetus hesitate, but so did most established pharmaceutical companies. They did not perceive early business opportunities for this technology, and decided that the best course of action was to wait and see. Unfortunately for them, this proved to be a poor choice.

In the meantime, Kleiner and Perkins became disenchanted with Swanson's obsessive focus on biotechnology and asked him to leave the partnership, not unlike what happened to Steve Jobs in Apple when he became too visionary. Now it was 1975 and Swanson was reduced to living on unemployment benefits. He applied to many companies, often having as many as three interviews a day for the next three or four months. No offers!

But Swanson was no quitter, and he was still very committed to the business possibilities of recombinant

DNA. So, in January 1976 he made an appointment to see Professor Boyer. He was given 10 minutes of Boyer's time. The 10 minutes extended to hours. Then and there they decided to work together, one providing the technical expertise and the other providing his business expertise. Each contributed $500 each toward the formation of a new company. Now, what would entrepreneurs of today estimate for the probability of success in a venture where the business foundations were so flimsy? But it worked! Swanson and Boyer agreed that the first product to focus on was human insulin—something that offered clear advantages over the animal insulin that was used at the time to treat diabetes. In addition, Swanson understood the marketing advantages. There were a large number of patients who could be potential buyers for the product, and the term "insulin" was already well known and did not need to be marketed.

In 1976 Swanson wrote a business plan for the new product and first presented it to his former employers, Kleiner and Perkins, because he knew that the partnership specialized in high-risk investments. But these investors were not yet convinced and asked to meet with Prof. Boyer. Boyer, with a clear and powerful presentation, convinced them of the potential of the technology. Kleiner and Perkins agreed to invest $100,000 each, a minuscule fraction of the millions of dollars needed to launch the venture commercially. But it was a beginning.

Most venture capitalists work in a hands-off way with companies in which they invest. This model is almost essential if later they do not want liability in case the investment fails. But Kleiner and Perkins, who were experienced businessmen, operated differently. As was their practice, they took seats on Genentech's Board and advised on business operations. They believed that this improved the chance of success of the ventures they invested in, although it increased the personal financial risk to these venture capitalists. However in this case, the active involvement by the partners didn't stop there. Kleiner and Perkins dissolved their partnership and joined Boyer and Swanson in the creation of a new company, Genentech; and Swanson was made President. At last Swanson was earning money again. It was 1976.

But the final goal was still far away, and there were several hurdles on the way to a commercial success. Licenses acceptable to Genentech had to be obtained from the universities whose names were on the original patents. Then there were critics who said university research, being paid for by the public, ought to see the benefits returned to the public, not used for commercial exploitation by one or even by a few companies. And there were people concerned about the safety and the containment effectiveness of the new microorganisms that were created during the research and production phases.

The book *Genentech*[9] describes the early hurdles and the actions required to bring the first product to fruition in the midst of a growing controversy on recombinant DNA. Suffice it to say, these hurdles came from many different sources, some with some very legitimate questions and others with purely political motivations. They ranged from obstacles created by various types of committees (political and academic) to legal questions on patenting, to priority questions on publishing, etc. And there was the intervention by the press that debated the ethical and moral issues of genetic engineering in the forum of public opinion, often focusing on using human embryos for stem cell research and the potential for genetically changing the human species.

In 1976/77, with Swanson's leadership, a new business plan was produced, partly based on facts and partly based on hope. And at that point Swanson was able to convince Eli Lilly and Company to contribute to the effort. Still cautious, the company provided limited financial support with a monthly payment.

Then, also in 1977, a critical experiment, without direct commercial value but with enormous scientific value, proved that the technology worked. A key contributor was Italian scientist Roberto Crea who had emigrated from Calabria in the South of Italy, first to the Netherlands and then to the United States where he joined the City of Hope Medical Center. In 1977 he was part of the joint research effort between City of Hope and Genentech that was able to construct the protein of a mammal by inserting an artificial gene into bacteria. We make this point here to lay the foundation for our later claims that multi-national and multi-laboratory approaches to science are decidedly advantages. (Note: In 1978 Crea was hired by Genentech.)

Finally, the efforts of Genentech's team of scientists, their ingenuity, and their very, very long hours spent working bore fruit. On August 21, 1978 they succeeded in producing **human** insulin in the laboratory—a world's first and a breakthrough with enormous commercial potential! But it was not yet the end of the road. The technology needed to be scaled up, commercialized, marketed, distributed and sold.

How had Swanson motivated his employees? He made sure that the company not only paid these researchers a good salary but also offered them stocks in the company, something most of them (coming from academia) did not fully appreciate—until they became millionaires. As a comparison, large pharmaceutical companies at that time usually only offered stock options to management and not to researchers.

Another event contributed to the 1978 Genentech breakthrough: the addition to the staff of a premiere researcher from the Netherlands: Herb Heyneker. He was leading a successful genetic engineering research team in Holland, when the Dutch government created what amounted to a research moratorium, due to the same fears that had been expressed in the United States. But in the US these fears did not stop privately funded research. Heyneker's joining the Genentech team was another example of the value of international research efforts.

After Genentech's August 21, 1978 success in producing human insulin, Lilly had no more reservations about subsidizing Genentech in a bigger way. On August 25 of that year Lilly and Genentech signed a multi-million dollar, long term R&D agreement with a licensing fee of half a million dollars, to be paid immediately to Genentech. The contract limited the use of Genentech's technology by Lilly to only producing insulin. But in return Lilly had the option of terminating the contract if certain (very optimistic) benchmarks were not reached by certain dates.

This agreement shows that Lilly had the foresight and courage to "jump" on the Genentech technology in the time window between when the technology was "possibly" successful and when it was proven to be successful—the time at which many others would join the race to buy the technology from Genentech. From the point of view of Genentech, the agreement had helped bridge the gap over the time interval between research and commercialization, where many good projects perish for lack of funds. To further bridge this gap, Genentech tendered an IPO in 1980, raising $35 million.

And then, the big milestone. In 1982, the FDA approved the Genentech insulin. This first-ever, recombinant DNA product, including production and sales was licensed to Lilly, providing a stream of revenue to Genentech for a number of years. Swanson's use of this strategy (licensing products once FDA approval was obtained) was repeated several times over the years to provide needed cash for R&D and operations.

With its first success, Genentech started pushing ahead with the development of a product that the company would produce and sell itself. This product, Protropin, a human growth hormone for children, was launched in 1985, after obtaining FDA approval. It was another first—the first recombinant drug product to be manufactured and marketed solely by a biotechnology company. And it was followed in 1987 by Activase, a recombinant tissue plasminogen activator (t-Pa) used to dissolve blood clots in patients with acute myocardial infarction.

By licensing its newly approved drugs, tendering an IPO, and finally selling its own products, the funding gap between research and commercialization had been completely bridged and Genentech was running on its own!

Afterwards, many other products were developed and marketed by Genentech, including: Pulmozyme (an inhalation treatment for children and young adults with cystic fibrosis), Rituxan (treatment for specific kinds of non-Hodgkins lymphomas), Herceptin (treatment for metastatic breast cancer patients), Xolair (a subcutaneous injection for moderate to severe persistent asthma), and Avastin (a monoclonal antibody for the treatment of metastatic cancer of the colon or rectum). And the list goes on and on.

Without question, Genentech owes much its existence and much of its success to Swanson's vision, determination, and ability to attract the "best of the best" to his startup venture. He served as Genentech's CEO from the beginning until 1990. Swanson had the unique ability to combine the best of two worlds for exceptional results—the resources of the corporate world with the ability of the academic world to carry out pioneering, basic research. And like other strong leaders, he used discipline and an intense focus on relatively short term goals to achieve exceptional success.

However Swanson left Genentech before it became today's superstar. He was followed by G. Kirk Raab, a "master marketer." Raab served as CEO from 1990 until 1995 when he was forced to resign under a cloud by

Genentech's Board. During his short tenure, Genentech benefited from Swanson's foundation, but the company became entangled in controversy and lawsuits. Raab was succeeded by Dr. Arthur Levinson, who served as CEO from 1995 until 2009.

Levinson was a molecular biologist who had never run a company, but he was what Genentech needed. He restored the company's reputation and re-emphasized research, thus revitalizing the new drug pipeline. But more important, he focused the company on oncology. This led to the impressive and sustainable financial growth that defines our Superstars.

Now the numbers achieved under Dr. Levinson's leadership.

Figure 5 below shows the overall dynamic growth of revenues for Genentech through 2009 (plotted on a linear graph, as we have done with the other companies).

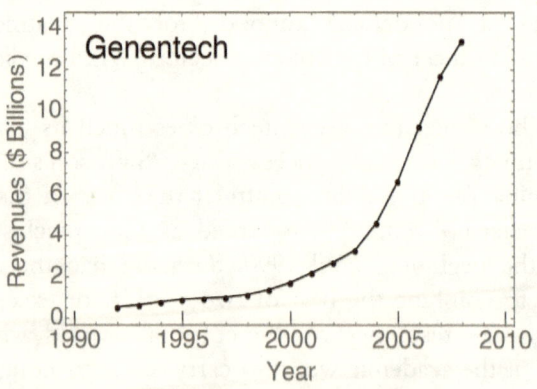

Figure 5. Genentech revenues on a linear graph

Figure 6 on the next page and plotted in the same fashion, shows profits. The data in both figures, indicating impressive and sustained exponential growth, allow us to call Genentech without reservation, a Superstar.

However it should be noted that it took Genentech longer

to achieve this status than the other Superstars, partly because it received no sales credit from its earlier licensed out products and partly because of the difficulties encountered in the early efforts to commercialize its new-to-the-world genetically engineered products. But in our view, as of 2009, Genentech was clearly a Superstar.

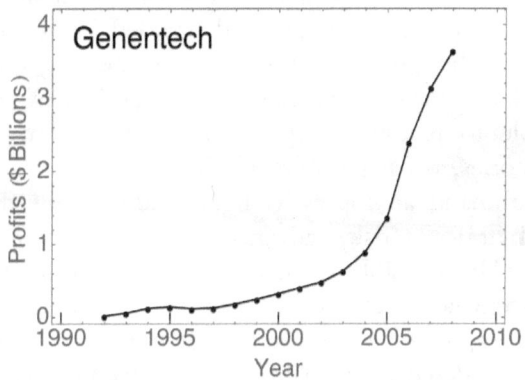

Figure 6. Genentech profits on a linear graph.

But what about today? In 2009, Genentech, Inc. merged with Roche Holding Ltd. and became a wholly owned but publicly traded subsidiary of that Group. In 2010, Ian T. Clark, with expertise in sales and marketing and extensive leadership experience in the pharmaceutical industry, succeeded Levinson as CEO.

And now Genentech is no longer independent. It is a part of Roche Pharmaceuticals. Thus this biotechnology pioneer has ceased to exist as a separate entity, not because of failure, but because of its extreme success.

If Genentech had remained a separate company, would it be a Superstar today? Probably, but we will never know. What we do know is that Genentech was truly the trailblazer that showed the way for many other biotechnology companies.

Because of its breakthrough pioneering efforts and

because it did once have Superstar performance, we include it in our list.

Amgen, Inc.[10]: Another Biotechnology Pioneer

William Bowles, then a financial manager and board member of the struggling biotechnology company Cetus, left his position there in 1980 and founded a new company based on the promise of genetic engineering—Applied Molecular Genetics (soon to be known as Amgen). Bowles was able to recruit George B. Rathmann from Abbott Laboratories, as Amgen's first CEO.

Rathmann, an impressive figure and a clear leader, was a good fit for a risky, advanced technology startup like Amgen. He was able to quickly raise significant funding from strategic investors and even more financing from venture capitalists. Then, under Rathmann's leadership, Amgen tendered an IPO in 1983. Altogether, Rathmann was able to raise enough capital for Amgen to survive the product development and commercialization phases without having to give up rights to its inventions.

But that isn't all. Rathmann, although originally a scientist, was business-oriented and ran Amgen's R&D operations with strict goals and timetables. He insisted that his researchers target only products with large potential markets—first forcing them to identify five potential targets, and then to focus on only one. And they were successful. They developed a breakthrough therapeutic drug for anemia that would later be sold under the name Epogen.

However Amgen was missing one more key capability—manufacturing. Rathmann had the insight to recognize this need and developed a strategic partnership with Kirin Brewery. The rest is history. Amgen's first genetically engineered drug, Epogen, became a blockbuster in 1989, followed soon by Neupogen, another blockbuster.

And that was just the start.

Today, Amgen sells a host of genetically engineered drugs for to diverse markets: Epogen for anemia, Neupogen for treating a common side effect of chemotherapy, Enbrel for arthritis, Prolia for postmenopausal osteoporosis, and Vectibix for colon cancer—to name a few that most would recognize.

From a risky startup in 1980 to a Superstar today— George Rathmann, clearly a strong leader, as we mentioned earlier, played a key role as Amgen's first CEO. It was under his leadership that many of Amgen's key discoveries were made.

But there were other leaders who also were very important: George M. Binder who succeeded Rathmann in1988 followed by Kevin W. Sharer in 2000 and finally Robert A. Bradway in 2012 (Amgen's current president and CEO). And as leadership changed, so did the growth strategies: from a focus on commercializing the discoveries of the 80s to efforts to broaden the indications for existing drugs to a series of acquisitions. All played a role in sustaining Amgen's exponential growth.

So what about the financials? Amgen first appeared on the Fortune 500 list in 1992. **Figure 7** on the next page shows the overall growth in revenues for Amgen from 1992 to the present, while **Figure 8** (also on the next page) shows profits over the same time span. These data are plotted in the same fashion as was done for the other Superstars and indicate exponential growth in revenues and profits, albeit with some departures from this extreme growth during the period from 2006 to 2010, departures that Amgen management attributed to the recession.

Forgiving those few years, the overall exponential increases in sales and profits over much more than a decade, including the current one, allow us to include Amgen among today's Superstars.

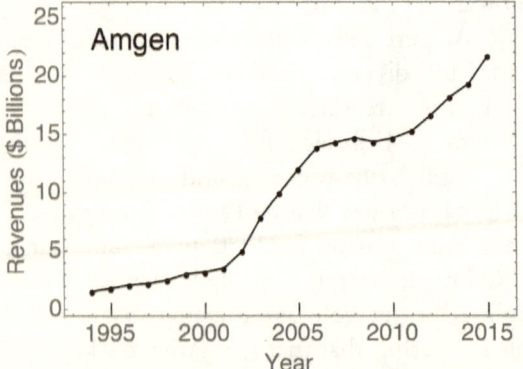

Figure 7. Amgen revenues on a linear graph

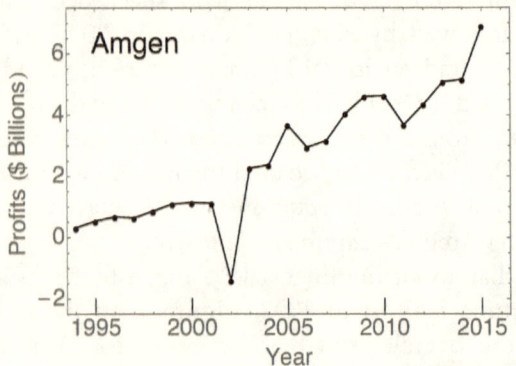

Figure 8. Amgen profits on a linear graph.

However, it should be noted that Amgen's growth in revenues for the last couple of years has slowed. This raises the question as to whether Amgen can maintain its status as a Superstar going forward.

Gilead Sciences, Inc.[11]: The Fastest Growing Superstar

Gilead Sciences is the fastest growing Superstar among those listed, with a growth rate about 10 times higher over a 15-year period than any of the others.

Revenues increased from $233 million in 2001 to $32.6 billion in 2015. Much of the growth is due to a number of excellent and numerous acquisitions, starting in 1999.

But back to the beginning. Gilead Sciences was founded in 1987 by Michael L. Riordan, who was 29 years old at the time, and had a somewhat unusual background. He had received a B.S.Ch.E. from Washington University in 1979 with a dual major in biology and chemical engineering.

He then was awarded a scholarship to spend a year working for the Ministry of Health in the Philippines at a malnutrition clinic. There, two things changed his career path. First, the extreme lack of health care opened his eyes to the economics of medicine. Second, he contracted dengue fever, and while seriously ill started thinking about the need for new viral therapies.

These experiences led him to pursue a medical degree (obtained from the John Hopkins School of Medicine) and an M.B.A. (obtained from Harvard Business School). From there he took a position with Menlo Ventures, a California venture capital firm. And his next step was founding Gilead Sciences. Overall he had an impressive and unusual collection of experiences and credentials for starting a company in biotechnology.

Riordan's vision was for his company to be focused on antiviral medicines. To this end, he assembled an impressive collection of collaborators and scientific advisers, including two Nobel Prize recipients—Harold Varmus, who later on became director of the National Institute of Health and the National Cancer Institute; and Jack Szostak, who in 2009, received the Nobel Prize for Physiology or Medicine.

In addition, Riordan proved himself to be a master at raising funds. In 1988 he was able to raise $2 million and another $10 million in 1989 from venture capital sources. And this was only the beginning. Then, with the licensing-in of key technology from the Czech Republic in 1991, he focused the company on small molecule antiviral therapeutics. He took Gilead public in 1992, raising $86 million. Then, after almost a decade of existence, Gilead introduced its first product in 1996—Vistide, a drug for the treatment of CMV retinitis in patients suffering from AIDS.

In that same year, 1996, John C. Martin succeeded Riordan as CEO and has had held that position ever since. Martin, with a Ph.D. in organic chemistry and an M.B.A., had joined Gilead in 1990 as its Vice President of R&D. As CEO, Martin continued the focus on developing and commercializing new antiviral drugs, and the list is impressive, including: Tamiflu in 1999 (discovery and early development by Gilead, late stage development and sales by Roche), AmBisome in 2000 (for the treatment of meningitis in HIV infected patients), Hepsera in 2002 (for treatment of chronic hepatitis B), and Macugen in 2004 (for age-related macular degeneration). And the list goes on.

However, Martin also pursued an aggressive strategy of acquisitions (14 and counting since 1999). The result? Under his leadership Gilead's growth exploded and the company has become one of the top creators of shareholder value in the world. Martin considers some of the keys to Gilead's success as: focusing on a pipeline of innovative products with high probabilities of success (whether they are developed internally or found on the outside), multidisciplinary team efforts in all areas, and the effective management of a global network consisting of both internal and external specialists.[12]

And now the financials.

Figure 9 on the next page shows Gilead's overall impressive growth of revenues. **Figure 10** (also on the next page) shows profits over the same time span. Again the data clearly show profitable, exponential growth in revenues for over a decade and still continuing, making

Gilead another Superstar.

However, it bears repeating that much of Gilead's revenue growth has been obtained through acquisitions. This doesn't make it any less of a Superstar, but it does raise the question about the sustainability of this high growth.

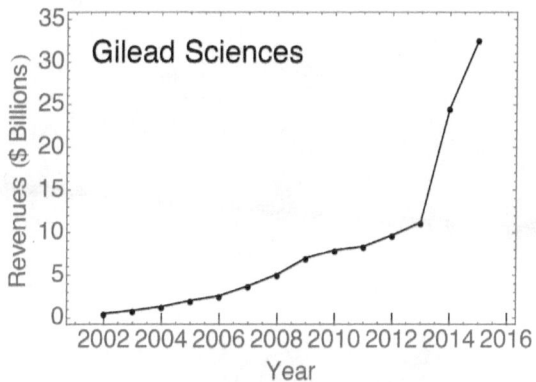

Figure 9. Gilead revenues on a linear graph

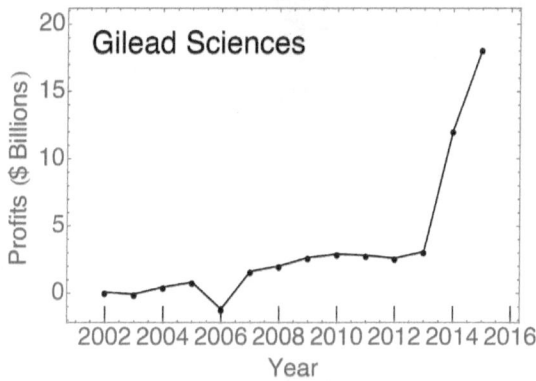

Figure 10. Gilead Scinces profits on a linear graph.

And one last set of questions to think about. Riordan and Martin were both strong leaders but with different strengths. Was just one of them responsible for making

Gilead a Superstar? If so, which one? Or were they both needed—each at a different stage of the company's development? No simple answers.

Three

OTHER EXCEPTIONAL COMPANIES

Superstars are not the only companies worth investigating as high growth businesses. In this chapter we focus on three other categories of companies with extreme growth—what we call Potential Superstars, Enablers, and Private Companies to Watch.

POTENTIAL SUPERSTARS

There are a number of companies that could be considered "Potential Superstars." However, we have chosen to focus on only two—Facebook and Google. These two large companies are clearly exceptional. They have demonstrated extreme growth, and share some common characteristics with the Superstars we identified in Chapter 2. However they are still "young."

If they are able to sustain or increase their extreme growth for a while longer while maintaining profiyability, they will clearly join today's elite group of Superstars. But they are not there yet, and nothing is certain in today's chaotic world.

Facebook, Inc.[13]: A Social Media Phenomenon

Facebook—an Internet based company that in 10 years went from "nothing" to an over $12 billion enterprise. The story of Facebook and its CEO Mark Zuckerberg is familiar to most, so here is a short summary.

In February 2004, a social networking service was launched by Harvard classmates Mark Zuckerberg (the computer programming student who developed it), Eduardo Saverin, Dustin Moskovitz and Chris Hughes. At the time, it was known as Thefacebook.com, and the website membership was only available to Harvard students. However, that rapidly changed. By 2006, membership was available to anyone over the age of 13 with a valid email address.

Thefacebook was incorporated in the summer of 2004 and operations moved to Palo Alto, CA. Zuckerberg never returned to Harvard. In 2005, his company officially became Facebook, and the website was facebook.com. As the website states: "Facebook's mission is to give people the power to share and make the world more open and connected. People use Facebook to stay connected with friends and family, to discover what is going on."

Early on, the costs for Thefacebook were covered by Zuckerberg and Saverin. But that changed in the summer of 2004. Venture capitalist Peter Thiel made a $500,000 angel investment in Facebook for 10.2% of the company and joined Facebook's board. And this was the beginning of many venture capital investments. The company was seldom short of funds for growth. For example, in October 2007 Microsoft bought a 1.4 % share of the company for $240 million, valuing Facebook at $15 billion.

Several lawsuits on the one hand and offers of acquisition on the other hand were no doubt somewhat distracting for the company's management, but the company kept its course and grew at an unprecedented rate. New users worldwide, expansion to new businesses, new services, and acquisitions such as Instagram and WhatsApp all contributed.

In May of 2012 Facebook's IPO raised $16 billion, making it the third largest public offering in U.S. history. In 2015, a little more than 10 years after Facebook's inception, its revenues were $17.9 billion and profits were $3.7 billion. Facebook's extreme growth since becoming a Fortune 500 company in 2012 is often attributed to the strong and unconventional leadership of Zuckerberg, and certainly qualifies it as a developing Superstar. Not bad for the creation of a college dropout! The challenge now for Facebook is sustaining its now exponential growth.

Google Inc.[14]: A Pervasive Presence on the Internet

Google is a very familiar and pervasive U.S. Internet-based company offering product and services such as online advertising, cloud computing, and software. It receives most of its profits from AdWords, an online advertising service that places advertising near the list of search results. Its products are well known to most, but its story is less familiar. Thus we provide some highlights.

Google was founded in 1998 by Larry Page and Sergey Brin while they were Ph.D. students at Stanford University. It was based in the garage of a friend. In its early years it successfully obtained significant venture capital funding. In 2001, Page and Brin recruited Eric Schmidt, then the CEO of Novell, to become Google's CEO. The company went public in 2004, with a market capitalization of more than $23 billion. At that time, Page, Brin, and Schmidt agreed to work together at Google for the next 20 years—and they are still together. That same year the company moved to new headquarters in Mountain View, California.

In an effort to maintain the company's unique culture after the extremely successful initial public offering, Google appointed a Chief Culture Officer, who was also the director of Human Resources. The purpose of this Officer was to develop and maintain the culture and work in ways to keep true to the core values that the company was founded on: a flat organization with a collaborative environment. This was a substantial departure from the business norm of those times and reflected the strong views of Page and Brin.

Google's extreme growth since incorporation (from revenues of $3 billion in 2004 to $75 billion in 2015) has been spurred by many products, acquisitions and partnerships. The names are familiar: the original product—Google Search, AdWords, Google Maps, YouTube, Google Chrome, Gmail, cloud storage service (Google Drive), an office suite (Google Docs), a social networking service (Google+), the Android operating system, and more. Google extended its business model to include communications hardware. For example it acquired Motorola Mobility in 2012 and installed a fiber-optic infrastructure in Kansas City to support a Google Fiber broadband business.

Besides high growth, a spectacular achievement of this Potential Superstar is how fast the brand value reached the top. According to Interbrand's 15th annual Best Global Brands Report,[15] Google reached the #2 position in this area in 2015, with a valuation of $107.4 billion! To clarify what this rating means, it's useful to understand that Interbrand's valuation was based on three factors:

1. The financial performance of the branded product and service.
2. The role the brand plays in influencing customer choice.
3. The strength the brand has to command a premium price or secure earnings for the company.

(Note: Among the other companies we highlight in this book, Apple is #1 with a valuation of $118 billion, Microsoft is #5, Intel #12 and Amazon #15.)

Google's strong financial results in a relatively short period of time and its impact on the world make it truly an exceptional company and are a tribute to its unconventional founders. However, although the revenue growth has been high, it's not exponential and it is slowing. Thus in 2015, under the leadership of Page and Brin, Google was reorganized, in order to "have their now-giant tech company feel once again like a scrappy startup, with Page focused on expanding the [core] businesses and Brin touting their most ambitious projects."[16] Specifically, a holding company called Alphabet, Inc. was created, with the core internet-related businesses of Google as its largest subsidiary—the new entity still called Google.

As in the case of Facebook and our Superstars, Google is an example of exceptional performance and strong and unconventional leadership. As far as the future, will the new Google become a Superstar according to our definition? What about Alphabet and the other subsidiaries?

THE ENABLERS

We call "Enablers" those high-growth companies that have provided and continue to supply to the Superstars key components that were and are essential pieces of the Superstars' products and fueled and continue to fuel their exponential growth. In other words, companies like Apple and Amazon and the others described in Chapter 2 would not have become Superstars without the technology and products created by the Enablers. And the Enablers have achieved exceptional growth, partly due to their symbiotic relationship with the Superstars. Without the Superstars these Enablers would not have a rapidly growing outlet for their products, and without the Enablers the Superstars might not be the exceptional companies they are today. Thus both sets of companies have benefited greatly from each other and that symbiotic relationship continues.

However, the revenues of the Superstars are growing exponentially while the Enablers' revenues are growing in a linear fashion—but that linear growth is impressive. By riding on the coat tails of the Superstars, the Enablers have been able to achieve revenue growth that significantly exceeds that of the median Fortune 500 companies. They are truly exceptional companies—for their growth and innovations. We have picked two of these high-profile Enablers to describe in some detail and illustrate our concept.

Microsoft Corporation[17]: The World's largest Software Provider

In 1975 Bill Gates and Paul Allen had the idea of developing software that would enhance new computer systems. Their first project was the development of a new programming language for the microcomputer Altair 8800, manufactured by Micro Instrumentation and Telemetry Systems (MITS). Thus they moved to Albuquerque (where MITS was located) and founded Microsoft in 1976. Bill Gates had dropped out of Harvard, where he was a student, to make this move which enabled him to follow his vision for a new kind of company based on computer programming. MITS distributed Microsoft's initial product, and the first year's sales were $16,000.

Four years later, Steve Ballmer, who would later become CEO, joined the company as a business manager. The following year, in 1981, IBM released its first personal computer, using Microsoft's newly developed operating system MS-DOS. That same year Bill Gates became president of the company and chairman of the board, and Paul Allen became Executive Vice President. From that point on, the company quickly became the leading vendor of cutting-edge operating systems and applications software for IBM PC compatible computers.

By 1983, Microsoft had reached $55 Million in revenues. Bill Gates, the chairman, stated at that time that his vision for the company was to be the leader in software applications, operating systems, and peripherals; which he said would make Microsoft "the IBM of the software industry." To that end, in 1983 Bill Gates announced in an advertising campaign that a new Microsoft operating system was about to be developed that would use a graphic interface. It was to be called "Windows," and would be compatible with all PC software products developed on the MS-DOS system. The announcement was a bluff, in that Microsoft had no such program under development. But as a marketing tactic it was sheer genius as it pre-empted newly advertised systems by the company VisiCorp, a company that eventually lost out to Microsoft.

November 1985 was a turning point for Microsoft because Bill Gates/ Microsoft did launch Windows, nearly two years after its announcement. Bill Gates' bluff had paid off. But think how frantically the scientists had to work within Microsoft to meet Gates' self-imposed deadline! Visually the Windows system looked very similar to the Macintosh system that the Apple Computer Corporation had introduced nearly two years earlier. However Apple had not patented their software. This left Gates free to introduce a software with a similar format to that of Apple's computers. Microsoft went public early the following year (in 1986), and from that point on was off and running.

Microsoft was a little late in utilizing the "explosion" of the Internet, but nevertheless by 1995, 20 years after the company's beginning, Microsoft had reached $6 billion in revenues (not quite fast enough to be classified as a superstar, but still quite impressive, without even "riding on the coat-tails" of the Internet). But the story continues.

The company started taking advantage of the Internet in the middle of the 90s decade. In 1997, Internet Explorer 4.0 was introduced (together with Microsoft Office 97), competing with Netscape, and by agreement with Apple Computer, Internet Explorer was bundled with the Apple Macintosh operating system as well as with Windows. Because of the intervention of the Justice Department, however, the bundling was later discontinued. In 1998 Bill Gates appointed Steve Ballmer as president of Microsoft but remained Chairman and CEO of the company until 2000 when Ballmer took over as CEO.

By 2015 Microsoft had reached revenues of $93 billion. Thus, since 1995 the company had grown its revenues more than 15 fold. Impressive performance! However, although the revenues increased rapidly during this time period, the growth was linear, **not** exponential. So Microsoft still is not a Superstar. But keep in mind that without Microsoft, the world of PCs and all of the businesses that depend on them (including Amazon and the biotech giants) would not be the same. So Microsoft is a true Enabler and an exceptional company.

But the story of Microsoft still isn't finished. In the past, even in the recent past, the company was highly focused on software products, as our brief history shows. However, under the leadership of the current CEO, Satya Nadella, this appears to be changing, as is demonstrated by the recent introduction of Windows 10 as well as a host of new hardware devices. According to Nadella, "We plan to invent new personal computers and new personal computing."[18] Will this significant change in direction be enough to elevate Microsoft to Superstar status? Only time will tell.

Intel Corporation[19]: A Global Leader in Semiconductor Chips

Intel Corporation is another exceptional company that supports the computer industry and grows with it. But it is more than that. Its many innovations enabled and fueled the age of microelectronics and all that entails.

Intel was founded in 1968 by Robert Noyce and Gordon Moore. It was no garage shop operation ($2.5 million in venture capital funding), and its founders were not young visionaries who dropped out of college. They were both experienced technologists with established reputations as pioneers in the semiconductor industry. They both held senior positions at Fairchild Semiconductor before they left to found Intel.

Intel's initial products included SRAM (static random access memory) semiconductor chips, which had modest success. However, in 1970 the company introduced their leading-edge DRAM (dynamic random access memory) chip, and sales took off. Intel went public in 1971.

During the 1970s DRAM chips became the industry's standard, and Intel's revenues grew as it expanded and improved its manufacturing processes and produced a wider range of memory devices. However, increased competition from Japanese semiconductor manufacturers had, by 1983, substantially reduced the profitability of this market. Then, the growing success of the IBM personal computer, based on an Intel microprocessor, convinced Gordon Moore (CEO of IBM since 1975) to shift the company's focus to microprocessors. Moore's decision to sole-source Intel's 386 chip played into IBM's success, and served as a catalyst for Intel and its microprocessors.

By the end of the 1980s, Intel had begun a 10-year period of unprecedented growth as the primary microprocessor supplier to the PC industry. Andy Grove, a businessman recruited by Noyce and Moore in the early days of Intel, became the CEO in 1987. Grove's business strategy focused on making newer microprocessors dramatically faster than previous ones. To accomplish this, Intel found new ways to manufacture chips with vastly more transistors in each device. Still today, Intel is recognized for its advanced chip designs and its leading-edge manufacturing capability.

In addition, Grove's strategy included a new marketing approach to increase brand awareness to manufacturers and consumers alike. Starting in 1991, by requiring computer manufacturers using Intel microprocessors to label "**Intel Inside**" on their computers, Intel was able to make its line of Pentium processors a well-recognized name. And the same "Intel Inside" labelling continues, although today Intel is a household name.

Then came the new century and a new leader. In the early 2000s, in the face of intense competition from AMD with its low-to-mid-range microprocessors, then-CEO Craig Barrett attempted to diversify the company's business beyond semiconductors. But few of these activities turned out to be successful—a lesson to be learned! However Barrett did have one success which had a significant impact on Intel. He convinced Steve Jobs to use Intel chips in Apple's PCs. Thus today, Intel and/or Intel compatible microprocessors can be found in essentially every PC.

Paul Otellini succeeded Barrett as CEO in 2005. He reorganized the company to focus its core businesses on platforms. This resulted in new products that provided a leap in processor performance, and allowed Intel to regain its leadership position. In addition to new products, since 2010 Intel has made a number of acquisitions. Thus its revenues, after a considerable dip, have started growing again.

So what have been Intel's financials for the past 20 years? To summarize, revenues increased from $16 billion in 1995 to $55 billion in 2015. While this is good growth, it's not exponential. So, as was the case for Microsoft, Intel is not a Superstar. But it clearly is an exceptional company that has changed the world with its advances in microelectronics.

Conclusions

Enablers are suppliers, and the fate of suppliers, even suppliers to Superstars, is somewhat uncertain. Ultimately the success of suppliers (including Enablers) is subject to the fortunes of the manufacturing companies which are their buyers, and in most cases depends on fighting off competitive suppliers. In addition, the markets for suppliers are companies, not consumers, and this limits their growth. However suppliers can be exceptional as Microsoft and Intel demonstrate. Both companies have performed exceeding well over the years. They were instrumental in fueling the microelectronics revolution, and developing the computer industry. And not to be forgotten, they supplied the building blocks for the growth of our Superstars.

SOME PRIVATE COMPANIES TO WATCH

This book focuses on publicly traded companies where complete financial information is made public and is readily obtainable. We have considered private companies as being outside of our scope because accurate financial results are difficult to obtain, particularly over a number of years. However, our Superstars were once private companies, and without question there are a number of exceptional private companies that are growing rapidly and have reached substantial valuations in a relatively short time. Such companies are being called "unicorns," a term popularized by Aileen Lee of Cowboy Ventures to denote a start-up company whose valuation has exceeded $1 Billion (a somewhat arbitrary number).[20] The names of some of these companies are familiar—companies like Uber Technologies, Airbnb, Dropbox, Snapchat, SpaceX, etc. In the future, we expect that a number of the fast-growing "Unicorns" such as these will become public, and a few will possibly become Superstars. Thus in this section we give a brief overview of three of the Unicorns—Uber, Airbnb and Moderna Therapeutics. We have chosen these three companies for their visibility (most people will recognize at least the first two), for their size and/or rate of growth, for their degree of innovation (in our opinion), and because two of the same, broadly defined technology platforms that enabled our Superstars (Internet and Biotechnology) enable them.

However, before we start, there are a few things worth noting about the Unicorns. First, if one looks at Fortune's 100 top-ranked Unicorns,[21] one finds that more than half of them are internet based or enabled by it. With their high valuations, this raises the question as to whether or not they are part of the next "tech bubble" (a question we do not attempt to address here). In addition, it is important to keep in mind that one innovation, no matter how disruptive, doesn't make a Superstar. All five of our Superstars have achieved their phenomenal growth by building on innovation after innovation.

Next, more than two thirds of the top 100 Unicorns are U.S. based, with China being a distant second location. This seems to support that the U.S. is still a "hotbed" of innovation and entrepreneurial spirit. However it also may reflect the availability of Venture Capital funding. In 2014, European start-ups raised only $8 billion while those in the U.S. raised $52 billion. This gap continued in 2015 (U.S. VC funding $72 billion versus European funding of $13 billion). This possibly reflects the fact that U.S investors are willing to take higher risks under certain circumstances.[22]

Finally, on a negative note, only five of the top 100 Unicorns have female CEO's. To us, this makes a clear statement about gender equality in the business world, but also reflects a societal issue.

Uber Technologies, Inc.[23]

Uber is a U.S. based, international, transportation network company headquartered in San Francisco, California. It developed and operates a mobile-app-based transportation service that allows consumers with smartphones to submit a trip request, which is routed by Uber to drivers who, using their own vehicles, will fulfill the request. The service has grown explosively in the U.S. and now has been extended to more than 70 countries and more than 400 cities worldwide. Uber keeps roughly 25% of every transaction, while the remainder goes to the drivers.

Uber was founded in 2009 as "UberCab" by two entrepreneurs—Travis Kalanick and Garrett Camp. The "app" necessary to submit a trip request was released in 2010, and the company was off and running. By the end of 2011, Uber already had raised more than $40 million in venture funds, and in subsequent years the company raised substantial additional funding. In total, since its beginning, Uber has attracted more than $18 billion in equity and debt. Today it valued at close to $70 billion, making it by far the largest of the Unicorns.

So who were these two entrepreneurs that created Uber? Travis Kalanick was born in 1976, and after high school enrolled in UCLA, to study computer engineering. However in 1998 he dropped out of UCLA with some of his classmates to found Scour Inc., a multimedia search engine, and Scour Exchange, a peer-to-peer file-exchange service. In 2000 he declared bankruptcy, probably to avoid legal complications connected with the business. But his entrepreneurial spirit was strong. In 2001 he formed Red Swoosh, another peer-to-peer file sharing company, which he sold in 2007 for $19 million. And then came Uber. Kalanick is Uber's current CEO.

Garrett Camp, a Canadian, was born in 1978; but unlike Kalanick, he completed his education. He holds an undergraduate degree in Electrical Engineering and Master's degree in Software Engineering from the University of Calgary. However like Kalanick, he had an entrepreneurial drive from an early age. In 2002, while still in graduate school, he co-founded a successful web discovery platform named StumbleUpon. In 2007 this company was acquired by eBay for $75 million, but he remained as its CEO. He still held this position when he co-founded Uber in 2009, using $250K of his own capital as seed money. He was Uber's first CEO. But Garrett's passion for start-ups remained strong, and he left Uber in 2013 to form a new venture.

So what does the future hold for Uber? Is its explosive growth sustainable in light of aggressive competition such as Lyft and Sidecar? Will it survive the legal challenges from the "taxi industry?" Can it capitalize on the move towards driverless vehicles? Can it successfully expand its logistics-like services into new areas such as food and package delivery? There are no answers yet, but Uber clearly is a company to watch.

Airbnb, Inc.[24]

Airbnb is an online marketplace that allows people to list, find, and/or book "nontraditional" lodging worldwide. It is a company that enables individuals to showcase and rent out extra space—space that now ranges from an extra room to an entire island. It has over 800,000 listings in thousands of cities and almost 200 countries. Users of the site must register and create a personal online profile before using the site. Every property is associated with a host whose profile includes recommendations from other users and reviews by previous guests. Founded in 2008 in San Francisco, California, the company is privately owned and operated.

It all started in 2007 with two friends, Brian Chesky and Joe Gebbia (both born in August 1981)—young, unemployed industrial designers rooming together in San Francisco who couldn't pay their rent. It also was a time when there was a hotel shortage in the city due to the many conventions held there. In desperation the friends purchased three air mattresses that they put on the floor of their apartment and offered them for rent (breakfast included). And a few people actually rented the mattresses.

In 2008, recognizing that they needed a good website to really have a business; they asked another friend who happened to have a degree in computer science (Nathan Blecharczyk) to join them. And AirBed & Breakfast (soon to be shortened to Airbnb) was born. They rapidly expanded the Airbnb business model—from beds and shared spaces to a variety of other properties including entire houses, igloos, and even private islands. And today, Airbnb grows not only by increasing inventory but also by increasing the numbers of hosts and travelers and matching them with each other.

The three co-founders of Airbnb remain with the company. They have grown it from nothing to a high visibility enterprise with a current valuation that exceeds $20 billion. Not as high a number as Uber's, but impressive for the short time it has existed. But what about the future? The questions are similar to those we raised for Uber: Is Airbnb's explosive growth sustainable? What will be the effect of legal/zoning challenges and renter (and neighbor) complaints? And of course, there is always competition—companies like HomeAway and others on the horizon. In any case, for now, Airbnb is a company to watch.

Moderna Therapeutics, Inc.[25]

Our third Unicorn, Moderna Therapeutics, is very different from Uber and Airbnb. It is a biotechnology company that does not yet have any products. What it does have is a breakthrough, patented technology worthy of a Superstar—if it works in humans.

Imagine a technology that helps the human body make the "medicine" it needs to fight disease. This is what Moderna is attempting to do with a technology based on messenger RNA (mRNA) science. As Moderna states on their website, it has found a way that mRNA can be modified and the ensuing mRNA Therapeutics:™

"...can be encoded for virtually any known protein and designed to be taken up by the cells in specific tissues and organs...Once delivered, like native mRNA in healthy individuals, mRNA Therapeutics™ act as cellular software directing ribosomes to express proteins or antibodies within targeted tissues—and have the power to catalyze the expression of hundreds to thousands of proteins for each mRNA molecule."

Just in case you didn't follow the details of the above explanation, the simplest way of describing Moderna's technology is to say that it is a way to reprogram cells to fight disease. Or, stated in non-technical terms:

"Moderna's approach is both simple and audacious: simple in that it taps into the most foundational way our bodies work, aiming to deliver instruction manuals for our cells to churn out proteins to reverse all kinds of diseases—from diabetes and heart disease to different forms of cancer. It's audacious because it has never worked in humans."[26]

Moderna's beginning is somewhat unusual. With initial funding from Flagship Ventures and based on university developed technology, Moderna Therapeutics was founded in Cambridge Massachusetts in 2011 by Noubar Afeyan from Flagship Ventures (currently Moderna's Chairman of the Board and CEO and Managing Partner of Flagship Ventures); Stephane Bancel (currently Moderna's CEO and a Senior Partner with Flagship Ventures) who left his position as CEO of bioMérieux to join Moderna; Kenneth Chien then of Harvard University and now of the Karolinska Institutet in Sweden; Robert Langer then and now of the Massachusetts Institute of Technology; and Derrick Rossi then and now of Harvard University and Boston Children's Hospital. Chien is a world-recognized leader in cardiovascular science and medicine and regenerative biology, Langer is regarded as the founder of tissue engineering in regenerative medicine, and Rossi is a stem cell biologist working in regenerative biology who made the basic discovery.

What stands out from the above description is that three of the company's cofounders never actually joined the company and the other two have senior management positions in both Moderna and another company (Flagship Ventures). Thus it is not only Moderna's basic technology that differentiates it from other Unicorns and biotech companies, but also its leadership team with their business backgrounds. This has resulted in a unique business model which the company calls the "Moderna Ecosystem" and describes it as a way to "simultaneously advance promising internal development programs, while also mobilizing an entire ecosystem capable of propelling the field forward for patients." Thus, according to Moderna's website:

> "One of the chief advantages that Moderna has over other early-stage biotech companies is that its

mRNA can focus on fighting multiple diseases at once rather than the typical and time-consuming path of defining and creating a drug therapy for each individual disease. The company already has 45 preclinical programs under way in cardiovascular disease, oncology and other areas and expects to be in clinical trials testing drugs and vaccines for a variety of therapeutic areas within the next two years."

How is this possible? The company has created a very dynamic outreach program for the simultaneous development and market introduction of many different products. This approach is divided into three different sub-programs. The first is Moderna Ventures. Moderna Ventures forms wholly-owned ventures to focus dedicated resources and staff in key disease areas. These include:

- Onkaido, formed as a wholly-owned subsidiary to develop mRNA drugs in oncology.
- Valera, directed towards the advancement of vaccines and therapeutics for the prevention and treatment of viral and bacterial infectious diseases.
- Elpidera, focused exclusively on the advancement of mRNA-based treatments for rare diseases.
- Caperna, focused exclusively on the advancement of personalized vaccines for cancer.

The second sub-program is based on **research collaboration**, currently with the Karolinska Institutet of Copenhagen where the focus is the treatment of serious diseases, and with the Institut Pasteur (headquartered in Paris) for the discovery and development of drugs and vaccines to fight infectious diseases.

The third sub-program relies on **external partnerships** where Moderna works with major companies in key therapeutic areas. As examples, the company has agreements with AstraZeneca focused on cardiovascular disease and certain oncology targets; Alexion Pharmaceuticals for the development of mRNA Therapeutics™ for rare diseases; and Merck for the development of vaccines and passive immunity treatments against viral diseases. To date, again according to Moderna's website, AstraZeneca and Alexion have initiated 36 unique mRNA research programs, greatly strengthening their impact beyond what Moderna could do on their own.

What is the business value of Moderna's multi-faceted outreach program and the consequent business model stemming from it? High leveraging of financial resources, commercializing more products faster, staying ahead of competition—at least these are the expectations. But it all depends on the technology. Whatever the future brings, Moderna Therapeutics is a company to watch.

REQUIREMENTS FOR A SUPERSTAR

PART II

Four

LAUNCHING PADS
The Foundation

As we have shown in Chapter 2, each of today's Superstars has had a major impact on the global economy, but their "stories" are each quite different. Thus it is not easy to answer the question as to what enables a start-up venture to become a Superstar. Clearly there is no simple recipe for creating such fast growing giants.

However there is a basic requirement. A company hoping to be a Superstar must make direct use of an extremely fast-developing technological area—what we call a technology **Launching Pad**. In other words, to be a Superstar, a company must be built on or enabled by a technology Launching Pad—Apple and Microelectronics, Amazon and the Internet, and Biotechnology for the others. Because these specific Launching Pads are so essential to the making of today's Superstars, this chapter is devoted to them. And because we believe future Superstars and most fast growing companies will be based on new Launching Pads, we devote the last part of the book to emerging developments in science and technology.

But first, what exactly is a technological "Launching Pad?" A technological Launching Pad is a broad-based, disruptive technology that is developing and expanding extremely rapidly. It is advancing **exponentially**. But it is more than that. It is a revolutionary technology capable of creating and sustaining new businesses, new industries, and even new societies. And it is a technology whose capabilities have already become pervasive enough and are growing fast enough to provide the foundations for Superstars. Hence the name "Launching Pad."

In this chapter we focus on the three Launching Pads that alone or together have enabled today's Superstars: **Microelectronics** (specifically integrated circuits), the **Internet**, and **Medical Biotechnology** (or more accurately Biogenetics).

MICROELECTRONICS: AN EXPLOSION OF DISRUPTIVE FORCES

Is Microelectronics-based technology (integrated circuits) THE basic Launching Pad, born in the latter part of the 20th century and continuing to strengthen in this early part of the 21st century? Does it give birth to or at least enable all other Launching Pads? It certainly is a building block for our other two Launching Pads. Think about it. The Internet wouldn't have the large impact on the world it does today without the rapid increases in speed and data handling enabled by advances in Microelectronics. And Biogenetics would not be making its radical breakthroughs without the advanced computers and digital equipment based on Microelectronics that it uses as tools.

However you look at it, Microelectronics has created a revolution. It is pervasive and changing the world as we know it due to rapid advances in the technology. But the advances in Microelectronics are not just rapid. They are being made at **exponentially** increasing rates as the doubling of microprocessor capabilities roughly every two years for the past several decades show. The resulting rapidly shrinking size of integrated circuits and the increased number of these tiny devices fitting on smaller and smaller chips has resulted in dramatic increases in computer processing speeds, hard disk capacities, and more—much more.

These radical improvements in digital electronics related to decreased size of integrated circuits coupled with increased packing density have irreversibly changed nearly every segment of the global economy. Large mainframe computers have been supplanted by small but highly powerful tablets, cell phones have become pervasive and morphed into smartphones, digital photography has almost completely supplanted film-based imaging—the list is endless.

Because of its pervasive and ever-increasing influence, we do consider Microelectronics to be today's most powerful Launching Pad. Thus, we provide more information on this technological revolution than we do on the other Launching Pads, and we use it as an example of what it takes for a fundamental scientific discovery to turn into a technological Launching Pad.

However, keep in mind that nothing is forever. If we had to make a prediction, we would pick the younger and more embryonic Launching Pad, Biogenetics, to be the successor to Microelectronics in the not too distant future. But the focus first is Microelectronics, and we start with a simple science lesson.

The Science behind Integrated Circuits

What is Microelectronics? To answer that question we focus on a basic scientific discovery arising from the study of electron and hole motion in solids that led to inventions in the area of semiconductors and integrated circuits— what we are calling Microelectronics. So, consider a solid.

To most people a solid is just a piece of material that can be handled with their fingers. But in reality certain solids have unusual properties that are defined by microscopic particles, the most common being electrons and holes. A rather abstract concept, is it not? If you were to come across it for the first time, how much would you bet that this would lead to revolutionary changes in our way of life? And yet, this is what happened.

The story in a nutshell: At the end of the Second World War, three scientists at Bell Laboratories, William B. Shockley, John Bardeen, and Walter Brattain were studying electron and hole motion in a particular kind of solid called a semiconductor. And in 1947 they discovered the "transistor effect" for which they were awarded the Nobel Prize in 1956.[27] This was the beginning—a world changing scientific discovery. But there was not yet anything capable of being useful.

From Science to Useable Technology

Moving forward from the "transistor effect," the Bell Lab threesome made crude prototypes of devices called transistors. A transistor is basically a switch that amplifies electrical signals. This innovation was the first step towards practicality. Next it was realized that by coupling transistors together one can build switches that control switches that control other switches, thus building up very complicated logic circuits.

From this came the integrated circuit. (also referred to as an IC, a chip, or a microchip)—an electrical circuit that consists of a set of miniature electronic components, including transistors, all on one small "chip" of semiconductor material, normally silicon. These IC's can be made much smaller than a discrete circuit composed of independent components, a factor that greatly enhances their performance.

In July 1959, Robert Norton Noyce filed for a U.S. Patent on "Semiconductor Device and Lead Structure," a first version of an integrated circuit.[28] But Noyce was not only an inventor. He was also a good businessman. He co-founded Fairchild Semiconductor in 1957 and Intel Corporation in 1968—companies that actually commercialized his invention and built upon it.

The next advance in what we are calling Microelectronics, involved placing increasingly larger numbers of smaller and smaller electronic components on a single chip, creating more and more complex "microprocessors." Very Large Scale Integration (VLSI), as it is called, started with chips containing hundreds of thousands of transistors in the early 1980s, and continues today with beyond several billion transistors on a single chip.

A Bird's Eye View of Progress in Microelectronics: Moore's Law

And now we stop, take a deep breath, and consider the past several decades of Microelectronics advances. The number of transistors on a chip provides a quantitative measure of that chip's capabilities so it is often used as an indicator of progress. And this number is "governed" by the so-called "Moore's Law," named after the scientist (Gordon Moore, co-founder of Intel) who first postulated it.[29] Moore's Law is the observation that, over the history of Microelectronics, the number of transistors in an integrated circuit has doubled approximately every two years—exponential growth! Remarkably, Moore's Law has continued to hold approximately for the past 50 years, and computer industry scientists predict that it will continue to be accurate for several more generations of integrated circuits, based on breakthrough developments such as IBM's research announcement of creating transistors as small as 7 nanometers, half the size of current transistors.[30]

Exponential growth. It's a characteristic of Microelectronics and of the Superstars that the technology enables. But what does that really mean? To put this huge level of growth in perspective, we use a simple example. Imagine that 40 years ago, you saw a small centipede in your home. Say that it was one inch in length. No big deal. But now imagine that you let it be, and the centipede grew with the same exponential law as the performance of integrated circuits. Today hat same centipede would be 200 miles long. Now imagine that it keeps growing for another 40 years at the same rate. The centipede would be larger than the earth, so large that it would be impossible to control. So, this example provides a preliminary answer to the question addressed in some detail in the next part: "Why are there Superstars today but not in earlier times?" It is at least partly because Superstars rely on sustenance from an exponentially growing centipede (Launching Pad), and in earlier times the centipede was too small to matter or didn't even exist.

However, exponential advances in technology raise another question. Although at some point exponential advances in a single technology will stop, what if such exponential development continues, first with one technology, then with another? Are we still going to be the masters of our technology-driven environment, or are we going to be its slaves in an unimaginably altered world? This is an issue we come back to in the Conclusion of this book.

Crossing the "Valley of Death"[31]

Now, returning to Microelectronics. It is the early 1950s, and the transistor has been invented. But it is still only the beginning. Just because a technology has become useable doesn't mean that it will develop into a world changing Launching Pad. The common barrier often preventing the advancement of new technologies to the point where they can have significant business impact has been called the "Valley of Death." The term "Valley of Death" is used to signify the large gap in funding between the end of the research and initial development phases for a technology and the beginning of the generation of funding for further development stemming from the commercialization of the initial products based on that technology. The name illustrates the belief that many good technology-based business projects die because they do not have adequate funds available during this critical, pre-commercialization time interval.

So how did transistors cross this deadly valley to become Microelectronics as we know it today? The answer is straight forward—government funding. And one of the main funders was DARPA (the Pentagon's Defense Advanced Research Projects Agency).

DARPA was created in 1957 to keep the United States technologically competitive with the Soviet Union. DARPA's contributions in many technological areas, including Microelectronics, are truly remarkable.[32] One of its first "products" was NASA, an agency that needs no description. One of its early projects was Arpanet—a war-fighting telecommunications network to electronically connect scientists and officials during and after a World War, that would eventually become the Internet, the next launching pad we discuss. And when the U.S. Air Force needed a way to guide its ballistic missiles towards military targets, DARPA funded a project that later became the foundation for the Global Positioning System (GPS) that is commonly used for navigation in cars and many other devices. And this list is only a start. DARPA has been and continues to be a key player in funding the development of life-changing inventions.

With respect to transistors, the DARPA programs and

other Navy programs supported the product development phase of the transistor for military applications; and then sales to the military provided funding that kept the technology "growing." These sales to the military accounted for the total $4 million integrated circuit market in 1962. Government funding continued, and as a consequence, additional new Microelectronics based products were developed, and their manufacturing costs continued to drop. The average price per integrated circuit dropped from $50 in 1962 to $2.33 in 1968.[33] At that point, several companies saw the opportunity to develop products for commercial markets, and integrated circuits began to appear in consumer products. The evolution of Microelectronics had become self-sustaining, and the explosive growth began. Microelectronics had successfully crossed the Valley of Death, thanks to government funding.

Stepping back and looking at the bigger picture, this example provides a partial answer to a question we address in Chapter 6: Why are today's Superstars based in the U.S.? Simply stated, in the last half of the 20th century, U.S. Government funds paid for basic research and initial development/commercialization in key new technology areas.

However that may be changing. In a New York Times article about his interview with Gordon Moore, Thomas Friedman writes that Moore stated: "I am disappointed that the government seems to be decreasing its support for basic research. That is really where these ideas get started. They take a long time to germinate, but eventually they lead to some marvelous advances."[34] And in a Fortune article entitled "Bill Gates Calls on the U.S. Government to Invest More in R&D," Gates is quoted as saying:

> "Government funding for our world-class research institutions produces the new technologies

that American entrepreneurs take to market... But while other nations like South Korea and China have drastically upped their R&D spending, the United States has essentially flat-lined... If the United States is going to maintain its leading role, it needs to up its game."[35]

Will the US now lose its technological leadership? In the future who will provide funding to cross the "Valley of Death" for basic science and technology and high risk start-up ventures where private investors and angel investors fear to tread?

All is not lost. Despite the cuts, DARPA has still a budget of several billion dollars, and has now started work on new technologies such as the brain-machine interface. As Washington Post editor Joel Garreau has noted: "What DARPA is doing by spending many millions of dollars (in this area alone) is to create what might well be the next step in human evolution."[36]

The Microelectronics Era: A Business Revolution

Finally, we focus on the Microelectronics **business** revolution that followed the invention and commercialization of integrated circuits. It started with Bell Labs having an important business realization, radical for those times: Development of the transistor (for which they held the rights) would move much more quickly if they opened up the field to other companies. So in September 1951, Bell Labs hosted a symposium to discuss the transistor and offered licenses to their technology.[37] Twenty-six companies, both big (such as IBM and General Electric) and small (such as the Texas Instruments of that time) signed up.

As a result of Bell Labs actions, the transistor radio, introduced in 1954, was the first consumer product based on their technology.[38] It was a joint project between the Regency Division of Industrial Development Engineering Associates and Texas Instruments (TI). However the product was discontinued after TI changed business direction. At the same time, a small tape recorder manufacturer in Japan called Tokyo Tsushin Kogyo had decided to devote their whole company to commercial products like transistor radios. This company was renamed Sony,[39] and the age of consumer electronics had begun, enabled by Microelectronics.

However, the mushrooming business and consumer impact of IC's wasn't quite that simple. A lot of the technology-based progress made after the original invention was due to making each new IC "invention" (generation) immediately and easily accessible to many other people who then provided a number of secondary inventions and thus multiplied the effect of the first. New examples of the power of such "collective innovation" or "piggybacking" are emerging every day, resulting in diverse advances such as 3D printers using advanced computer capabilities and ANSYS engineering simulation software for personal computers.

In summary, today an astonishing stream of new products, new companies, and new capabilities has already resulted from the Microelectronics business revolution.[40] And that revolution is still young. But now, couple Microelectronics with the Internet, our next Launching Pad, and the world is forever changed.

THE INTERNET[41]: CREATING AN INTER-CONNECTED WORLD

The Internet: Then and Now

Think back to the world of the late 1990s and early

2000s—the first decade or so of the public Internet:

> "...mobile cellular devices ('smartphones' and other cellular devices), which today provide near-universal [Internet] access, were used for business and were not a routine household item owned by parents and children worldwide. Social media in the modern sense had yet to come into existence, laptops were bulky and most households did not have computers. Data rates were slow and most people lacked means to video or digitize video so websites such as YouTube did not yet exist, media storage was transitioning slowly from analog tape to digital optical discs (DVD and to an extent still, floppy disc to CD)....various software frameworks, which enabled and simplified speed of web development, largely awaited invention and their eventual widespread adoption.
>
> The Internet was widely used for mailing lists, emails, e-commerce and early popular online shopping (Amazon and eBay for example), online forums and bulletin boards, and personal websites and blogs, and use was growing rapidly, but by more modern standards the systems used were static and lacked widespread social engagement."[42]

Now fast-forward to the current day. The evolving Internet, coupled with high-speed Wi-Fi and expanding cellular networks, has changed almost everything. It has fueled the rapid shift from magazines and newspapers to online news and social media, from physical storefronts to online retailing, from simple spreadsheets to big data and analytics, from device computing to cloud computing, and more. The world has rapidly converted from all analog to digital almost everything and has become irreversibly interconnected as a result—enabled by the Internet.

Think about Internet induced changes from a

communications standpoint. Cell phones have become smartphones which can connect to the Internet. Thus they not only often replace landlines, but also provide the ability to communicate with and readily access information from almost every corner of the world. Social media, enabled by the Internet, gives much of the population of our planet a way to communicate instantly with each other. And the powerful combination of smartphones with social media has the ability to create significant political action, such as the insurgences of the so-called "Arab Spring" and the not-so-desirable spread of ISIS around the globe.

Put all of this together, and it is clear. The Internet is a key part of our global societies' infrastructure and a Launching Pad in its own right.

The Creation of the Internet

So what is this un-seeable, untouchable Launching Pad that is called the Internet? The simplest explanation is that the Internet is a high-speed, often wireless, way to transmit digital data over long distances. It is a vast global system of interconnected computer networks used to link several billion devices worldwide. It consists of millions of private, academic, business, and government networks, linked by a broad array of different networking technologies. As most people today understand it, the Internet provides the capability for an individual using a computer (or tablet or smartphone) which is connected to the network to access and/or transmit information across the network for a variety of purposes—email, instant communication, information gathering, advertising, retail purchasing and much more.

Unlike the transistor, the Internet is not a "thing" and had no single inventor. It is a capability that has evolved over time. The inspiration (or vision) for the Internet is attributed to J. C. R. Licklider, who proposed in his January

1960 paper: "A network of such [computers], connected to one another by wide-band communication lines [which provide] the functions of present-day libraries together with anticipated advances in information storage and retrieval and [other] symbiotic functions."[43]

Then, as we described above in Crossing the Valley of Death, development of the DARPA funded ARPANET was started in the late 1960s, based on this vision. The original goal for ARPANET was to create an academic network that would allow users of a "research computer" at one university to "talk to" research computers at other universities. The military interest, and hence DARPA funding, was because messages could be routed or rerouted in more than one direction. Thus the network could continue to function even if parts of it were destroyed in the event of a military attack or other disaster. This was viewed as a critical capability in the Cold War era.

ARPANET, once realized, was then expanded in the 1980s with additional government funding (more help in crossing the Valley of Death) from agencies such as the National Aeronautics and Space Administration (NASA), the National Science Foundation (NSF), and the Department of Energy (DOE). But it was the declassification of the ARPANET in 1989 that led to worldwide participation in the development of new networking technologies that led to increased Internet utility.

However new networking technologies were only a start. Like with Microelectronics, it took innovation upon innovation to create today's Internet as a Launching Pad. The first breakthrough: In 1991 a computer programmer named Tim Berners-Lee introduced the World Wide Web (www), changing the Internet from just a way to send files from one place to another to something that was itself a "web" of information that anyone on the Internet could retrieve. Then in the 90s came the development of web browsers and a government act that allowed commercial use of the Internet. E-commerce was born and with it came the dot.com boom (and then bust).

But this still wasn't the pervasive Internet of today. The changes that would propel the Internet into its place as a global social system took place during a relatively short period, starting around 2004. Key advancements included:

- Powerful laptop computers becoming less costly and widely available
- Increased capacity and miniaturization of memory devices—from floppy discs to hard drives to solid state drives
- Higher speed data transmission
- Wider Internet access at lower prices
- The emergence of social media and websites such as Twitter and Facebook

And then came the "mobile revolution" which put the Internet into the hands of much of human society, of all ages, as they moved around their daily lives. Microelectronics developments had enabled high levels of computing activity on small handheld devices leading to Internet enabled smartphones and tablets. This allowed much of humanity to share, discuss, and continually update and respond to each other.

Together, all of this has created an Internet that interconnects and reshapes our world. But will it continue? One of the technologies responsible for the explosion of the Internet relates to faster and faster data transmission through optical fibers. According to Gerry/Gerald Butters the former head of Lucent's Optical Networking Group at Bell Labs, there is a "law" called Butters' Law of Photonics, which parallels Moore's law.[44]   It is based on the technology that enables the transmission of large amounts of data at the speed of light—optical fibers. Butter's law says that the amount of data coming out of an optical fiber is doubling every nine months. Thus, the cost of transmitting a bit of information over an optical network decreases by half every nine months. There is no question that this kind of increase in capability will help fuel the Internet's capability as a Launching Pad. But for how long? That probably depends on the emergence of a few more innovation building blocks.

For now, just remember what we described in Chapter 3. More than half of today's Unicorns are built on or enabled by the Internet. Impressive numbers for a clearly healthy Launching Pad.

MEDICAL BIOTECHNOLOGY (BIOGENETICS): THE RAPIDLY EMERGING NEW FRONTIER

Biotechnology[45]

Biotechnology, in general terms, can be defined as: the manipulation of living organisms or their components to produce (manufacture) useful products such as pest resistant crops, new bacterial strains, or novel pharmaceuticals. Today this includes things such as the use of bioreactors in manufacturing, microorganisms to degrade oil slicks or organic waste, genetically engineered bacteria to produce human hormones, and monoclonal antibodies to identify antigens.

But Biotechnology is not new. Humans have been manipulating living organisms to improve their way of life for millennia. It goes back to early societies in which people collected seeds of plants with the most desirable traits for planting the next year. There is also some historical evidence that Babylonians, Egyptians and Romans used these same types of selective practices for breeding cattle. And even as far back as 6000 B.C., humans produced beer, wine and bread using fermentation, a process in which the biological activity of some living bacteria is critical.

Jump forward to the mid-19th century. It was then that Gregor Mendel used experiments with seeds and plants to develop his principles of inheritance that described the transmission of genetic traits—before anyone knew physical genes existed. Mendel's work became the cornerstone of modern genetics, and it was the first step in the transformation of Biotechnology to the more focused Medical Biotechnology (Biogenetics) that we have identified as a Launching Pad.

But it wasn't until the mid-20th century that researchers focused their efforts on the physical nature of genes and the connection between genes and proteins. Once they did, they found a direct relationship between mutations of a gene and the sequence of amino acids in a protein. Then, in the 1940s and early 1950s, experiments pointed to DNA as the portion of chromosomes (and perhaps other nucleoproteins) that held genes. The discovery of the double helical structure of DNA in 1953 by James Watson and Francis Crick was a flash point. It formed the foundation for today's era of molecular genetics that revolves around DNA.

Medical Biotechnology (Biogenetics)

Although our Superstars and the Unicorns from the medical field are called Biotechnology companies (and we will continue to refer to them as such), the more accurate name for the technological area that is their foundation is Medical Biotechnology, and more specifically Biogenetics. As we explained in Chapter 2, Medical Biotechnology can be defined as the science of using living cells and cell materials to produce pharmaceutical and diagnostic products that help treat and prevent human diseases.

Today, the process commonly used in Medical Biotechnology is genetic engineering. Genetic engineering refers to scientific procedures that allow the direct manipulation of genetic material in order to alter the hereditary traits of a cell, organism, or population. Thus Biogenetics, our Launching Pad, is the broad technology area that uses genetic engineering to alter genomes of living organisms.

As we highlighted in the last section, the actual evolution from Biotechnology to Biogenetics started with the discovery to the 3-D structure of DNA. Key events from that point on are summarized in the "Timeline for Medical Biotechnology" found on the Amgen (one of our Superstars) Website,[46] so we won't repeat them here. However, there is one key breakthrough that stands out from the others.

In 1973, Stanley Cohen and Herbert Boyer performed the first successful recombinant DNA experiment, using bacterial genes. They were able to insert a recombinant DNA molecule (rDNA) into a foreign cell and have it replicate—gene cloning.

What is rDNA? It is a form of DNA that has been created (genetically engineered) by combining at least two segments of DNA (genetic material) from at least two different species, creating sequences that would not otherwise be found in the genome. Finding a way to insert such rDNA into a foreign cell and have it replicate was the fundamental discovery that served as the catalyst for the age of genetic engineering and the foundation for Biogenetics. In 1980, Cohen and Boyer were awarded a U.S. patent for this world-changing invention.

The first licensed drug generated using the Cohen/Boyer recombinant DNA technology was human insulin, developed by Genentech. And the rest of the story is the one we told in our Chapter on Superstars. Biotechnology companies have become big businesses and

Superstars.[47] As Fortune magazine states regarding Biotechnology (Biogenetics) companies:

> "Over the past decade the market value of Fortune 500 pharmaceutical companies has nearly doubled to $ 1.5 Trillion, thanks largely to the explosive growth of Biotechnology firms. …. These have a combined market cap that is fast approaching that of the old guard Pharma companies."[48]

Clearly, whatever you call it—Biotechnology or Medical Biotechnology or Biogenetics—this technologically rich area qualifies as a Launching Pad, and perhaps an even greater one than Microelectronics. It's hard to predict since Biogenetics is still in its infancy, with new potentially breakthrough advances being made at an ever increasing pace. At this point it is not clear if these new discoveries will just be the fuel for the Biogenetics Launching Pad, or whether one or more will become Launching Pads in their own right. Four of these emerging areas—cloning of genes and organisms, stem cell research, TALENs, and CRISPR—appear to us to be the most promising. Therefore we address each in more detail in Chapter 14 as examples of embryonic Launching Pads.

AMPLIFYING THE POWER OF LAUNCHING PADS

The three Launching Pads described in this chapter are the essential building blocks for today's Superstars, but these technologies don't exist in isolation. We are in the midst of a technology created "perfect storm" where the explosive advances in Microelectronics, the Internet, and Biotechnology are intersecting and amplifying the power of one another. This is creating an explosion of innovations and changing the world as we know it. And it appears that it is these symbiotic relationships that are fueling the creation of Superstars.

Perhaps the most obvious example of the power of a symbiotic relationship between launching pads is the marriage of Microelectronics and the Internet by Microsoft. In the section devoted to this company in Chapter 3 we stated: "Microsoft was a little late in utilizing the 'explosion' of the Internet, but nevertheless by 1995, 20 years after the company's beginning, Microsoft had reached $6 billion in revenue (not quite fast enough to be classified as a superstar, but still quite impressive), without even 'riding on the coat-tails' of the Internet."

But then things changed. As we further described: "The company started taking advantage of the Internet in the middle of the 90s decade. In 1997, Internet Explorer 4.0 was introduced (together with Microsoft Office 97), competing with Netscape, and by agreement with Apple Computer, Internet Explorer was bundled with the Apple Macintosh operating system as well as with Windows." Would Microsoft have become a Superstar of its own if it had not delayed "joining forces" with the Internet? Of course we cannot judge history in hindsight, but it is a fair question to ask.

Microsoft is not the only company that benefited from synergy between technological launching pads. As we alluded to above, it's actually a characteristic of all of the Superstars we have discussed. Apple is a company owing its success to the symbiosis between the Microelectronics Launching Pad (small devices like iPhones) and the Internet (worldwide connections). Amazon is no different. For this company the Microelectronics-enabled high speed Internet broadband capabilities coupled with software developed for the Internet enabled a small book seller to become an Internet retail giant. The synergy of Launching Pads for the Biotechnology-based Superstars isn't quite as obvious, until you think about it. But without the advances in Microelectronics, Biogenetics as we know it today wouldn't exist.

However, there are numerous important advances, that are happening right now as a result of the this technological symbiosis. These are described as future Launching Pads in Chapters 14 and 15. As a preview, consider the field of Nanotechnology and the nanomedicine stemming from it, where breakthroughs will be made because of the intersection of nanodevices with biological matter. Or, look further into the future. Think about the possibilities that could arise from a symbiotic relationship between studies on the human brain with the field of complexity science. And this is only the beginning. Bottom line, in today's interconnected world, rapidly developing technologies are also interconnected.

Five

ACT OF CREATION
The Spark Starting it All

Being propelled forward by a Launching Pad is not sufficient for the development of a Superstar. Another absolutely critical factor (and a more obvious one) is the Act of Creation. This "act" may be an individual's flash of insight that leads to the creation of a new business concept or it may be a technical invention that stems from a Launching Pad or some combination of both. For example, how much of Apple's explosive success is due to new technology versus speed of introduction of ever more innovative new products, versus creative marketing? The specific answer doesn't matter. What is clear is that without significant and repeated Acts of Creation there would be no Superstars, only companies that are followers.

But what is this critical spark that leads a talented individual to originate truly innovative new ideas and turn them into a world-changing business? Where does the spark come from? And why are the resulting Acts of Creation that give rise to Superstars concentrated in the United States? When you examine creativity in arts and sciences, you find that it is distributed fairly evenly throughout the globe. But not so with business creativity, at least for now. We won't attempt to provide definitive answers to these questions. Instead we use examples to give insight into this intangible thing called the Act of Creation. Why do we bother? Because it is through such acts that all new and great things start.

THE ORIGIN OF IDEAS

The sources of breakthrough ideas are described in the classic book by A. Koestler where he discusses the origins of the act of creation.[49] In the Forward to that book, Professor Sir Cyril Burt writes:

> "If there is such a thing as creativity...then it is clear that civilization must owe much, if not everything, to the individual so gifted." And: "The greater the number and variety of genuinely creative minds a nation can produce and cultivate, the faster will be its rate of progress." And finally: "...in these egalitarian days it requires some courage to pick up the pen and defend the concept of 'creative genius' against the onslaughts of the scientific sceptic."

We can support the idea of the existence of particularly gifted individuals with a personal example. One of us (Ennio Fatuzzo) used to live in Zurich: "On many days I took the public trolley car to go from my office to ETH, the Zurich Polytechnic. Every time I passed by a church that was on the way, I looked at the clock on the church tower and used this information to adjust the time on my watch, which was not very accurate." Well, once upon a time, Albert Einstein took the same route on the same trolley car when he was traveling from the patent office, where he was working, to his home. But going by the same church and looking at the same clock tower made him wonder not whether his watch was accurate, but whether time on his trolley car was affected by the motion of the car. And this spark of creative thinking led to his breakthrough theories.

Why such a difference in thinking, besides the obvious fact that Einstein was a genius? Part of the answer can be found in an opening sentence in the 2003 Annual Report of Amgen that in our opinion describes very well the act of creation:

> "It starts with a flash of insight
> A potentially life-changing discovery
> And then the really hard work begins"

Yes, there is a lot of hard work involved, but it all starts with a flash of insight by an individual that in one particular moment sees the world differently.

Going back to Koestler's book, he argues that the scientist's insight is the same as the artist's act of creation. Almost 50 years later one can see that this general concept of creativity involving a flash of insight is still valid by looking at the evidence in the world around us. For example, any manager who has headed a research laboratory can attest to this by observing the best scientists at work. But we also believe that the act of creation in business is the same as in science and art. All such acts originate from the creativity and flashes of insight of individuals.

BARRIERS TO CREATIVITY

The question still remains as to **how** any of these creators come up with their breakthrough ideas. Does the flash of insight occur in group meetings, so popular today? Probably not. In pursuit of an answer we first briefly review how this "act" often happens in the scientific world.

We start by examining one key barrier to the creation of

radically new ideas—the kinds of ideas necessary for a breakthrough discovery or invention. This is the barrier that stems from all the new interactive activities typical of today's life. Specifically, the more we are engaged in communicating, as spurred by the developments stemming from the progress in Microelectronics, the less time we have for ourselves—alone—to think and create completely new ideas.

A recent article in Physics Today describes the importance and power of silence and solitude in setting the stage for an act of creation.[50] And the article goes on to explain that Silence and Solitude are becoming precious commodities. They are "being crowded out by the hurrahs in favor of collaboration, engagement, outreach." Examples of famous new ideas in the field of physics and how they were created in silence and solitude are given in the article. "Speaking of silence and solitude," the article states, "Isaac Newton craved it. So did Albert Einstein. And Henry Cavendish and Paul Dirac positively exuded it. Silence and its companion solitude seem to be a recurring feature in the history of physics."

Another, albeit mixed example, led to the creation of Schrodinger's equations. A few days before the Christmas of 1925, Schrodinger, a Viennese-born professor of physics at the University of Zurich "took off for a two-and-a-half-week vacation at a villa in the Swiss Alpine town of Arosa. Leaving his wife and children in Zurich, he took along de Broglie's thesis, in addition to...a former Viennese girlfriend and two pearls. Placing a pearl in each ear to screen out any distracting noise, Schrodinger set to work on wave mechanics. When he and the mystery lady emerged from the rigors of their holiday on Jan. 9, 1926, the great discovery was firmly in hand."[51] Thus here too, silence and a sort of solitude played an important role in setting the stage for the act of creation.

However, as expressed above, today there is a real

danger that the conditions necessary for stimulating all of this creativity in individuals are being crowded out by group activities and the almost constant interactions that may be socially desirable but certainly do not spur the creation of breakthrough new ideas. Having said that, it is important to keep in mind that such activities and interactions are often desirable (or even essential) in the development phase of an invention. They just are not helpful in the creation of a basic concept. One other point: It is important not to confuse solitude with loneliness, which Mother Theresa once described as "the most terrible poverty of all." At times we crave solitude, but we always fear loneliness. Thus when solitude turns to loneliness, it becomes a barrier to creativity.

And now we move from scientific creativity to the act of creation in business. One of the most familiar examples of the creation of completely novel and breakthrough business ideas is that of Steve Jobs and Apple. Brett T. Robinson, visiting professor of marketing at the University of Notre Dame, has published a book that details how Jobs intermingled the technological and the transcendent.[52] In his book, Robinson argues that religion—from Zen Buddhism to Catholicism to mystical futurism—defined Jobs' design methodology and approach to business. Robinson adds:

> "Jobs' Zen master Kobun Chino told him that he 'could keep in touch with his spiritual side while running a business.' So in true Zen fashion, Jobs avoided thinking of technology and spirituality in dualistic terms. But what really set him apart was his ability to educate the public about personal computing in both practical and mythic ways. The iconography of the Apple computer company, the advertisements, and the device screens of the Macintosh, iPod, iPhone, and iPad are visual

expressions of Jobs' imaginative marriage of spiritual science and modern technology."

And certainly none of this is the result of consensus meetings or marketing panels! In other words, it appears that spirituality can be added to silence and solitude as factors encouraging the act of creation.

One additional example of the act of creation in business is Jeff Bezos' flash of insight that resulted in Amazon.com. As we described in Chapter 2, Bezos daydreamed about such a company during a long, lonely drive from New York to Seattle, in 1994. And when he arrived at destination, he had already written a business plan for the initial embodiment of Amazon. This seems to be a clear example of the importance of silence and solitude for creativity.

There are other examples of business flashes of insight that we could provide, but the above well-known stories illustrate our points. One conclusion that we can draw is that the act of creation for a breakthrough business revolves around silence, solitude and contemplation, just like the creation of revolutionary scientific theories. Teamwork and consensus meetings, email and Facebook are not part of this process.

And a broader conclusion supports the premise we stated in the beginning of this chapter: Without repeated acts of creation by a special individual, there wouldn't be any breakthrough businesses, there wouldn't be any Superstars. But keep in mind that creativity and leadership don't have to reside in the same person. Yes, that creative individual may be the exceptional leader that creates the Superstar, such as Jeff Bezos. However, Gilead Sciences provides an example showing it can be just as effective for the driver of commercialization, in partnership with the inventor(s), to create a Superstar.

Six

OTHER KEY ATTRIBUTES
OF SUPERSTARS

Yes, Launching Pads and Acts of Creation are essential requirements for creating Superstars, but together they still are not sufficient. Today's Superstars have other characteristics in common that should be considered. In this chapter we highlight four of these characteristics that we believe are key: leadership, unconventional approaches, market focus, and availability of funding.

However, it is important to keep in mind that while the exploration of these points of intersection may be informative and provide guidance, such comparisons also have limitations. Specifically, we highlight only a few commonalities while neglecting others.

Nevertheless we believe that we have identified certain attributes that can lead to a higher-than-average chance of successfully creating a Superstar. Therefore, in the following sections, we proceed with our look at key characteristics of Superstars in hopes that they provide insight as to why the Superstars are enjoying such unprecedented success, against the backdrop of the "average" corporation.

EXCEPTIONAL LEADERSHIP

Much has already been written about the importance of leadership in general, and the leaders of today's Superstars more specifically. We highlighted some of this information in our brief histories of the Superstars in Chapter 2. Drawing on this information and our own experiences and research, we provide here a short summary of some of the common leadership characteristics that we believe are essential for Superstars.

First, an intelligent, strong-willed leader whom people will follow (not necessarily like) is required. This leader must be a risk-taker who is unafraid of making mistakes, and who enthusiastically embraces the unconventional, ranging from unusual management styles to untested business models. This leader also must be able and willing to rapidly reinvent (or support and partner with those creative individuals who can reinvent) everything again and again as circumstances dictate—from business models and business definitions to entire product lines.

To say this in a different way, to create a Superstar a leader must be able to think and act "outside of the box." Does this mean that these leaders have to have that nebulous ability called "vision?"

Our answer is: not always. Remember that some of the "visions" of leaders like Steve Jobs or Jeff Bezos led to actions that were clearly mistakes. But these same leaders also made correct decisions repeatedly, year after year. Clearly, in some cases the vision of a strong leader can create and drive markets.

One last commonality among Superstar leaders. The leaders must have exceptional commitment, persistence, and stamina to be able survive seemingly disastrous occurrences in their business and personal lives without declaring defeat—incidents we highlighted such as getting fired, ending up in hospital for stress, or having to work impossible hours, sometimes for no compensation. How many people are willing and capable to endure all of that to end up winning in business? The answer, of course, is only a few—those few capable of leading their enterprise to Superstar status.

EMPHASIS ON THE UNCONVENTIONAL

In the previous section, we described leaders of Superstars as enthusiastically embracing the unconventional. But it's even more extreme than that. Our perhaps controversial conclusions: First, today's Superstars, as businesses, did not follow the precepts of typical Business Schools, but rather developed from multiple innovations coupled with unconventional approaches in all aspects of business and business management. We believe that if you follow conventional business wisdom you can create a very good or even great company, but you cannot create a Superstar. Superstars are synonymous with innovation and nontraditional approaches to everything.

This leads to our second observation and conclusion. Today's Superstars all began as small, independent, start-up ventures. This allowed them the freedom to be different. Thus we conclude that it would be very difficult, if not impossible for an embryonic Superstar to develop within an existing, large corporation. And our own experiences with innovation in large corporations support our view.

Moderna Therapeutics, one of the Unicorns we highlighted in Chapter 3, is an example of unconventional management coupled with technical breakthroughs in a way that is unique. As we described, the company uses an unusual business model (the "Moderna Ecosystem") that allows it to simultaneously advance numerous internal and external development programs. Is Moderna's new approach the beginning of a revolution in business management that others will follow? Only time will tell, but we believe it has a good chance to succeed.

MARKET FOCUS

Another key common characteristic of the Superstars is Market Focus, and we mean specifically "market" **not** "marketing." Of course the Superstars have demonstrated varying kinds of marketing innovation, but one thing they have in common are the characteristics of the markets they address. First, their markets are truly global. Yes, each started in the U.S., but each quickly expanded to foreign markets. If that were not the case, they never would have been able to achieve and sustain their explosive growth. Large as it may be, a U.S. market alone wouldn't have been large enough.

Next, the customers of the Superstars are the end users. As we alluded to in Chapter 3, suppliers can be exceptional companies, but their market is limited to and by other companies. Superstars, on the other hand, whose products address individuals or the needs of individuals, have orders of magnitude greater possibilities.

Last, the markets that today's Superstars address, were initially uninhabited. In other words, the Superstars either created their own markets or were the first to market with their new-to-the-world offerings. No fast follower or copycat has yet become a Superstar.

ACCESS TO FUNDING

The last key characteristic that we call out is "birthplace." All of our Superstars (and the vast majority of Unicorns) were started in the United States. Why? It's not an accident. We could say that there is more freedom for innovation/creativity in the United States. Or we could say that there is more support and encouragement in the U.S. for **young** university researchers to invent and become involved in founding new business ventures.

These may be contributing factors, but we focus on another, perhaps more important reason: financing. As described in Chapter 4 in the section on "crossing the valley of death," larger amounts of cash have been and still are more readily available in the U.S. than in the rest of the world for funding high-risk ventures. Some of this financial support comes from venture capital firms and from angel investors. In addition, in a number of areas, particularly those driven by technology, significant government funding is also available. That's not saying any of this funding is easy to get, but it is out there for U.S. based enterprises and not accessible to start-ups in other countries.

WHY SUPERSTARS ONLY NOW?

PART III

Seven

THE PAST
Trailblazers, Not Superstars

Today, whether companies are Exceptional or Superstars, their stories almost always start with technology-driven, **revolutionary** change. But this kind of disruptive change and its impact on business isn't new. So why were there no Superstars in previous times?

To answer that question, this chapter describes the birth and early development of several "exceptional" companies from the past that, in their times, outperformed most other companies in their Industries in sales and profit growths. Why did these "trailblazers" not grow fast enough to become Superstars? Would they have become Superstars in today's business environment? To address these questions, we start with a brief history of technology-driven, revolutionary changes. Then we turn to examples of actual companies.

TECHNOLOGY-DRIVEN REVOLUTIONARY CHANGE: A BRIEF HISTORY

Of course, technology revolution is certainly not new. Since the beginning of human civilizations, there have been many technology-driven revolutionary changes. Early examples, as early as prehistoric times, are the inventions of fire-making and of the wheel. However more recent technology revolutions are more relevant to the making of exceptional companies. Thus we start by taking a quick look at the "Industrial Revolution."

Today, in industrialized nations, products are manufactured swiftly by the process of mass production, on assembly lines, using power-driven machines. People of older times had no such products or systems. The Industrial Revolution[53] is the name given to the collection of technology-based inventions which enabled this current way of life. The key driving forces for this revolution were 1) the invention of machines to do the work of hand tools; 2) the use of steam, and later of other kinds of power (e.g., gas, oil, electricity), in place of the muscles of human beings and of animals; and 3) the adoption of the factory system.

Starting in the late 1700s, and continuing through the early 1900s, this technology-driven revolution was characterized by things such as the building of railroads, large scale iron and steel production, large factories taking the place of small shops, widespread use of machinery in manufacturing, and the coming of age of oil. These disruptive developments totally changed the way of life of large masses of people, by providing employment for many (albeit not always with good working conditions) and enabling the production of goods in large quantities at low cost, thus making them accessible to many. But these technology-driven changes, although revolutionary, were slow to develop, at least by modern standards. They took over two centuries to evolve.

Moving ahead to the 20th century, the invention of the vacuum tube and its impact on telecommunications and the birth of companies like RCA, based on this original invention, led to the era of electronics, in general, and consumer electronics specifically. Again this is an example of a technology-driven revolution that has had and continues to have a very large impact on our way of life and the way we do business. And this time the revolution only took a few decades. Yes, electronics was a broad-based, disruptive technology; but it did not develop and expand as rapidly as those technologies we have called Launching Pads.

But it is not just about speed. There is another aspect of technology-driven disruptive change that is important to consider. Clearly, some basic inventions have long-term consequences radically different from others. Some are like cannon shots that cause great turmoil, but are not followed by a sweeping "tail" of progress on many different fronts. Such cannon shots awaken people to new, albeit constrained horizons, and then leave them free to explore new areas of technology and business, but only within those horizons. However, other types of basic inventions involve technologies that keep propagating, and have an effect more similar to that of a rocket with continuous propulsion.

The technologies and businesses stemming from the Industrial Revolution (power first from steam, then oil, then electricity) are examples of multiple "cannon shots" of their times, based on multiple technologies. The invention of the vacuum tube could be viewed as a specific and more recent "cannon shot." However this particular invention was more than that. It was the beginning of the era of electronics—a time where simple electrical circuits became more and more powerful, fueled by a stream of disruptive technologies involving active electrical components such as transistors and diodes. Thus unlike the Industrial Revolution, Electronics can be viewed as a rocket with continuous propulsion and the vacuum tube as its first disruptive technology.

Was the Electronics of the 20th century a Launching Pad? It certainly provided the basis for a number of exceptional companies. However the technology propagation was not fast enough to produce Superstars. Something was missing. To provide some insight, we highlight several "almost Superstars" from the 20th century.

TRAILBLAZERS IN THE 20TH CENTURY

In the first part of the 20th century, tsunamis of disruptive change, technology-driven and/or otherwise created, were pervasive. They provided an environment where exceptional companies were born and flourished. To try to understand why these Trailblazers from the past didn't reach the heights of today's Superstars we provide four examples.

Ford Motor Company[54]: The Birth of the Automobile Industry

The invention of the automobile at the beginning of the 20th century was not enough at first to create great successes. The gasoline-powered engine had been invented in Europe, and Karl Benz and Gottlieb Daimler of Germany incorporated it into the first automobile. However, it was in the Ford Motor Company that the vision of "assembly line production" was developed. Ford designed a car and built a factory based on this new concept.

In 1908, this factory produced the Model T Ford, a car much less expensive to build than any other at the time, which made it the world's first "affordable" car. Ford's manufacturing-based innovation quickly led to the birth of the modern automobile industry, the death of the "horse and buggy" era, and the rise of the Ford Motor Company as an industry leader. Its birth and growth were the brainchild of Henry Ford and were not greatly affected by the economy, or by the First World War. However, the company did have a **profound effect** on the economy, first in the US and later worldwide, so that the economic landscape was not the cause of Ford's success, rather it was shaped by this success. We will see later in other examples that the birth and initial growth of several other companies were tightly interwoven with the economy of that time, while others were not.

Yes, the Ford Motor Company was a business started by a technology-enabled act of creation that resulted in extreme growth and worldwide impact. But the basic technology foundation was more or less a single "cannon shot." After its first explosive disruption it evolved incrementally. It provided Ford with excellent growth, but that success took decades.

McDonald's[55]: From Cars to Fast Food

No name is quite as synonymous with convenience and mega-success as McDonald's. The first McDonald's was a drive-in restaurant opened in 1940 by two brothers, Richard and Maurice McDonald. Revolutionary for that time, McDonald's customers were able to remain in their cars to order and then eat food delivered to them by servers known as "carhops." The brothers were successful with their new drive-in concept, and it wasn't long before they decided to expand.

To accomplish this, the McDonald brothers developed a new type of restaurant based on a combination of several concepts: assembly-line food preparation using unskilled and lower-paid workers instead of cooks; a limited menu with items that could be prepared ahead of time; disposable "dinnerware" (paper and plastic), and self-service where for the first time customers had to stand in line to order and wait for their food. This combination of concepts allowed the brothers to produce large quantities of food for a low price, less than half that of competing restaurants, and to serve it fast. The prices were important to the restaurants' success because World War II left many families with far lower incomes than in the past. In addition, the brothers marketed hamburgers as the food of choice for kids, instead of promoting them as cheap fare. The first "McDonald's Restaurant" based on these innovations opened in 1948, and was a huge success. This was the beginning of the fast-food revolution that ultimately led to a dramatic global success for McDonald's and the creation of an entirely new multi-billion dollar industry that continues to have far-reaching effects on the world's economy, health and social norms. It is interesting to note that the jump-start of MacDonald's was helped rather than hindered by the hard economic times of the post-World War period.

A business act of creation in a world changed by war and technology-driven industrialization. Although there was no clear technology base, this business disruptive change ultimately resulted in extreme global success. But again, it took decades.

Radio Corporation of America (RCA)[56]: A Technology Driven Giant

Next, turn back the clock to the first half of the 20th century and focus on RCA, the then great (but now defunct except for its trademark) electronics manufacturing company. In its time, RCA invented many disruptive new technologies; and the company used these radical innovations to reach great heights of success. With its revolutionary radio and television products, RCA created an entire new industry—consumer electronics. Innovation clearly was the driving force and the key to success. However we are not talking about unbridled innovation.

RCA had a powerful and visionary leader, David Sarnoff.

It was the clearly articulated visions of Sarnoff that started RCA on its quest to create the future. Sarnoff passionately believed in the revolutionary potential of three not-yet-invented products for markets that didn't exist at the time: commercial radio, black-and-white television, and color television. There was essentially no market research to support these product concepts, and the technologies needed did not exist. But that didn't faze Sarnoff. He told his laboratories directly what specific products were to be invented. He did not specify how to design them, but he did dictate exactly what the final products had to do for the customer. None of these directives were questioned by the organization. After all, times were different then; and Sarnoff was the President.

To say it another way, in the early days of RCA, David Sarnoff made most key decisions with only minimal input from his organization or management team. He alone decided the direction of the company and which programs would be funded. This visionary leadership approach led to great successes for a while—when RCA was the primary developer of the disruptive technologies and when management missteps and program inefficiencies were not important because there was no meaningful competition.

What happened? Well, David Sarnoff did have a vision for another disruptive product—the video recorder. And he communicated this vision to his company just before he retired. But then, new leadership that "followed the rules" took over, and RCA became a different and more traditional company. Serious competition appeared, and many management "mistakes" were made (no clear direction, unwise financial investments, constantly changing technology choices, etc.), leading to disaster and eventual death of the company.

Technology-driven revolutionary change again and again, a visionary and unconventional leader, and multiple acts of creation created an electronics giant. But the world still changed rather slowly back then, preventing RCA from becoming a Superstar in the days of David Sarnoff. Then, moving closer in time to today, the giant lost its way and disappeared. However, during its prime, RCA stands out as a different kind of Trailblazer. It appears in many ways similar to today's Superstars (particularly Apple). One wonders what would have happened if RCA had travelled a different path in the post David Sarnoff years. Because of what "might have been" versus what actually happened we devote the first chapter in Part IV (Chapter 9) to a more complete story of RCA in hopes of providing additional insights into the making of today's Exceptional companies and Superstars.

FedEx Corporation[57]: A Global delivery Giant

Federal Express, now FedEx Express, is a subsidiary of FedEx Corporation. What began as a simple logistics company has grown into a multi-faceted import/export company owning one of the largest airlines in the world. However, that growth has had a checkered past.

Fred Smith's original disruptive concept (developed while he was studying at Yale University) involved the creation of an air transport company to deliver parcels overnight. He founded Federal Express in Arkansas in 1971 based on this concept. Lack of support from the local airport caused him to move his operation to Memphis, Tenn. in 1973—a fortuitous move. It was in that year that the oil crisis and the recession it caused hit the U.S. economy. As a result, some businesses were under intense pressure to make deliveries on time, but could not afford to use their own fleet of airplanes. At the same time, Smith's rapid delivery service started experiencing sizable increased—demand from manufacturing companies that required fast delivery of electronic parts for their "just-in-time" manufacturing processes. Finally, the business was growing.

Despite these successes, the company experienced cash flow difficulties. In order to save his now growing company, Fred Smith went to Las Vegas to play blackjack in the hope of winning what was needed to keep the company afloat. Probably to his own surprise, he won $27,000, which he reinvested into his business, allowing Federal Express to survive. Going to Vegas when you need cash is not a good business plan, but starting a business when there is a need, without being deterred by the recession...is... But Smith's desperate actions allowed Federal Express to survive and ultimately become a global powerhouse.

Airplanes, an oil crisis and recession, the explosion of electronics, and business acts of creation and desperation. A long and rough ride to growth and global impact. For sure a Trailblazer, but not a Superstar.

THE EMERGENCE OF SUPERSTARS

What do these companies have in common? Ford, McDonald's, RCA, and FedEx are examples of how technology and sudden and disruptive changes in the business environment can have a dramatic impact that reaches far beyond one company or one industry, just like the brainchild of gifted inventors can have a similar effect on a segment of the economy. And the two occurring at the same time can change the industrial landscape substantially. We call these major disruptions, whether they are man-made or caused by economic turmoil, "Business Tsunamis." Just like tsunamis in the ocean, Business Tsunamis are powerful (sometimes devastating) waves of change that irreversibly alter the business landscape. They can range from tidal waves such as recessions or technology-driven revolutions to more localized waves such as the invention of a focused new technology or a new marketing concept. Business tsunamis can create new companies and industries, provide dramatic growth for existing companies, or lead to the demise of a company or an entire business segment.

However, not all Business Tsunamis are created equal, nor do they arise in the same way. In the case of RCA the Business Tsunamis it created were triggered by its multiple inventions of disruptive, electronics-based technologies. In the case of FedEx, the company created its tsunami by fulfilling a need to keep some businesses alive with the quick and relatively low-cost delivery of increasingly valuable electronics components. Thus its impact was technology enabled (air transportation and electronics), not technology based. In the case of Ford and early automobiles, its Business Tsunami was not caused by new technology or by a product invention, but by a manufacturing innovation: automobile mass production. For McDonald's and the fast food industry, the Business Tsunami was the result of applying a combination of service, marketing, and manufacturing innovations to an existing business.

As these examples show, Business Tsunamis can be vastly different from each other in many ways. On the one hand, there are Tsunamis that are strong but relatively short-lived. On the other hand, there are Tsunamis that are slow at their onset but with lasting long-term effects, such as those caused by new "disruptive" technologies. When these two superimpose, the results can be terrific. In the past, this led to the creation of Trailblazers, but today there is a difference.

As described in Chapter 4, three recent and ongoing technology-driven revolutions are serving as Launching Pads for today's Superstars and their cascading Business Tsunamis: Microelectronics, the Internet and

Biotechnology. But there is a fundamental difference from the technology-driven revolutions of the past. These three technologies today are evolving exponentially (with ever increasing speed), and it is because of this that they are able to propel companies based on them towards Superstar performance. The disruptive technologies of the Industrial Revolution (and those of much of the 20th century) did not propagate at such an incredibly increasing pace. In other words, the exponential growth of technology did not yet exist. This is one of the reasons why there could be no Superstars in previous times.

But there are other factors that have come together to create today's fast-paced, global environment where Superstars can flourish. In the next chapter we highlight some of these "Agents of Change," without which there would be no Superstars.

Eight

THE PRESENT
Agents of Change

In the previous chapter we addressed the question: "Why were there no Superstars in the past?" As we concluded, part of the answer was the lack of broad-based technology advances being made at exponentially increasing rates (Launching Pads). But there are other key differences between the present and the past, differences that today are creating a world forever changed and still changing. There are sweeping forces that we call societal "Agents of Change" that together with the Launching Pads have created a new environment where it is possible for Superstars to exist.

Step back for a minute and reflect on today's new environment. Almost "instant" communication and global "interconnectivity" are real. Their coupling is creating global market dynamics that increase not only the size and types of new business opportunities, but also the scope, speed of reaction, and intensity of competition. As a result, business risk in general, the negative consequences of wrong or slow management decisions, and the importance of intellectual property have dramatically increased. But because of this altered landscape, the possibility of creating

Superstars is real.

Therefore, in this chapter we explore the business implications of several key Agents of Change that make the "Present" very different from the "Past." Taken individually, much has been written about each of these "Agents," but here we bring together a review of the key forces that in the aggregate provide stepping stones for the creation of Superstars.

THE PACE OF BUSINESS: FASTER AND MORE CHAOTIC

Wouldn't it be simple to conduct business at the pace and rhythm of past times when progress was gradual, and when only simple changes in business practices were necessary to keep pace with the sedately evolving business world? A world without computers or smartphones. A world where everything, from using human resources to making critical decisions was deliberate and relatively straightforward. A world where the skills required of workers and leaders did not change much with the times.

This was the business environment in the not-too-distant past. Communication consisted of face-to-face meetings or documents written or typed one at a time and delivered by surface mail or messages sent by telegraph. Because of costs, goods and people could be transported only by ship if the destination involved crossing an ocean. Collecting and analyzing data, including competitive intelligence was a time-consuming, labor intensive process.

As a result, markets and competitors tended to be "local" and competitive reactions were slow. For example, "yesterday" there were neighborhood grocery stores, not today's giant supermarkets. And people ordered products by phone or mail from the Sears catalogue instead of by Internet from Amazon. In this world of the past there was plenty of time to develop business plans, make decisions, and commercialize new products and services. The flow of the river of business was "slow" and forgiving of mistakes.

However now, fueled by new discoveries and driven by an exponential wave of digital technology advances, there are several key differences in the business environment. In their book *Chaotics*,[58] Kotler and Caslione detail the increasingly rapid and pervasive changes impacting business in the past few years and conclude that this increased pace of change is here to stay, becoming an integral part of everyday life, causing chaos and creating an "age of turbulence," but also giving rise to huge new opportunities.

We have already highlighted several of these pervasive changes based on digital technologies. What are some of the others that are having or will soon have major impacts on business?

Today, using satellite transmission, communication is almost instantaneous, whether it is through television, Internet or mobile technologies. Rapid and relatively low-cost transportation is available for both goods and people using jumbo jets. Personal computers, tablets, and smartphones are pervasive. Combined, these technology-driven advances result in immediate access to global information and the ability to reach quickly (physically or electronically) almost any part of the world, and even influence it, as is shown by the next agent of change that we consider.

The results? These advances are catalysts for creating entire societies where the pace of life is becoming faster and faster, expectations for immediate actions are increasing, and needs and wants are changing frequently.

As for business, these advances are fostering the development of dynamic global markets and providing rapid access to up-to-date customer information and competitive intelligence. Thus rapid and effective competitive responses anywhere in the world are possible. All of this has created a business environment where speed is a significant competitive advantage and often is the key to business survival and success.

But that is not all. In this faster paced world, the entire lifecycle of businesses also is speeding up. Lifespans of "great" companies are getting shorter and shorter while the creation and growth of new enterprises are faster and faster.[59]

How real is this? Just think about the intense battles in the smartphone arena among Apple, Samsung, and Blackberry. In this war Apple often has been first with new capabilities, but Samsung has followed quickly. Blackberry, however, has been slow to respond. And the consequences? Apple is a leader and a Superstar, Samsung is a healthy rival, Blackberry is on a downward spiral and resorting to desperate measures.[60]

Digital technology advances also provide numerous opportunities (and the capabilities) for businesses to tap expertise from around the world. This is allowing them to give life to new products and services much more rapidly and cost effectively than in the past by drawing on truly the best skills and resources available and by incorporating the least expensive materials, solutions and processes. Because of its far-reaching implications, we treat this kind of product-related "global interconnectivity" as a separate agent of change and consider it in more detail in a later section.

Extrapolating into the future, one can see easily how the pace of change in business will **continue to increase**. This is partly due to new technology-assisted methods that are being created and refined to perform basic business operations. For example, suppose the right kind of global competitive and market information was available to make good business decisions at twice the speed of today's decision-making processes. Corporations could revise strategies more quickly and effectively. Then they could act rapidly to start essential research and development (R&D) programs, make major strategic investments, and implement focused marketing plans. This is one of the promises of analytics/big data.[61]

Next, suppose that the pace of R&D was increased by using artificial intelligence (AI) applied to analysis of large amounts of data, saving months or even years in the development of products—a capability already used by the pharmaceutical and biotech industries. Now suppose that **global** networks of technical experts existed that could be easily accessed to rapidly augment a company's internal capabilities.

Or suppose that new manufacturing equipment was delivered in half the time it takes today and was immediately operational because of advanced computer-assisted design and prototyping and even manufacturing using 3D printing—already more than a possibility.[62]

Technology-enabled data collection and analysis, rapid and effective decision-making, computer-aided design and manufacturing, 3D printing of physical objects, and rapid global interconnectivity. All of these things and more are becoming not only possible but common today, and each advance increases the pace of business. This has made **speed** much more than just a strong competitive advantage. It is now a key to the survival of the corporate "species" and has enabled the development of Superstars. The 21st century belongs to those companies that can adapt to this rapidly increasing pace of business and the "chaos" that surrounds it.

But why is the increasing pace of business accompanied by chaos? Business is like a river. When the "current" is slow, as it often was in the past, it creates a laminar flow that is predictable and orderly—a calm stretch of water where there is time to correct mistakes in action and direction. However, in today's river of business, the speed of the current is rapid and ever increasing, causing widespread turbulence and treacherous rapids. In these chaotic waters, business dynamics are governed by completely different and rapidly changing rules.

The message for business leaders who want to successfully "navigate" the turmoil in this raging torrent with its turbulent waters: Beware! Too much has changed to be able to rely on business practices and knowledge from the past. Only those businesses that are adaptable and keep up with the increasing pace of everything will survive or perhaps even become Superstars.

SOCIAL MEDIA: A RAPIDLY DEVELOPING GAME CHANGER

The world is not just moving at a faster and faster pace. It also is becoming more interconnected through digital technology. The Internet provides easy access to a wealth of information. Tablets and smartphones enable instant global communication and sharing of text, pictures, audio, and video. These capabilities have given rise to a new agent of change, the phenomena of "social media."

What are social media? By now, everyone is familiar with this area to some extent, but we want to be clear about how we are using the term. There are many definitions, but here is one that is brief, but clear: "Social media essentially is a category of online media where people are talking, participating, sharing, networking, and bookmarking online. Most social media services encourage discussion, feedback, voting, comments, and sharing of information from all interested parties. It's more of a two-way conversation, rather than a one-way broadcast like traditional media. Another unique aspect of social media is the idea of staying connected or linked to other sites, resources, and people."[63]

In other words, social media is an Internet-enabled website service that allows the users to interact with both the website and other visitors to the site almost in real time. It provides new ways to communicate instantly and globally between organizations, communities, groups, and individuals; and its popularity is exploding. Literally millions of people are using today's most popular social media such as Facebook, Twitter, YouTube, Instagram, Pinterest, and more. As a result, some social media providers have become big businesses themselves.

Social media usage has become pervasive all over the world, and the effect has been earth-shaking in some areas. Consider, for example, the Arab Spring—the revolutions in the Middle East that began in Tunisia and toppled governments. The most publicized use of social media that spring was during the Egyptian Revolution where thousands of demonstrators took to the streets at the same time, assembled by and coordinated through messages on Twitter. Social media also was used extensively by these demonstrators to provide news and videos of the events to the rest of the world and to try and gain support for their movement.[64]

And there are new examples every day. Remember the impact of social media in Hurricane Sandy where it provided real-time reporting and support for those affected.[65] Or think about the killing of Michael Brown in Ferguson, MO, and the role of social media in the visibility of that event and the protests that followed.[66] Or what about the growing practice of posting video from law enforcement body cameras on YouTube? And even more recently, consider how Erdogan's use of social media helped him foil the coup attempt against his government in Turkey.[67]

These are just some examples of how social media can enable simultaneous, multi-way communication with thousands of people, all sharing the same goals, or the same interests, and do that with the speed of light (well, almost). With an agent of change this powerful, surely companies other than the social media providers should be able to harness it in order to substantially strengthen their business, or create new businesses. But the results in this business arena, in the beginning, were unremarkable.

Yes, businesses started using social media a few years ago, but primarily as a basic marketing tool—a one-way promotional channel focused on increasing awareness and/or reputation of an organization or brand in a way that is less costly than traditional advertising. As one business leader stated in a 2010 Harvard Business Review study: "Social media is a big ocean and we are pulling into a little bay where we are most protected."[68]

Why such a specific focus? In reality, it is not that surprising. As we have described, many break-through capabilities start with a **core of disruptive innovations** followed by a **myriad of secondary innovations** that build on the first and then are applied in **different and often unrelated arenas** by visionary leaders.

As an example, consider the Internet, which we have described as a Launching Pad. Many businesses and services have sprouted from this technology/capability, with more emerging every day. But it has taken years for entrepreneurs to couple developing needs with innovative new ideas and harvest the bonanza of business opportunities. Amazon.com is an excellent example. In the relatively early days of the Internet (1994), it was only an online bookstore. Today, it is an international, multi-billion dollar, e-commerce Company—a Superstar that uses the Internet in ways never envisioned in its early days.

Now let us return to the social media environment of a few years ago. It was almost as embryonic from the business perspective as the Internet was in 1994. So it was not surprising that its promising future for business didn't happen immediately. However, things changed rapidly.

Companies started to explore expanding their use of social media beyond the obvious avenues for advertising. Their first step often was focused on obtaining company and product feedback by connecting directly to customers (or potential customers) in two-way or multi-way dynamic dialogues. And social media soon proved to be a powerful marketing force for things like creating brand awareness, targeting audiences, and gathering business intelligence.

Today, over 90% of companies are active on social media networks; and it is fair to say that social media has changed how many of these companies do business: "Around the world, social media is quickly becoming standard operating procedure at companies. Facebook, Twitter, Instagram, LinkedIn, and other networks have fundamentally changed how companies reach and interact with customers, offer products and services, communicate with employees, and—in a nutshell—do business. And that wave hasn't even begun to crest."[69]

Currently, business is starting to use social media for internal networking and communication as well as recruitment. Longer-term benefits springing from these kinds of social media-enabled connections could range from designing and testing new products through distributed R&D to "crowd-inventing" new products. And companies could move from monitoring trends to creating new trends and initiatives. There could be an avalanche of business applications as innovative new capabilities are developed.

Bottom line, today social media is becoming a "game-changer" in the business arena. And, just like with the Internet, as more and more innovations occur; social media is likely to become an even greater agent of change for business. In a business world moving faster and faster, it shouldn't take long. Moreover, as social media continues to develop, those companies that lead the way will be the winners. Those that are sitting back and watching are likely to be the losers.

GLOBAL-SOURCING: ENABLING
NEW BUSINESS PRACTICES

New products used to be developed/designed and completely manufactured/assembled by one company, usually in one location. Although this often was a lengthy and expensive process, it didn't matter. Those were the times when the business focus was domestic, the pace of business was slow, and competition frequently was embryonic. The early production of the Ford Motor Company's Model T automobile provides a good example of this "everything in-house" and "owning the whole supply chain" practice.[70]

But the world changed, and competition intensified. Low-cost manufacturing became the driver for successful new, mass-produced products. This led to the first and still best-known embodiment of outsourcing—overall product design by one company that then farms out the manufacturing of parts or even its total products to another company, either domestic or foreign, which is a lower cost producer. Nike outsourcing the manufacturing of its clothing to Bangladesh[71] and Dell outsourcing production of components and sometimes entire computers[72] are just two of many examples of companies seeking low cost solutions. Of course, as with any major change in the supply chain, there are negative implications for some, positive for others. In the case of outsourcing, the displaced workforce bears the brunt of the negative impact, but the moves are beneficial for the average consumer.

Now we turn to today's world, where the pace of everything is even faster, and the playing field is global. Although cost is still important, speed of commercialization is in the driver's seat for many products and services. For example, Apple designs its iPhones internally but outsources manufacturing all over the world to wherever the needed capacity exists.[73] But that is just the beginning. The promise of speed and increased capabilities through global interconnectivity is driving a revolution in the practice of outsourcing. Technology has created the capability for disruptive business practices that we call "global-sourcing." The following four examples illustrate the breadth and power of global-sourcing.

We turn to the construction arena for our **first** example of global-sourcing. There are a growing number of companies that construct/assemble complex building modules for installation in power plants, gas refineries, and more. These companies are located wherever the cost structure and expertise is appropriate, and the finished modules are shipped worldwide for final assembly in major construction projects. All of this is possible due to global interconnectivity created by digitally-enabled, "instant" global information exchange and computer-aided design. An excellent article in Bloomberg Business Week gives specific descriptions of several such "construction global-sourcing" projects.[74]

Next, Boeing provides our **second** example with its "product global-sourcing" in what-was-then a trailblazing approach to the design and manufacturing of their Dreamliner. To summarize, the design and manufacturing of components for the Dreamliner was spread out across the world, depending on where the best technology could be found. These subassemblies were then shipped to a Boeing plant for final assembly. To illustrate the concept more clearly, the readers can fast-forward to Chapter 12 and read a more detailed account of Boeing's approach to its advanced-concept Dreamliner. To summarize here: Despite delays due to problems with subassemblies from different subcontractors not quite "fitting" together and performance issues such as the highly publicized battery and wing crack problems,[75] today the Dreamliner is flying high.[76] The conclusion? All revolutionary approaches to new systems and products have teething problems. But Boeing's ambitious global-sourcing concepts based on global interconnectivity demonstrated a way of achieving more rapid and cost-effective product commercialization.

The Indian company Infosys is one of the crown jewels of the Indian information technology industry and provides our **third** example—the global-sourcing of software and information technology services. What this comprises and how it came about is clearly described by Nandan Nilekani, one of the founders of Infosys, as reported in the book *The World is Flat* by Thomas Friedman:

> "What happened over the last [few] years is that there was a massive investment in technology, especially in the bubble era, when hundreds of millions of dollars were invested in putting broadband connectivity around the world, undersea cables, all those things. At the same time, he added, computers became cheaper and dispersed all over the world, and there was an explosion of software: e-mail, search engines like Google and proprietary software that can chop up any piece of work and send one part to Boston, one part to Bangalore and one part to Beijing, making it easy for anyone to do remote development. When all of these things suddenly came together around 2000, Nilekani said, they created a platform where intellectual work, intellectual capital, could be delivered from anywhere. It could be disaggregated, delivered, distributed, produced and put back together again— and this gave a whole new degree of freedom to the way we do work, especially work of an intellectual nature...."[77]

Interconnectivity enabled by digital technology has

leveled and globalized the playing field for software-based development and services.

Our **fourth** example of global-sourcing goes a giant step beyond Nilekani's concept of outsourcing just intellectual capital to the broader outsourcing of Research and Development (R&D). The first movement in this direction was the outsourcing of non-strategic R&D operational activities such as product testing. This was primarily for cost savings or to meet local regulatory requirements. Next, multi-national corporations started establishing R&D sites in strategic global locations to access local talent and expertise, to provide proximity to and knowledge of local markets, and to gain flexibility in resource allocation. Today this is common practice, but it is not enough to be competitive. In our fast-paced economy, no single site and no single company alone can possess all the ideas, knowledge, and capabilities required to bring new innovations to the market.

Advances in digital technology, however, have made rapid and easy access to external sources of innovation and distributed R&D possible. It is no longer necessary for a project team to be co-located or to have actual contact to be effective, and it is no longer enough to rely only on internal idea generation. Moderna Therapeutics, one of the Exceptional companies described in Chapter 3, provides a good example of global R&D outsourcing with what they call the "Moderna Ecosystem." As described in Chapter 3, Moderna combines research collaboration with Universities, external partnerships with major drug companies, and their own internal development programs. This enables them to move forward on many fronts at the same time.

Thus, whether it's through locating proprietary R&D activities in other countries or through arm's-length relationships with an array of customers, suppliers, governments, universities and other research organizations, a vast global network of R&D activities is becoming a key to business success. Global companies such as Pepsi, GE, and IBM recognize this and routinely work with other companies in different industries, in different places, and with different cultures to develop and commercialize complex and innovative new products. The obstacles, however, are significant; so succeeding requires new approaches and leadership skills. Defining boundaries and crossing them, combining and separating activities, insourcing vs. outsourcing, onshoring vs. offshoring, shared information systems, and more are just a few of the challenges.[78] But, despite the difficulties, global-sourcing of R&D (and everything else) is the business path to the future.

GLOBAL COMPETITION: THE "SNAKEHEAD" INVASION

Snakeheads are amazing and fearless fish, native to Asia, that can breathe air and teach their young to do so by pushing them out of the water. In one episode of the TV series "River Monsters," Jeremy Wade shows a dramatization of a snakehead stalking an unsuspecting baby Chihuahua—a scene that catches your attention! And now these formidable predators are invading the waters of North America, aggressively destroying native species even though they are far from their home environment, in the waters of another continent.[79] Sound familiar? Substitute some well-known foreign corporations for Snakeheads and you will have a picture of emerging and aggressive global competition.

Why is this happening? All of a sudden, enabled by new technology, a **global** corporate "ecosystem" and a **global** economy have become realities. Because of this globalization, many more companies are now in the same race for survival and/or dominance. And, as in the wild, competition among these "species" becomes more and more aggressive as they all chase after growth and profits in shorter and shorter time frames. They all are scrambling to outperform each other—to invent better products, to develop and produce them more quickly, to market them more efficiently, and to meet the higher and higher quality levels that customers have come to expect, and to invade and conquer each other's markets.

But each company, although now fighting on a global battlefield, originated and developed in its own unique ecosystem (country or region), giving rise to capabilities, business practices and goals that are different from one competitor to the next. So, when one of these "predators" attacks outside of its own ecosystem, its "victims" often do not have the defenses or the experience to protect themselves, and sometimes don't even recognize the danger until it is too late. Thus the attacker becomes dominant.

Consider Toyota. In the late 1950s, when Toyota first appeared in the United States, Elvis was king of rock n' roll, big American cars with big engines and tailfins were "in" and postage stamps cost just 3 cents. Toyota's entry into that market was their "Toyopet" Crown Sedan. It was a high quality, reliable vehicle; but was woefully underpowered, under featured, and overpriced for the American market. However Toyota quickly adapted to the new environment and introduced the "Corona" in 1965. It wasn't big, but it met the American desires for power, automatic transmission, low price, and special features. However Toyota didn't stop there. The company aggressively used their core competencies and values and in 1969, with the Corolla, introduced Americans to the previously undiscovered pleasures of high quality and reliability in a vehicle that had good performance and was reasonably priced. By continuing to build on their engineering strengths, manufacturing innovations such as kanban ("just-in-time"), dedication to quality and continuous improvement (kaizan), and ability to adapt, Toyota has become a leader in today's global automotive industry.[80]

But global competition is more than just a clash among diverse cultures. Globalization through a fast-paced, interconnected world has changed the overall competitive landscape forever. There are many more players involved, and they are quick to act and react. Consequently, staying ahead is more difficult than it has ever been. When Ford led the automobile revolution, there was no thought of Japan. However today, Japan and Korea are formidable forces shaping the automotive industry. And it used to be that when someone said television, you thought RCA. But as we chronicled in the RCA story, the company no longer exists. So today you are more likely to think Sony or Samsung. And what about...? The list is endless. Business competition has changed. It is global and aggressive.

And there is another important difference. Foreign competitors often play the business "game" with different rules and different expectations. One good example of this is the drive for "immediate profits" by many US companies versus the focus on obtaining higher market shares by some foreign companies. This is one reason for the increased practice of "dumping"—foreign competitors charging a lower price for products in US markets than in their own country to obtain market share. And sometimes, although it is illegal in the U.S. and other countries, that price is even below the cost of producing or obtaining the product; so the foreign company makes no profit. There are numerous examples of "dumping" by foreign companies into the U.S.: China and solar cells and steel, Korea and steel pipes and tubes, multiple countries and office paper, and more.[81] This is just one aspect of global competition where the players have different goals and their time horizon for winning is longer.

What are the consequences of all of this? Today, it is essential for businesses to recognize the possibility of alien corporate invasions from any part of the world and make plans accordingly. What does this mean? Let's return to the saga of Snakeheads. These strange fish are considered a delicacy in some countries, but not in the U.S. Here they are viewed only as a menace. The U.S. has been forced to acknowledge their presence but has not accepted it as desirable or permanent. Maybe it is time to reassess the situation and find ways not only to protect against "snakeheads" but also to accept what they have to offer and coexist.

INCREASED BUSINESS RISKS: THE CHALLENGES OF GLOBALIZATION

In spite of the chaotic world around us, the risks involved in playing some types of games haven't changed. For example, playing roulette, whether it is Russian roulette or the more civilized version in Monaco, is the same as it always has been. However, the game of business has become a much more dangerous venture. Developing a new business or expanding an existing one involves a whole new dimension of risk. Specifically, creating or entering new markets is a bigger and much more complex endeavor (hence much riskier) than in the past, partly due to the developing global economy and partly to the consequences of global competition.

On a positive note, globalization significantly increases potential market sizes, creating extremely attractive and visible business growth opportunities. Just think about the worldwide explosion of smartphones, or the rapid expansion of wine import and export businesses, or the huge potential for a new cancer drug. Even water is now a global opportunity, as the recent history of San Pellegrino shows. Twenty years ago it was a relatively unknown Italian mineral water. Today, it is distributed worldwide to more than 120 countries on five continents.[82]

However, on the risk side for individual companies, highly visible, big growth opportunities create new global competitors that were never before seen as threats—Korean car manufacturers, Indian software developers, Chinese computer and internet-based companies, European appliance manufacturers, and more. The bottom line: more companies around the world are likely to be pursuing the same specific growth opportunity at the same time. Therefore, the risk of failure for any single company is high—significantly higher than in the past.

Conversely, a company's probability of winning is significantly lower than in the past when it had a reasonable possibility of being the only company pursuing a good new opportunity that was unrecognized by others. Yesterday there were many single-company big successes: Kodak and silver halide film, IBM and computers, Motorola and cell phones, RCA and consumer electronics. But in today's dynamic global economy, due to growing interconnectivity and the faster pace of everything, there will not be many "lone pioneers" such as these.

Also on the risk side, pursuing today's larger global opportunities requires greater resources than what were needed in the past to be successful in smaller, "local" opportunities. This results in the **financial** risk being much higher, sometimes high enough to place an entire company at risk. If a project fails, for whatever reason, that failure is costly. Kodak having to declare Chapter 11 bankruptcy as a result of its late and failed attempt to become a major player in digital photography is a good example of today's high cost of failure.[83]

And there is another kind of risk involving resources. In

the past, under-resourcing a project or underestimating the amount of needed resources or using resources ineffectively did not matter as much as it does today. Today, any of these "mistakes" will slow down progress; and in a faster paced and more competitive business world, this decreased speed will almost certainly create a significant competitive disadvantage. This, in turn, greatly increases the probability of a costly failure in the marketplace.

On the other hand, not all companies want to create new businesses or enter new markets. Some are satisfied with their current business arena. That was the initial position of Kodak, when faced with the competition from digital photography. In such cases, it is easy for a company to become a slave of its past and continue to pursue business as it always did. But strategies and business methodologies and products that were once successful may not be applicable in a business environment that has changed significantly; and pursuing them unchanged may lead to disaster.

But that is not all. There is yet another dimension to the risk involved in managing to performance levels of the past. What once was good enough is no longer acceptable. In reaction to today's rapidly changing and more risky business world, stockholders are increasingly demanding **higher** and **more consistent** profits in **shorter** time frames. And their patience with visionary leaders and longer term investments is limited unless the payback is assured. In other words, if companies do not rapidly produce expected or promised results, business leaders are likely to be replaced. Two high visibility CEO examples of this are Apple's Steve Jobs and Twitter's Jack Dorsey. Both were forced to leave the companies they founded. Although both were re-instated later on, this is not the usual outcome when someone is fired.

This stockholder "impatience," along with the impact of

globalization and the increasing pace of business has totally changed the business "game." Together, these factors significantly augment the risks of trying to maintain the business status quo. Today, "staying the course" instead of pursuing new opportunities is more likely to result in corporate death, and thus this may end up being the riskiest choice of all.

And finally, because of today's need for speed, failure not only is connected to making wrong or bad decisions but also frequently is the result of making good decisions too slowly or projects taking too long. Kodak's eventual management decision to pursue digital photography was a good one, but the delay in making that decision was a major contributor to the effort's failure. BlackBerry's major delays in introducing the BlackBerry 10 line of phones were a major contributor to that company's financial problems.

In a highly competitive, global business environment that is rapidly changing, **a slow decision will almost always be a wrong decision**; and being late to the market almost always assures failure. Just as in nature, a slow company will become prey for the faster, more aggressive one.

INTELLECTUAL PROPERTY: THE RISE OF THE GEEKS

As technology advances on many fronts, more and more businesses and services increasingly are turning into "high-tech" operations. In this new kind of business environment, intellectual property considerations have increased in corporate visibility and importance and must be factored into both product-related and total business decisions.

It's unlikely that companies like Intel and Apple would be as strong as they are today if they didn't have extensive portfolios of patents to protect their inventions against competition. And without a portfolio of patents covering inventions needed by others, companies like Samsung would be behind, struggling with the followers, not bargaining and playing with the leaders. It's clear. Sustainable business success in today's technology-shaped world requires **continuous** product inventions as well as re-inventions of the business itself. And these inventions, whenever possible, need to be protected.

What makes patents and other forms of intellectual property (e.g., copyrights, trademarks, design rights) so much more important in technologically rich environments? When rapidly evolving new technology is the basis for products and/or for basic business operations, a continuing flow of patents can nurture and protect the business, can help create and sustain new businesses, or can block others from **rapidly** capitalizing on disruptive innovations. Essentially, by preventing direct copying, patents force competitors to find alternatives. This decreases their efficiency and often increases the costs of their products and services. This always has been and continues to be the value of patents. However, today there are other benefits. In the current business environment where speed is a key to success, patents can be effective weapons for **slowing down** the competition. And sometimes, that makes all the difference.

There is yet another reason for the growing importance of patents in our fast-paced, technology driven world. It's a little like a card game. The winning players are those who have the right Intellectual Property "cards" to play—to license and collect significant revenue, to cross-license for strategic gain, to negotiate, or even to sell.

Looking at it another way, patents are emerging as a new currency, and they are driving mergers and acquisitions. One good example is the Google purchase of Motorola Mobility: "The Google deal highlights the growing significance of patents in mobile and the steep prices that companies are willing to pay to keep them from rivals."[84]

Given the growing importance of patents, there is one additional important consideration. In order to have "good" patents (unless one acquires them) one must be **first** in the race to develop new technology or make new inventions or recognize and acquire promising start-ups. This consideration forces businesses to look for ways to hasten technology and product development.

So, as the race for new technology and new patents intensifies, it causes an increase in the rate of technological advances that in turn increases the potential for disruptive change, an ever-increasing spiral into a chaotic and exciting future. Geeks of the world unite! Your time has come!

CONCLUSIONS

As we have described, it is no longer business as usual. Being good (or even great) in the past doesn't guarantee success today or in the future, and certainly won't result in Superstar performance. As we have highlighted in this chapter, in today's digital age, powerful agents of disruptive change, together, are irreversibly altering the business landscape, creating new frontiers where technology is pervasive and turbulence is the new normal. Nothing is stable, and the rate of change is accelerating.

But this isn't the end. There are many new technology-driven agents of change lurking on the horizon—biotechnology, advances in particle physics, new science and technology advances that we haven't even imagined yet (some of which we will describe in Part V). And who knows how all of this will affect business. Only one thing is certain. Entrepreneurs who aspire to create Superstars must learn to quickly adapt to our chaotic environment by understanding, embracing, and effectively using technology-driven, societal Agents of Change.

One last comment. As Agents of Change rapidly evolve and intersect with Launching Pads, they affect not only business but also society and humanity in general. Many of these impacts are positive, but others, such as displaced workforces, can cause harm and are likely to become bigger problems in the future. What is the best the balance between success for a company and its impact on human lives? We do not know, but business bears some of the responsibility for seeking the answer.

A LEADER'S PATH TO SUPERSTARS

PART IV

Nine

THE RCA STORY
Insights from the Past

It is hard to imagine the downfall of companies like Apple, Amazon, Microsoft, or Intel. Yet not that long ago, it was just as difficult to imagine the downfall of RCA, a powerful symbol of the technological revolution that began at the start of the 20th century. But today, the name RCA is only a marketing trademark. However once upon a time, RCA was a very large and vibrant manufacturing company whose world-class laboratories invented many new disruptive technologies. As we highlighted in Chapter 7, with its revolutionary radio and television products, RCA even created a new industry (consumer electronics). And the company perceived itself to be invincible. But business invincibility is not like a diamond. It does not last forever. Whatever happened to RCA?

In this chapter we tell the story of how RCA reached great heights but then fell to its death.[85] RCA's early successes are described briefly to provide background and show how leadership and "new-to-the-world" concepts (both marketing innovations and disruptive technologies) led to world-changing business success. Similarities to today's Superstars are apparent. Then, RCA's failures are chronicled to show how these same things can lead to business failure—if not used correctly. The last episode in the life of RCA (video players) illustrates the complexity of corporate survival in a rapidly changing business landscape such as exists today. As a conclusion, we take a step back and focus on the lessons that can be learned from the story of this Trailblazer of the not too distant past about creating exceptional companies today and turning good companies into great ones.[86]

THE EARLY VICTORIES: THE DAVID SARNOFF ERA

The Radio

RCA (Radio Corporation of America) was founded in 1919 as the American spin-off of Marconi's Wireless Telegraph Ltd. (Marconi), a British company founded by Guglielmo Marconi to commercialize his invention of wireless transmission, better known as the radio. From the start, there was a disagreement between the leaders of RCA and those of Marconi over how to commercialize the disruptive new radio technology. Marconi wanted RCA to focus its efforts on the application of radio technology to the niche of wireless telegraph and telegraphic equipment mounted on ships for the military.

But RCA's leader, President and CEO General David Sarnoff, had a bigger vision. He dreamed of creating a new and much larger market by selling a radio to every home. Although this strategy was risky because it focused on a non-existent market for a product that had yet to be developed, Sarnoff made this choice. RCA commercialized the product; and the market did develop, fueled by RCA's purchase of radio broadcasting stations, by its formation of the National Broadcasting Company (NBC), and later by its acquisition of the world's largest manufacturer of phonographs (the Victor Talking Machine Company). By the late 1920s, with no significant competition, RCA had become the world leader in sales of radios. Sarnoff's vision and business strategies coupled with RCA's development of the disruptive radio technology had created not only a new market but also the beginnings of an entire new industry—consumer electronics.

But RCA's path to this early success was rocky. The company's organization was unstable and without clear reporting lines. Sarnoff alone made all important decisions. Costs for product development and time to commercialization were grossly underestimated, and capacity planning was inadequate due to grossly inaccurate sales forecasts. But RCA was a **lone pioneer**, so in spite of all this, RCA's disruptive new product was a wild success.

Black and White Television

Well before RCA achieved great success with radio, Sarnoff had the vision that black and white "television" could be RCA's next major new blockbuster product. Again this was a case where neither the product nor the market existed. But in 1923, in spite of the risks, Sarnoff made the decision to proceed.

There were three possible technical approaches: two mechanical systems and a more complex system that was completely electronic. Sarnoff chose the all-electronic system, which was the hardest to implement, but also the most difficult for competitors to copy. Once he had decided, he concentrated all of RCA's resources on this **one technical path**.

However it wasn't until 1945 that RCA finally introduced the black and white television to the consumer market—many years after Sarnoff made the decision to develop it. The delays were partly due to the technical challenges, partly due to internal RCA issues, and partly due to World War II. But in the end, none of that mattered. Sarnoff's choice turned out to be the right one. The sophisticated electronic system had significant performance advantages, and the technology complexity kept the competition at bay. Thus, as with the radio, RCA had great business success by coupling disruptive technology with market creation.

However, like with the Radio, RCA's path to success with television was full of mistakes, including grossly underestimating costs. This mistake could have sunk RCA, but it didn't because RCA had **big financial reserves**, the **ability to raise cash**, and **little competition**. As before, David Sarnoff's visionary leadership and strong personal direction were responsible for continuing the extreme growth of RCA.

Color Television

In the late 1940s, based on the success with black and white television, Sarnoff decided that a color television product should be RCA's next disruptive innovation. On the surface, this appeared to be a somewhat less risky endeavor than black and white TV since there was a developing consumer market for television, and color TV was only a small technology step from black and white—or was it?

We will not describe the series of missteps that preceded the eventual market introduction by RCA of color TV in 1954. Suffice it to say, again there were numerous delays which gave other companies with different proposed video formats the opportunity to compete with RCA for government approval. However in 1953, RCA's version of color TV was adopted by the government as the U.S. standard, and the way was cleared for RCA's product introduction. By the mid-1960s, RCA had become the undisputed leader in color TV—another great business and technology win for RCA.

But this time, success was much more difficult for RCA. As it had done before, RCA had failed to accurately forecast expenses, underestimated time for market development, and overestimated early sales volumes. With the less costly black and white TV, these "mistakes" only caused minor problems. However in the case of color TV, these mistakes resulted in a lengthy and expensive introduction phase. Nevertheless, in the end, as with radio and black and white TV, RCA management only saw the ultimate success of color TV and felt invincible.

COMPUTERS: A SHORT-LIVED AND EXPENSIVE FAILURE

Still enjoying its success with black and white TV and concurrent with its development of color TV (the early 1950s), David Sarnoff became attracted to a developing market/industry: computers. Since computers were based on electronics and Sarnoff viewed RCA as the leader in electronics, he decided it would be easy for them to quickly dominate this arena and expand their business successes. But this was very different from RCA's previous endeavors. It meant undertaking a significant **technology catch-up** effort in digital electronics just to be a follower in the current technology of computers instead of being the leader with a proprietary new technology. And it meant competing with **established companies** in an **existing marketplace** instead of creating that marketplace. However Sarnoff was undaunted and decided to proceed.

By the early 1960s RCA had indeed become a major computer company, though not the leader. However RCA's computer business lost money from the beginning, and the effort needed to support it diverted significant internal resources from other potentially promising programs. As the decade of the 1960s came to a close, RCA enjoyed continued success with color TV, but saw the financial losses from its computer business mounting. It was on this note that the "David Sarnoff Era," which had seen wild successes with radio and television, officially ended.

In 1970, David Sarnoff retired and was succeeded by his son **Robert** Sarnoff whose leadership style was very different from that of his father. Robert's approach was management by consensus instead of directives from the top.

It was only as the massive losses of the computer business continued, that his management team was finally forced to take a hard look at the situation. They reached the conclusion that to compete head-on with IBM, major changes in their own product design were needed. By mid-1970 this had become RCA's highest priority, and half of its formidable laboratory staff was assigned to the project.

The renewed "surge" in the RCA computer effort was short-lived. As corporate financial losses rapidly increased, RCA management finally became convinced that they could not win the "computer war." All efforts were discontinued in 1971, and the existing computer business was sold. This resulted in a write-off of $250 million, a huge amount for the times. Many resources had been wasted in a hopeless battle, and now RCA found itself facing its next and even bigger challenge with a **significant financial handicap**.

VIDEO RECORDERS: RCA'S FINAL CHAPTER

The Video Recorder story starts in the early 1950s and continues through the final years of RCA. It overlaps in time with the wild years of RCA's TV success and computer failures. This part of the history of RCA highlights issues often arising in today's challenging corporate environment. It illustrates how the dynamic and competitive nature of a truly global economy can result in the death of a company once considered great as well as the creation of new giants. So we tell this episode in some detail to illustrate the complexities and difficulties of surviving in a fast-paced world of technology-driven disruptive change.

The "Vision"

It is 1951, and David Sarnoff (then RCA President/CEO) is celebrating his 45th anniversary with RCA. In a highly publicized speech to his staff he asked his laboratories to give him three "presents" for his 50th anniversary in 1956. One of these "presents" was a "videograph" (video recorder). This was Sarnoff's vision for creating RCA's next major "Business Tsunami" based on a new RCA disruptive technology.

Behind for the First Time

Sarnoff's envisioned video recorder (or video player) was a device that recorded video and then played it back in some fashion. He believed that with such a product RCA could replace the "old" technology of silver halide film, which was used at that time to record movies and TV shows.

When Sarnoff presented his challenge in 1951, RCA was in the midst of developing its TV and computer businesses. So, available resources for the video recorder program were limited, and progress was slow. In the past, when RCA had little competition, under-resourcing programs hadn't mattered much; so management wasn't concerned.

But the business environment was changing. At the same time that RCA was slowly pursuing the video recorder, there was another company with a similar goal and a similar approach—something that frequently happens in today's dynamic world. This small, unknown company (Ampex) successfully developed and in 1954 commercialized the world's first practical video recorder. It was based on magnetic tape. Ampex had beaten RCA in the technology game—something that had never happened before.

RCA was behind for the first time, and Ampex had **protected its technology** well with patents. So in 1956, RCA entered into a cross-license agreement with Ampex that allowed RCA to sell Ampex video recorders.

The Race to be Different

The Ampex video tape recorder (VTR) was very large; and thus it was suitable only for broadcast and professional use, such as in television studios. This left ample room for the invention and development of a system truly designed for home entertainment. This became RCA's goal— creating a **consumer** video player.

RCA's consumer video player efforts started in earnest in the mid-1960s with various groups within RCA pursuing different technology approaches. Each technology approach had its own champion or group of champions in Management. Thus the different video player programs continually jockeyed for position and resources, resulting in a great deal of in-fighting—very different from the times of David Sarnoff when there was only one direction.

Attempting to resolve the conflicts, management first chose one video technology for focus, then another, then another, and then back again. These **frequent changes in priorities** led to confusion and slow progress on all fronts.

Struggles and Turmoil Within

As described earlier, Robert Sarnoff did not have the "vision" and assertive style of his father. His "consensus" approach resulted in years of almost continuous organizational re-structuring, management indecision, and constant strategic re-direction. These factors, combined with the defocusing effects and costs of numerous unrelated acquisitions (Banquet frozen foods, Random House books, Hertz rental cars, etc.), caused RCA to become a company of erratic change and limited progress in many areas, including that of the consumer video player.

And also unlike his father, Robert tended to delegate major decisions to committees of lower-level staff. As a consequence, a staff organization called "Venture Group" became responsible for the consumer video player project, including technology choices. This group had expertise in finance and marketing, but was inexperienced in commercializing technology-based innovations.

Once again the project's technical direction was changed frequently and resources increased or decreased as technical problems were encountered and/or management of the Venture Group changed. This led to even more limited progress in most areas and the "death" by attrition of several video technologies that might have been viable.

No Longer Alone

By 1970, there were only three technology contenders left in RCA's video player arena. Two were truly disruptive technologies ("Holotape" holographic tape and "VideoDisc" capacitance-based video disc). The third was an evolutionary technology ("MagTape" based on magnetic tape). The Venture Group finally chose a single approach, and "Selectavision I" based on Holotape was announced as RCA's soon-to-be marketed consumer video player product. But management had misjudged the technology readiness. The ensuing delays, re-organizations, and management changes **opened the door for foreign competition**.

The early 1970s saw the commercialization and explosion of a new kind of magnetic tape based VTR—the video **cassette** recorder (VCR), a development largely unanticipated by RCA management. This VCR revolution was started by Sony in 1971 with the introduction of its "U-matic" system which used magnetic recording tape in a cassette instead of wound on an open reel. It was smaller, lighter, and less expensive than open reel VTRs; and businesses and educational institutions quickly adopted it. But the U-matic system still was not easily transportable or cheap enough to be widely accepted as a consumer product.

However the VCR approach (magnetic tapes in a cassette) appeared so promising that the playing field rapidly became crowded. Most of the VTR players from the 1960s actively pursued VCRs and were joined by a host of additional companies such as Sanyo, Quasar, Panasonic, Thompson, and JVC. RCA finally recognized the potential, cancelled its Holotape program, and joined the VCR race with its "Selectavision II" MagTape effort. But the Japanese had a significant head start. RCA was **too late with too little**, and in 1974 Selectavision II was cancelled.

Now there was only one RCA technology left—the capacitance-based, pre-recorded VideoDisc.[87] In early1975 RCA announced "Selectavision III" based on this technology as its consumer video player system. Unfortunately this announcement came just after Phillips-MCA had announced a video disc system. And, not much later, Teldec (Telefunken-Decca) actually introduced its video disc system in Europe. Now, RCA would not be first to market with a consumer video disc player, and it appeared that they might not even be second. RCA management finally became concerned about competition—but only European competition. Although they were aware of Japanese VCR developments based on magnetic tape, they did not consider these to be threats to RCA's VideoDisc. But they were wrong.

Japan Leading the Race[88]

Concurrently with developing U-matic, Sony was developing a **consumer** magnetic recording system—"Betamax." Sony offered U.S. marketing rights for this system to RCA, but RCA rejected the offer, convinced that their own VideoDisc technology was superior. Therefore Sony went ahead on its own, and in 1975 its Betamax system was launched.

At the same time Sony was developing Betamax, JVC (owned by Matsushita) also was working on a consumer VCR system. JVC's system, like Sony's Betamax, used magnetic tape and was being designed specifically for the consumer home market. JVC set clear technical and performance requirements for the product at the beginning of the program. Unlike what happened numerous times in RCA, **these requirements did not change** from the inception of the program until its commercialization—despite sometimes limited resources. This new JVC system was called "VHS."

1976 saw the market introduction of VHS, as scheduled; and it was accompanied by the introduction of a compatible video camera. In addition, JVC gave licenses to a number of other Japanese hardware manufacturers (Hitachi, its own parent Matsushita, Mitsubishi, and Sharp) for producing VHS hardware. This committed these large companies to supporting the JVC format and provided additional manufacturing capacity.

RCA now had two formidable video player competitors, both selling consumer systems based on magnetic recording technology. And by 1977 it was clear (even to RCA) that Sony and JVC had successfully created the Consumer Video Tsunami. RCA's years of management vacillation, changing technology approaches and priorities, and program delays had been costly. Now RCA was forced into an intense global race for the technology and market dominance.

And on the RCA front, things still were not going well. Despite product demonstrations for management, the RCA VideoDisc was not yet on the market. Although some of RCA management believed they had to accelerate the VideoDisc program to provide an effective counter-attack to the Japanese, the new CEO (Griffiths) did not and placed the VideoDisc program on hold pending solutions by the laboratory to what he saw as serious technical shortcomings.

At this point RCA's Consumer Electronics Division, frustrated by the lack of an RCA-manufactured video player product, licensed and introduced JVC's VHS system as an RCA product. This quickly became an important part of the RCA video business. An interesting question (which we can only speculate about but cannot answer) is whether this action by RCA (supporting the Japanese VHS format) was in part responsible for the later defeat of the RCA VideoDisc system.

VHS Going Down the Home Stretch[89]

Now that the Consumer Video Tsunami had been created, the challenge was to ride this giant wave to business success. For JVC, ultimate success for VHS (and failure for Sony's Betamax) depended on factors **unrelated to the technology**. Almost immediately the VHS format gained great acceptance, penetrating more than 20 percent of the market for consumer video players by early 1977. But then an unexpected event occurred. Sales dropped to almost nothing.

At this point JVC aggressively pursued their "systems" approach through the then innovative concept of **consumer education**. They set out to teach the consumers about video cameras, thereby convincing them to purchase the entire system—player and camera. This was clearly a new approach to marketing; and it worked, in a sense creating a "marketing" Tsunami.

In parallel with its consumer education effort, JVC looked for companies in Europe that would license and manufacture VHS recorders. Thomson in France, Thorn in England, and Telefunken in Germany signed on, joining a growing list of companies in Japan. This strategy of gathering a large number of companies "pushing together" for the success of the VHS format was an essential piece of winning the "format war" with Sony. This was another part of riding the Consumer Video Tsunami to success that didn't depend on technology (whether disruptive or not).

And JVC did win the video battle. By 1980, sales for the VHS format had surpassed those of Sony's Betamax—a huge success for the relatively small team that **kept their focus on the same goals** for the duration of the program. And there still was no VideoDisc product.

Too Little, Too Late: The End for RCA

In 1980 RCA was in a clear leadership position in the color TV market, and its financial situation was once again solid. And the VideoDisc technical advances gave management confidence that the now re-designed system could give RCA total leadership in the consumer video market—surpassing VCRs (including JVC's VHS system) and defeating any of the other emerging video disc contenders. Therefore the VideoDisc commercialization program was re-initiated. And RCA management, finally recognizing that timing was crucial, established an aggressive (and costly) plan for market introduction.

In 1981 the RCA "Selectavision VideoDisc" system was introduced to the market. In the next two years, in spite of a seriously worsening company financial situation, RCA forged ahead with its costly VideoDisc effort. RCA was successful in lining up various Videodisc "partners" for player manufacturing, programming, disc production and distribution, and consumer sales. RCA also made numerous price decreases in both players and discs. But all of this did little to stimulate VideoDisc sales. Why? Because at the same time, the prices of VCRs and recording tapes had decreased even more, and the **new business of renting pre-recorded video tapes** had emerged. VHS sales skyrocketed, and no company's video disc program survived.

In 1984, **twenty years** after its start of research on video recorders, RCA was forced to admit defeat. Production of its VideoDisc players was discontinued, and the company was forced to take a $175 million write-off (a huge amount for the times) that accelerated the company's deteriorating financial situation. RCA did not survive for long. Between 1984 and 1986 parts of the company were divested, leading to the takeover of RCA by GE in 1986 and the final breakup of the company. Thus the company that was once the leader in consumer electronics was now nothing more than a casualty of the innovative marketing and technological developments of its global competitors.

LESSONS LEARNED

At the beginning of the era of the video recorder/player and just before its demise, RCA had moved into unfamiliar territory—more like the business environment of today. It had entered a business "game" with new rules played on a **highly competitive, global** battlefield. Management's reaction was unfortunate and ultimately fatal. They reacted the way people often do when they walk into a dark room. Their first reaction was to freeze (no action, no decisions). Then they wandered around aimlessly (deciding and reversing decisions frequently). What could or should RCA have done differently, and how can today's entrepreneurs and business leaders learn from RCA's successes and failures?

Unfortunately, there are no simple answers. Despite attempts to do so, one cannot use examples of business events such as those just chronicled to develop a generally applicable "formula" for creating Superstars or corporate success in a rapidly changing world. The dynamic complexity of creating, managing, and growing a company in a disruptive business environment makes it necessary for leaders to develop their own specific plans for survival and growth. However RCA's experiences do provide invaluable lessons applicable to the management in a rapidly changing environment and technology-driven revolutions in general. We have highlighted some of these insights throughout this chapter, but for emphasis we summarize them in a different way below.

The Burden of the Past

It is easy for a company to become a slave of its past and continually pursue business as it always did. But strategies and business methodologies that once were successful may not be applicable when the business environment has changed significantly. From the successes of radio and TV, RCA's leadership had developed three basic beliefs. Their strategy for the video player battle was based on these beliefs, but these "old" approaches to business no longer worked.

The first belief was that "vision" is the only necessary ingredient to create successful disruptive technology-based businesses. After all, the radio was an idea not requested by the consumer and not identified by market research. Instead, the need was created and "pushed" onto consumers by RCA's Chief Executive. But RCA's Radio Tsunami, created by Sarnoff's vision, did not destroy existing businesses. It created a new market where the consumer had no pre-conditioned expectations. So, there was time to make and correct mistakes. Pursuing David Sarnoff's vision of a video player in the same way led to a negative outcome for RCA. In the 20 years it took to realize this video player vision, the business environment had changed dramatically, but RCA had not.

The second belief was that disruptive technologies will always win—no matter what the timing. This was true in the case of radio, and RCA leadership saw that it was eventually true in the case of TV. Therefore, they were convinced that their disruptive video disc technology would win in spite of the Japanese successes with magnetic tape based VCRs. But it was too late. By the time RCA had commercialized its VideoDisc product, global competition with VHS products was entrenched. The timing and the market were not right for another new consumer video technology—no matter how disruptive.

The third belief (closely related to the second) was that when the technology is good enough, business success comes despite mistakes and corporate inefficiencies. Indeed, during RCA's rise to prominence its new product commercialization skills were lacking, development cost overruns often were large, program delays were the norm, and sales forecasts were grossly off the mark. In spite of all this, in these early days, RCA's disruptive new products eventually were introduced and provided great successes for the company. Excellence in operational skills was not important when RCA was "a lone pioneer." It was with this mindset that RCA leadership approached the video player battle. However, now there was capable global competition that had "changed the rules." Creating a sweeping Business Tsunami was no longer enough. Riding that Tsunami more skillfully than others had become a requirement for success, and RCA did not recognize this until it was too late. And at that point, RCA did not have the capabilities needed to be competitive in this way.

The ultimate lesson learned: Look to the future, not the past! Make sure you are aware of and understand the implications of new technology advances and evolving Agents of Change on the business environment.

Understanding Competition

When RCA was the pioneer and dominant market leader (as it was during the development of radio and TV), competitive understanding was not a requirement for its business success. However, by the time of the video player episode, things had changed. A number of other companies, not all U.S. based, had developed the technology capability to be serious contenders in the consumer video arena. During the early 1970s, although RCA leadership had started to appreciate the importance of knowing about competitive activities, their focus was on threats from the U.S. and Europe. They totally discounted Japan.

It was only in the mid-70s that RCA was forced to recognize the substantial threat from Japan, and that awareness came only because Sony and JVC had commercialized consumer video products, and they (RCA) had not. At that point RCA finally acknowledged the technical capabilities of Japan but did not appreciate the additional threats posed by Japanese business methodologies and strategies. By that time, RCA had competitive awareness, but did not yet have competitive understanding.

Japanese "hi-tech" firms, on the other hand, had a

detailed understanding of American industry. They used this understanding to develop a new approach to business. They saw that they would be unable, at least in the short term, to "out-invent" the United States with respect to disruptive technologies. However, they believed that if they could build exceptional competence in the engineering and manufacturing arenas, they could be competitive with products based on existing technologies. Their assessment was that the advantages these competencies would provide them in time-to-market (elapsed time from the inception of work on a product to the actual product launch), in cost, and in quality would allow them to compete and win against the West.

JVC's success with VHS is a clear example of the effectiveness of this "Japanese" approach. JVC focused on improving an existing technology (magnetic tape recording) and making the engineering and manufacturing innovations necessary for its product to be first to market and competitive. Conversely, RCA management chose to develop a disruptive technology (VideoDisc), even though they knew it would take longer, cost more and most likely would have performance/quality issues in the beginning. RCA was not the first, and won't be the last, to underestimate the importance of market presence, quality, and cost.

However JVC didn't rely just on a well-engineered product. The company also used innovative new marketing concepts (bundling the video player with a video camera, renting rather than selling pre-recorded tapes, and consumer education) to increase the attractiveness of VHS to the consumer. RCA's focus on competing only with technology left it surprised and unprepared to deal with these marketing innovations. Ultimately, RCA's lack of appreciation for the power of innovative new business practices and methodologies and disruptive marketing had fatal consequences.

The lesson here: Look for new competitors and new types of competition, direct and indirect, wherever it might exist. And this includes business innovations as well as product inventions.

Resources

A disruptive technology-based growth strategy is costly. It's true that revolutionary ideas may be difficult to create, but usually ideas are not expensive. However an idea alone is far from sufficient to create a business success, especially when there is active competition. Creating and unleashing a Business Tsunami based on a disruptive technology requires a clear vision for the challenges ahead and a well-defined path to follow. But in a highly competitive environment such as the one that developed in the video arena that is not enough. Success also requires good financial management, enough resources to make timely progress, and adequate cash reserves to cope with the unexpected. Underestimating resource needs and/or under-resourcing efforts is likely to lead to failure as RCA learned the hard way.

RCA entered the video player battle in earnest just after having "wasted" a quarter of a billion dollars on its failed adventure with computers. Cash reserves were inadequate for an aggressive video player effort, but RCA felt it had no choice. Management believed if the video player program was delayed until the company could completely recover financially, they would be too far behind their competitors to be successful. They were probably correct in their assessment of the situation, but the way they managed the video player program made the situation worse. As we have described, the multiple changes in technology and product focus led to costly delays (both competitive and financial), but the resource drain didn't stop there. Extensive marketing campaigns made necessary by the competitive battle with VHS further depleted RCA's resources. When RCA finally withdrew from the market, its financial situation was beyond repair.

Could RCA have minimized the financial losses by focusing on one technology/product to shorten the time-to-market? Would that have been enough to "save" RCA? There is no way to know. But what if RCA had concentrated all of its resources on one technical approach (e.g., VideoDisc) from the beginning? Then RCA's video player could have arrived first to the market. In the end, timeliness and disruptive technology might have allowed RCA to win the race and regain dominance in the developing consumer video industry.

And the lesson: **Speed** is critical in today's technology-driven business environment. This means adequately resourcing projects, focus, and state-of-the-art development and commercialization skills are essential.

Innovation

In the video recorder part of the RCA story, there were many potential disruptive inventions originated by competing companies. As we chronicled, some inventions were commercialized, but others were not. Some of those innovations created Business Tsunamis, some did not. Some of the players involved won in the business arena and others ended up in defeat. Now, by looking at these events through the lens of time, several important concepts relating to disruptive innovations can be identified.

Why is the choice of which innovation to pursue so critical? One answer is that if the product doesn't excite the customer the business will not be successful. On the other hand, if the product takes too long to develop and scale-up to manufacturing, there is likely to be strong competition in the market to contend with. In other words, the choice often boils down to: What is most important—product sophistication or timeliness of market introduction?

As we have described, RCA management finally chose a disruptive technology for product sophistication (VideoDisc), in spite of the fact that the technology wasn't totally developed. However, by this time RCA was in a race with foreign competition, and the timing of market introduction was of paramount importance. If RCA had understood this, they might have made a different technology choice, or they might have managed the program differently. But they misjudged the importance of time-to-market. In other words, even a product based on the best "disruptive technology," when introduced too late into the market place, loses its commercial impact. And this was the final, deadly lesson RCA learned.

WHAT MIGHT HAVE BEEN

Could RCA have been more than a trailblazer? Could it have become a Superstar? Of course it is easy to identify RCA's "mistakes" in hindsight. But given the complexity of the changing business environment and the intertwined forces affecting any company's business, there is never just one correct way to proceed. So we will never know, but:

> "If RCA had resisted the lure of the computer and avoided the curse of the conglomerate, if it had continued to concentrate, as did its Japanese competitors, on the consumer electronics market, the one that it knew best, then it might have remained the industry's path definer. Instead, RCA failed and the Japanese quickly ascended as the dominant commercializers of consumer electronics."[90]

Ten

BARRIERS BY TRADITIONAL MANAGEMENT

To repeat what we stated as one of our key assumptions in the Introduction: "Today, business practices in most companies are developing very slowly compared to other areas of knowledge such as Microelectronics or Nanotechnology. Thus these practices in general, and business management more specifically, are not benefiting from advances in these other faster moving areas—a situation that needs to be corrected soon to prevent a further "fracture" between business management and the scientific foundations of the industrialized world.

In other words, the Microelectronics revolution and the resulting increasing pace of change in the world today have not yet resulted in a **revolution** in business management, but merely in a few modest changes. In this Chapter, as a first step towards understanding how this constrains innovation and smothers embryonic Superstars, we explore and critique some typical business management practices of today. A key point we make is: "What is being taught in many business schools and by many consultants (and therefore being commonly practiced) is traditional business management which is not in sync with a fast-evolving and technology rich future.

To illustrate the outdated way business management often operates, we do not give a treatise on the subject, but instead provide examples. Although the first example is not terribly recent, it is still relevant since business management is evolving quite slowly (as can be seen by comparing the teachings of many of the business books published recently with those published 10 years ago).

MANAGEMENT APPROACH

Now, the first example. In July 2006, prior to the most recent economic recession, there was an interesting article was published in *Fortune* magazine by Betsy Morris.[91] Jack Welch, the legendary CEO of General Electric turned "guru" after retirement, at that time, had spoken widely and written about his management rules for business success, at least for his company. Welch's rules, as listed in Morris' article, were:

1. Big Dogs own the Street
2. Be No. 1 or No. 2 in your Market
3. Rank your Players: Go ahead with A's
4. Shareholders rule
5. Be Lean and Mean
6. Hire a Charismatic CEO
7. Admire my Might

But Morris considered Welch's rules to be obsolete and proposed her own "new" rules to replace Welch's "old" ones. These were:

1. Agile is Best; Being Big can Bite you
2. Find a Niche, Create Something New
3. Hire Passionate People
4. The Customer is King
5. Look Out, Not In

6. Hire a Courageous CEO
7. Admire my Soul

In the article, Welch's reply to Morris was that some of her "new" rules were consistent with his "old" rules. So he agreed with those. However he strongly disagreed with some. For example, in support of his rule No. 3 (weeding out the weakest employees) versus Morris' new rule (hire passionate people), he stated: "The Red Sox and the Mets are playing tonight. Guess what? They are fielding their best team."

Considering Welch's "old rules" and Morris' "new rules" from a broader perspective, there is the issue of whether these rules are meant to have a short-term or a long-term effect on financial results. This is left somewhat unclear in the debate, so it contributes to the difficulty in judging who is correct: Jack Welch, the experienced retired CEO of a very large company, then a top consultant to many diverse corporations; or Betsy Morris, the business journalist without direct experience in managing a large business.

In a sense, one can say that both are right and both are wrong, depending on the definition of business success, the timeframe being considered, and your view of business management. For example, if you "manage by words" rather than "managing by numbers" the above sets of "rules" are compatible with each other for the most part, and both are right. The trouble is that today's stockholders are not interested in "words." They are interested in immediate results measured **by numbers** such as sales, sales growth, Profit & Loss, Return on Capital, Return on Equity, etc. And without stockholders' confidence, a company cannot do well. Therefore, from this view of business success, it is essential to "manage by numbers." And from this viewpoint both Welch's and Morris' rules are wrong.

As early as 1994, this "words" versus "numbers" issue in business management was recognized. Consider the short article written by Maurice Ramsey,[92] a then retired senior lecturer in physics at Northumbria University in the UK. In this article he described the three main activities of the "education establishment," which he called the "three cultures." Examples he gave of these "three cultures" were: 1) scientific (exemplified by the Schrodinger equations), 2) artistic (exemplified by one of William Shakespeare's sonnets), and 3) business management (an area where teachings are only expressed in general words). His conclusions about this "third culture" are rather harsh. He writes that: "The third culture seeks not to enrich and enlighten but to control and self-propagate." And he posits that the "words only culture" is one that is often propagated by business consultants.

The point we are making with these examples is that in today's environment where speed, adaptability, and accuracy are keys to business survival, one cannot manage a company by basing actions **only on words**. The common problem? Although the business objectives are always stated in numbers, only words are used to plan how to reach them. Thus in our fast paced, technologically driven, exponentially changing world, the challenge for business management is to **bridge the gap** between words and numbers—to manage, not just measure, the business by numbers. Please note that we said "manage the business" (which includes strategy building and decision-making) and did NOT say "manage the employees," which is a very different proposition.

To summarize, while the world is radically changing around them, today's business management is not proactive in coping with these changes and thus is NOT keeping pace with the technological and economic realities of the times. Bottom line, **business management today is obsolete.** It is being practiced as a slowly developing "art" or even worse, guided by fads that come and go, devoid of major, permanent leaps. The result—missed opportunities to ride the tsunamis of technological change to extreme growth.

TREATMENT OF INNOVATION IN LARGE COMPANIES

The innovation that is promoted in large corporations is mostly technical innovation. Yes scientists are encouraged to invent and to file patents on those inventions that are assigned to their companies. But management (and corporate culture) channels these efforts towards making **evolutionary** technical advances that will contribute to the existing business. In addition, business creativity is often ignored. What is the problem with this? Imagine that a young person within a large company wants to start a new-to-the-world business using state-of-the-art technology that is readily available. What would commonly happen to that person and the idea? To illustrate the issues, we create a **fictional** example.

Suppose that a young woman, whom we will call "Mary Smith," had an idea for a revolutionary social networking business, similar to Facebook but somewhat earlier in time, and wanted to develop it into a business in the large corporation where she worked instead of trying to start the business herself. Full of enthusiasm, she approached a middle manager in her big company. And, as is often typical, Mary received little encouragement. But she was an adventurous and committed young entrepreneur. Hence she found a way to get an appointment with the company's President to try and interest him in her idea.

Now, let us focus on the President. He (not she) is in his early 60s, not far from his retirement for which he is guaranteed a nice pension—provided nothing awful happens in his company before he retires. He has been picked by the Board and the stockholders specifically to keep the company on a steady course, with sales and profits increasing at least 5% per year and **no surprises**— something that was proving to be extremely challenging. In addition, the Board and the stockholders have made it clear to him that they do not like negative publicity, particularly the kind that would be connected to a "bad" (or risky) investment.

Continuing our story, Mary Smith is escorted by the president's executive assistant (certainly not just a "secretary") into the president's **corner** office (it always is a corner office if the President is someone of value). The scheduled meeting is very short because the president has to leave soon, first for an "important" meeting on the golf course and then to prepare for the next day's Operations Committee meeting, where possible new investments will be discussed. Although he does not have much time for Mary, he is very polite.

Mary is a little nervous, but is committed to her idea and makes a good presentation. The president thinks that it is more than a little farfetched and certainly risky, but says he is willing to consider it—in principle. He then asks Mary a couple of questions: Have you debated this idea with your peers within our company? Have you worked with our marketing department to do any marketing research? Do you know what kind of investment is required and what the estimated return is? Her answers in short: all "no." The president then replies: "Well Mary, I praise your initiative, but you need to proceed in an orderly fashion. First, meet with your peers within the company, and if they support your idea, then come back to me with a detailed market research plan."

A few days later, Mary tries to make another appointment with the president, but his first available slot is much later. Although impatient, Mary is persistent, and a month later they meet again. The dialogue goes like this:

"Well Mary, what have you found?"

"You see, Mr. President—"

"No, call me John. We are all on a first name basis in this company."

"Yes, John. I met with a group of my peers in our company. Although most of them did not like my idea, a few were strongly supportive and excited."

"Well I'm sorry Mary, but in this company we **manage by consensus.** If you do not have a consensus, maybe your idea is premature or not well thought out or just plain not good."

Although the president desperately needed a promising new opportunity for his company, he did not appreciate that a consensus decision is very often going to involve following the same, familiar road, and this is usually the worst decision in a time of crisis or when something new appears on the horizon. To avoid disaster or to have a chance to capitalize on something new, a leader has to quickly make the decision to change direction, and determine the new path to follow.

To continue with our story, the president (John) then asked Mary: "Have you checked with our marketing department?"

"Yes, Sir—John, but all they did was to ask a Panel that was meeting for another assignment a few questions relating to my idea. The Panel thought that nobody would be interested. But I strongly believe they are wrong."

"Well Mary, I will support you making one more attempt. A famous consultant who is expert at evaluating businesses will be visiting us in two months' time. I will set up an appointment for you with him to discuss the merits of your idea."

Two months later the now very impatient Mary explained her idea to the consultant. "Well, Ms. Smith," says the consultant, "there are millions of ideas in this world and it is difficult to identify the good ones. But it is possible. Have you read my book B *How to win, win, win, win at business?*"

"No, sir, I have not read it."

"No?!" Well, buy it and read it. Then we can discuss your idea intelligently. One can predict with 98% accuracy whether any business can be successful. But one must use the system taught in my book"

Back to a meeting with the president, yet another month later: "You see, Mary, not all ideas are good ideas. But you are talented, and I want to give you an opportunity to learn about business. I have decided to assign you to a business manager's group so you can learn the realities of the business world. Then, if you can support your idea with data, we can discuss it again."

Mary is totally frustrated, but not willing to give up, so continues to work on her idea from her new position.

A year later, it is time for a "performance appraisal." The Human Resources manager sits with Mary's new manager to evaluate her performance. "What are her weak points?" he asks.

The Supervisor replies: "Well, there are many. Mary is not a team player. She thinks too highly of herself and her idea, and does not pay attention to consensus opinions from her team. She does not ask for advice from the marketing department, does not want to listen to our expert consultant, and has come up with unrealistic market expectations for her idea. Who could possibly believe that her idea could lead to a multi- billion dollar business within 10 years?"

And Mary was rated as a "C-," below the requirements for the job.

Mary had had enough. After telling her manager what she thought of his leadership and the leadership of the company, she quit. But she didn't give up. She started her own company, found appropriate investors, and aggressively pursued her revolutionary idea. Will she succeed? Only time will tell. But one thing is clear. If she had not left the big company, her "act of creation" would not have amounted to anything.

Our point with this story? Today there is no space for the Marys, Mark Zuckerbergs, Steve Jobs, Jeff Bezos, etc. in the life of a major corporation. Even if an innovative idea or a new technology offers the potential of multi-billion dollar sales (and good profits) within 10 years, the risk is too great. If one doubts that this story represents the culture often found in large companies, we suggest reading the book *Tough Choices* by Carly Fiorina.[93] We do not wish to enter the debate as to who was right and who was wrong in her disagreement with her Board or make any reference to her politics. We merely wish to point out that, in our experience, her description of corporate life is generally accurate.

But the problems for disruptive innovations in large companies start even before personnel are hired. We also suggest reading the article "Elite Universities Are Turning Our Kids into Corporate Stooges,"[94] which describes recruiting practices by large companies.

So what is today's alternative to "Corporate America" for pursuing breakthrough ideas and technologies? **Start your own business**. We have all been impacted by the business that Mark Elliott Zuckerberg started on his own. He and others like him have been able to succeed because of financing from private investors who were **really** interested in supporting revolutionary, albeit risky ideas. They were willing to take risks, because they individually judged that the potential payoffs were sufficiently high. And equally important, the creator and trailblazer leading the way is not hampered by the culture and common practices of many of today's large corporations.

THE LACK OF EVOLUTION TO
NEW LAUNCHING PADS

As we explained in Chapter 4, we define "Launching Pads" as the basic science or technologies from which entire new industries are born—industries created by advancing the technologies and using these advances in the commercialization of revolutionary new products. But why do the initial breakthroughs often happen outside of the major corporations that would have the resources to bring the commercialization to fruition?

This is a question for which we have provided a partial answer in the previous section, but there are some additional factors that come into play. Why did Kodak not start developing internally a **microelectronics based** imaging platform while they were in the lead in photography? Why were many established pharmaceutical companies so reticent to seriously develop Biogenetics? Why was the iPhone not developed inside an established mobile telephone company? It appears that not many large companies have the will to re-invent themselves and enter the future with completely new technologies and business models.

What is the problem? We believe that, when a **completely** new Launching Pad is developing, any attempt to implant it inside an established large company creates a "crisis of rejection," just like implanting a new organ into a body where the immune system does not want to receive it. When people (scientists included) are faced with something completely new that they do not quite understand, their first reaction is to reject it. By the time they realize that they cannot ignore it, it is often too late to catch up.

But there is another problem. Large companies, even if they have sizable research departments, generally do not have sufficient resources for generating enough of the right breakthrough technology advances within their own company to lead to substantial growth. And companies cannot afford to import numerous **potentially** good ideas from the outside (even if they were able to survive the inside "barrier of rejection") because in reality many of these fail when one tries to turn them into products. But large companies could be more open to importing ideas from the outside when their business validity has been proven with reasonable probability. The time window to act is short (window between the proof of the business validity and the financing by angel investors), but it can be done. Unfortunately, this does not happen very often. Can this problem be solved in the near term, to give new life to established companies? Some directions to pursue are explored in Chapters 11 and 12.

COMPANY "ATMOSPHERE"

We have described, with a few examples, some of the differences between the "normal" companies of today and the Superstars. However we would be remiss if we did not mention the "atmosphere" that exists in most Superstars. We can get a few glimpses of the working environment in a Superstar by watching a few video programs that have been produced and a few accounts by papers and magazines. But let us summarize by saying that informality characterizes these environments, from more informal dress codes to personal interactions, to the excitement of being at the forefront, to young and enthusiastic management, to extremely long working hours volunteered with personal pleasure. In other words, there is an excitement and electricity that starts at the top and invades every corner of the company. If we only could replicate this excitement in most large Fortune 500 companies!

Eleven

SCIENCE-BASED
BUSINESS MANAGEMENT

In the previous chapter, we focused on some of the ways that traditional business management is hindering the creation of new Superstars. However, as we stated, there is another and more serious aspect to the problem: business management is advancing linearly in an exponentially changing, technology driven world; and the gap is widening. This is a serious problem for the survival and success of companies in the future, as well as for the creation of new Superstars.

What needs to be done? That is the key question that this chapter addresses. The answer revolves around the need for the "art" of business management to transition to the "science" of business management. More specifically, we address one important leadership skill that is often ignored: the ability to make effective decisions rapidly. How does a business leader accomplish this? We believe such actions require science-based management methodologies and tools.

In this chapter we provide brief overviews and our assessments of what we believe to be the most usable and progressive forms of science-based business practices that are available (or almost available) today. These are the first steps toward practicing business management as a science instead of an art.

SCIENCE-BASED DECISION-MAKING

As we have stated several times, in a rapidly changing, disruptive environment, business survival and growth depend on "speed." And this means making the best decisions and making them quickly. If leaders use a logical and data-based process and have rapid access to the right information, they can anticipate the reactions of others and proactively make better choices. This is what we call science-based decision-making, and it increases the chances for business success.

Science-based decision-making starts with the **scientific method**. The scientific method is a logical, data-based approach to investigating phenomena and developing new knowledge. This method consists of the collection of data through observation and experimentation, followed by the formulation and testing of theories based on that data. If the experiments "validate" the theories (i.e., the results are reproducible and in accordance with the theories), the theories are then used to predict future results.

Use of the Scientific Method is not new, and the explosive advances in technology and science of the past 100 years have been made by applying this logical and **quantitative** approach to what was once an empirical world. The initial leaps forward were made when science started tackling simple problems that could be solved by the deterministic approach typical of the 19th century and earlier, but not yet to problems of increased complexity. Then, during the 20th century, it was shown that probabilistic theories, using advanced computer-based technologies (initially in the field of military strategy), could be applied to problems that were previously thought to be inherently impervious to them. Specifically it was shown that problems where one could not guarantee a direct connection between cause and effect for each **individual** event could be treated rigorously by looking at the aggregate of many events. This is one of the break-through advances that will lead to methodologies and tools that have the potential to change business management and the business landscape. The only question is when.

In today's business world, those businesses that are technically oriented already have embraced some scientific methodologies in the operations arena (research and development, engineering, manufacturing, finance, and to some extent marketing). But, as will be discussed in the following sections, many business leaders are still using empirical (or even intuitive) approaches in making **total** business decisions. However, the new science-based management tools and methodologies that are starting to emerge will allow management to apply quantitative techniques to business decisions rather than relying on intuition and experience, and—most important—to do so in the short timelines required by the "new business speed." In addition, these new tools provide a way to quantitatively analyze risk factors in shorter time frames, leading to **both** better and quicker decisions.

However, the most advanced techniques are rather complex and require an effort that small to mid-size companies often cannot afford. The good news is that simpler techniques and simulations for evaluating alternative strategies are available. Therefore in the next section we focus on computer-based methodologies that could be used today, but often are not—specifically techniques for computer assisted business **optimization**. Then, in the remaining sections, we address business analytics and big data and computer assisted business **planning**.

COMPUTER ASSISTED BUSINESS
OPTIMIZATION (TODAY)

Cost cutting, pricing optimization, sales promotions, new products, new businesses, new strategies, new... What is the right mix of actions and directions for a business? That depends on business performance and objectives, and those depend on many interrelated variables. For example, pricing, advertising, product quality, and competitive position all affect sales; and sales affect manufacturing utilization which affects costs. And of course profits depend on sales and total costs. And what about cash flow? This extremely important business metric depends on many variables—income, depreciation, investments, inventories, receivables, accounts payable and more.

As one can see, today it is not straightforward to optimize simultaneously all of the interrelated factors considered important in a business in order to obtain the best results. Too often business management focuses on a single, easily identifiable and changeable factor (e.g., pricing), and actions are taken based on "what if" scenarios created using simple spreadsheets. Then the focus moves on to the next single factor and its impact is calculated. Yes, such basic computer modeling could be called computer assisted business optimization, but it is extremely limited, because it does not take into account the mutual interaction between different variables; and it often is based on very limited actual data.

But even a relatively simple computer model can do better. How do you proceed if you want to develop such models? In our book *Survival in the Sea of Economic Chaos*[95] we provide several examples, limited in scope but better than a single variable analysis. In one case, the dependence of units sold (and hence sales) on selling prices is plotted using the price elasticity of demand, (determined from separate studies). Another example models the effect of selling prices on profits by incorporating a plot of costs versus units produced.

However the relatively simple models described above still do not take into account many other relevant, interrelated variables. Furthermore, measures other than profit sometimes can better represent a company's financial performance. For example, return on assets can be more important in the case of the grocery stores business. Or accurately determining cash flow may be essential when there is the possibility of a shortage of cash or if excessive up-front investments have been made. In these cases, simple calculations, such as those described in our book referenced above, are not sufficient, and a computer model better representing the **whole business** is preferable and possible. But developing such a model requires some programming expertise. Variables needing to be incorporated into the model include:

- Those which can be assessed by appropriate market research (e.g., expected sales volumes, price elasticity, cost and effectiveness of advertising and promotion)
- Those which can be determined by appropriate internal audits (e.g., fixed and variable manufacturing costs; the probability of success, the returns, and the timing of both R&D programs and manufacturing/process improvements)

Although it is desirable, one can see that the effort in producing a complete computerized model of a company's business is quite work intensive. In practice, as mentioned above, only a mid-sized or a large company may be able to afford it. For smaller companies we suggest that the examples referenced in this section provide a good starting point. However to be competitive in the near future, companies of all kind and sizes will need to have business intelligence systems and expertise to drive reporting and descriptive analytics and to embrace "data science" as described in the following section on business analytics and big data.

BUSINESS ANALYTICS AND BIG DATA

Business analytics refers to "the extensive use of data, statistical and quantitative analysis, explanatory and predictive (computer) models, and fact-based management to drive decisions and actions."[96] The rapid development and adoption of advanced business analytics technologies is already altering the business landscape.

Big data refers to data sets too large for traditional data processing. These data sets have the potential for "huge new benefits—but also heartaches."[97] The explosive emergence and availability of such huge, fast-changing, unstructured data from various old and new sources, mostly external to a business, and attempts to analyze them, has created the "age of information"—an age where knowledge is power. But in many companies these unwieldy data sets have also created an "analysis bottleneck" that limits their usefulness.

But now it is possible to combine big data with advanced business analytics. Unparalleled and real-time access to vast quantities of data and the ability to rapidly analyze them in meaningful ways are already realities. Business management is being challenged with the rapidly growing technical capability of harnessing the vast potential that is hidden in multiple sources of massive data/information.

Today many companies already are analyzing big data to achieve significant competitive advantages—to improve products and services, cut costs, attract repeat customers, and more. An IBM Global Business Services Executive Report documents several big successes: "Companies like McLeod Russel India Limited completely eliminated systems downtime in the tea trade through more accurate tracking of the harvest, production and marketing of up to 100 million kilos of tea each year. Premier Healthcare Alliance used enhanced data sharing and analytics to improve patient outcomes while reducing spending by $2.85 billion. And Santam improved the customer experience by implementing predictive analytics to reduce fraud."[98]

Still embryonic though, are advanced analytical methodologies that can be applied to big data to build useful models for predicting and optimizing future outcomes. Such tools would enable leaders to make better decisions and make them faster and with lower risk; and might even help scientists make fundamental discoveries. This is the promise of the emerging field of data science, the marriage between big data and advanced analytics, the former providing the information, the latter supplying the tools that can be applied to that information to develop insight and guide action.[99] However, there is one giant caution for business leaders. Big data and analytics, no matter how sophisticated and expertly used, will not replace or necessarily even predict disruptive innovations. Analyzing the past and extrapolating to the future is not likely to accurately predict a future shaped by unparalleled disruptive and exponential change.

COMPUTER ASSISTED BUSINESS PLANNING (THE FUTURE)

As we have stated, we advocate a greater use of scientific methodologies in business management, especially for developing new and better strategies and plans and for rapid and more effective decision-making. However there is a problem. To be specific, today data on the performance of a company can be analyzed in great detail using simple business analytics in the form of conventional computer-based tools. Examples include the Profit and Loss statement, the Balance Sheet, and analyses of Cash Flow and Return on Investment. And, more recently, as described in the last section, computer analyses of big data are becoming common as the field of data science develops. But these all are **analyses of the past—** past data, past performance of a company.

When it comes to projecting alternative possibilities for future performance in a rapidly evolving and competitive world, different tools and methodologies are necessary. In other words, planning based on a linear extrapolation of a company's existing data into an exponentially changing future is no better than planning based on intuition. New science-based approaches and tools such as Game Theory or ABMS or something not yet invented are needed. Although these tools have not yet been developed to the point where they are readily usable and reliable enough for broad applications, we describe them in this section. Why? Because we are confident that these and/or related technologies will be developed in the near term that will give management the ability to model electronically possible alternative futures for a specific business, including its financial results as the result of different strategies, tactics, and competitive actions.

However, before briefly describing some of the developing approaches, it is important to understand the degrees of validity that are exhibited by various models. There are many different definitions of the degree of validity of different models, but we will adopt the definitions that have been used by the military, for which trying to predict the future strategies of opponents is of vital importance. Specifically, models projected towards the future can be catalogued as having one of three kinds of validity: Descriptive Validity or Structural Validity or Predictive Validity.

Descriptive Validity means that a model is able to explain **after the fact** the events which took place during an "engagement." In business, common examples of this kind of model are case studies—models which are aimed at trying to explain (in most cases qualitatively) business results after they have occurred. Such descriptive validity models are generally not computer-based and are not useful in accurate business planning.

Structural Validity means that the model is an approximate description of the situation one wants to study and has appropriate characteristics which describe **in principle** the real world situation. However the accuracy of this description is limited and may be inadequate to derive operational decisions. An example of this kind of model is the prediction of the weather or of the stock market. In a business example, the dependence of sales volumes on selling prices used in a structural validity model can describe the correct trend (higher prices yield fewer sales) but not the *exact* relationship between these two variables. This may have some usefulness when accurate market research is unavailable, but again is not adequate to support accurate business planning.

Predictive Validity means that the model can **predict fairly accurately** (and even quantitatively) a complete competitive scenario or parts of this scenario. For example a model showing the dependence of sales volumes on selling prices (to stay with the same example as given above) can have predictive validity if it is based on market research data which describe "real-world" market forces and quantitative expectations of sales volumes. These are the kinds of models that will be useful for science-based decision-making in the future. Thus, in the remainder of this section we will briefly describe evolving computer-based methodologies that are being used to develop models with enough predictive validity to be useful for the planning and the management of business operations.

Use of "War Games" in Industry: A Model with Some Predictive Validity

The application of the principle of war games to business competition is still in its infancy, in that very few companies do so with the full complexity of similar military games. Commonly, for applications to business, there are games which are based on a one-player model or on non-interacting multi-player models, as opposed to mutually interacting multi-player models. As an example of these games, one can build a model where business decisions are "played against" a computer with an embedded business model. In this type of games one team decides prices, investments and other types of business decisions, and the computer gives the outcome in sales and profits **regardless of how the other players decide to play their hand**. There is a winning team in this type of game, but there is no interaction between how one team plays the game and how the other teams react. Therefore frequently this type of game does not maintain constant the size of the market. For example, if all players decide on the same **low** selling prices, then the aggregate of the sales is much higher than if all decide on a different and higher price. Although in the real world there are varying degrees of price elasticity and therefore there are some instances where this technique is still applicable, usually this type of game does not represent well those businesses where the main effect of price wars is to take business away from each other.

Games with the full complexity of what we call "War Games" are exercises so designed that the **outcome depends not only on one's own decisions** but also on the decisions freely taken by the competitors. In both military and business applications, this employs some of the principles of Game Theory—the subject of the next section.

Game Theory[100]

Game theory is "the study of mathematical models of conflict and cooperation between intelligent rational decision-makers."[101] It can provide a powerful science-based approach to creating models that can reasonably accurately evaluate alternative "futures." This branch of applied mathematics has been used in disciplines such as economics, biology, and computer science. Specifically it attempts to mathematically model behavior and predict results in competitive situations, where the outcomes of an individual's choices depend on the choices of others. It was initially developed to analyze competitive situations (including combat) where one individual does better at another's expense (the so-called "zero sum" game), but has been expanded to other competitive and/or cooperative situations.

This methodology, when applied to business, creates a "game" that consists of: a set of "players" (competitors), a set of "moves" (rational actions) available to those players, and a mathematical model that predicts the "payoffs" that players might receive for each combination of actions. By "playing" this game, a leader can evaluate possible alternative outcomes of encounters with competing organizations that may have parallel and/or conflicting goals. In other words, Game Theory can help leaders make better strategic decisions in complex situations by predicting the probable consequences of the collective actions and reactions of all the players.

Although the full use of game theory involves complex mathematics, the basic principles can be applied qualitatively to provide general guidance. We call this **qualitative** game theory. This is a logical process that uses the basic concepts of Game Theory (but not the complex mathematics) to create simple models of competitive business situations. The model framework is developed by establishing: the players, the goals, the possible actions (assumed to be rational), and the constraints (including timing). Sometimes just having this information is valuable. The game is "played" by answering logically "what if and then what" questions for all possible actions by the players. Visualization of the game is helpful and is often accomplished by using a matrix approach or a "decision tree" diagram.[102] Usually this type of "game" will clearly identify some options that are undesirable and others that deserve further consideration. Therefore, although the guidance is general, qualitative Game Theory can be a useful decision-making methodology when timing is critical and mathematical experts unavailable.

One early example of this type of application of game theory in business was given in an article by Raymond W. Smith, CEO of Bell Atlantic, where he explains that the value of game theory is to "analyze different scenarios, exploring interdependencies and changing strategies mid-course."[103]

According to Smith, game theory, as applied to his business, requires "placing yourself in the shoes of your opponents to understand how they will counter your tactical moves" and if necessary change direction.

In Bell Atlantic they had a number of techniques to compare the merits of alternate strategies prior to the final implementation. Smith's article quotes three named "Fish Bowl" (debate of different ideas), "Red Team/Blue Team," similar to war games, and "Future mapping" to identify, among many possible strategies the one which offers the highest returns with the smallest risks. Smith points out that this way of operating requires management skills and practices which are different from those prevalent in the past. Of course, human nature is such that these new approaches invite resistance within the organization, and therefore we expect that they can only be implemented if they are driven "from the top."

While such a qualitative approach to game theory can be useful, a full quantitative model is needed to predict with some accuracy outcomes in today's complex and dynamic economic environment. However, this is not simple. Developing quantitative models with predictive validity requires the use of advanced mathematical tools that are not common knowledge among business leaders. Therefore leaders must find and rely on appropriate experts for model development and application (game playing). Even though this approach is complex, it can be worthwhile for a large company or a complicated business situation. The good news is that there are a number of consultants and experts available who have experience in successful business applications of this methodology.[104]

Since published examples of actual applications of quantitative versions of Game Theory to business are very rare, we have no way of knowing which and how many corporations use these more advanced versions of this technique. However, there is an excellent published example from several years ago—an article entitled "Scientific Management at Merck."[105] We summarize this article below.

Merck is a company that in most of its history has shown relatively fast growth, coupled with excellent profits. And all this has been achieved in an industry that has very long lead times between decisions and results, partially due to government regulations and to the approvals required in the pharmaceutical field. It's important to keep in mind that such long lead times make forecasting and scenario studies that much more difficult, because the more distant is the future, the more difficult it is to predict it correctly.

However, according to the article, a number of quantitative predictive tools based on game theory have been used successfully by the management of this company. Why did they resort to this expensive and complex methodology? According to the article, on average, at that time, it was taking $359 million and 10 years to bring a drug to market. Then, after market introduction, 70% of the products did not repay the investment. Therefore the company leadership decided that it was essential that future numerical predictions be made with the highest possible degree of predictive accuracy. This was being made even more difficult because, in addition to the evolution of markets, a number of possible but not yet certain developments were appearing on the horizon, including the possibility of significant health care reform, the growing demand for generic drugs, and new discoveries in the field of biogenetics.

Given this situation, Merck recognized that it was not sufficient to plan for the **most likely scenario**, but was essential to develop a sophisticated, quantitative, contingency planning methodology. Many companies, given this scenario, would have become very conservative in their investments, because after all it is the easiest path to follow. But Merck went in the opposite direction. In the article, Merck leaders were quoted as saying: "The route to success is to put **more** money at risk." And "Success ... won't result from the quality of the scientists alone ... but will also come from the quality of the thinking about where to invest."

In the authors' opinion this scenario will become more pervasive to other types of industry, because, as technology development becomes more sophisticated and more expensive, even non-medical products will take longer to develop and will require an increasing amount of scarce capital to invest in new enterprises.

However Merck didn't just employ Game Theory. The

article describes other quantitative, science-based models that the company used for decision making: a "Research Planning Model" which is based on a simulation technique used in physics and known as "Monte Carlo Simulation," and a "Revenue Edging Model" which minimizes the effect of those financial events over which Merck has no influence. In both of these models the programs used computer simulation coupled with Game Theory to work out different scenarios with their consequences, probabilities, maximum risks; and to predict the best course of action based on these and other factors.

As can be seen from these examples, advanced computer simulation (modeling) can be a reasonably accurate methodology (to the same degree as the inputs are accurate) that rapidly works through a large number of scenarios. It can point to the strategy which combines a high probability to achieve the desired outcomes, (usually best financial results) and least downside risk. However, as in the case of Merck, the use of game theory is most useful when it is applied to situations when there are many players (as most often is the case) and when management wishes to see the business from the point of view of each of the players over a period of several years rather than as a point-in-time event.

In other words, Game Theory is particularly useful for exploring alternatives when there are multiple players, conflicting goals, and many action options. However, one should be cautious: the more complex the business situation, the more complex the mathematics. In addition, Game Theory assumes that the players always make rational choices, and that doesn't always happen in the real world. Bottom line, Game Theory is on the verge of becoming a useful tool.[106] However, it takes investment— in time and in people. The hope is that future developments will make this more readily useful to the broader business management community.

"Agent-Based Modeling and Simulation"[107]

Although Game Theory provides an excellent logical framework for simulating business situations (as well as for developing military strategies), as we have mentioned, the complexity of the "real world" makes the development of rigorous models difficult. Therefore, a number of experts believe that the decision-making methodology known as Agent-Based Modeling and Simulation (ABMS) is often a better science-based choice.

ABMS is a computer-enabled methodology that describes (and predicts) the evolution of dynamic systems by simulating the behavior of their constituent "agents" (individual parties or players). In other words, ABMS is a modeling technique that rapidly converts knowledge of a large number of individual behaviors into an understanding of overall system-level outcomes. To do this, it combines elements of Game Theory and Complexity Science (see Chapter 15), and uses Monte Carlo methods to introduce randomness.

More specifically, with ABMS, a system (e.g., your market) is modeled as a collection of entities called Agents. Each Agent individually makes decisions and acts based on a set of rules appropriate for the system it represents (e.g., producing, selling, buying). ABMS can create thousands of individual Agents rapidly, and it allows "learning" and repetitive interactions among those Agents to occur. This enables the system to evolve, and unanticipated behaviors to emerge (emergent phenomena). This adaptive feature allows ABMS to explore complex system dynamics, which are out of the reach of the pure mathematics of Game Theory. In other words, ABMS has the ability to predict possible outcomes such as—in the case of business—market shares, sales, and profitability and to provide strategic insights into future marketplace behavior. To summarize, the key features differentiating ABMS from Game Theory are:

1. ABMS builds the market (and predicted outcomes) "bottom" up from many individual interactions.
2. ABMS can use data in many forms from many sources.
3. ABMS can analyze multiple scenarios rapidly.
4. ABMS does not require every party to take rational actions and allows for adaptive behavior.
5. ABMS allows for unanticipated emergent phenomena.

Thus, like a number of experts, we believe that ABMS is the best developing science-based methodology for helping leaders make decisions about problems with many interrelated but unpredictable elements. However, it is important to keep in mind that, like Game Theory, the complexity of use deters many business leaders from using this technique, and that models, no matter how sophisticated, can only project probable outcomes, not actual reality. Therefore, it is up to the decision-maker, the business leader, to use those tools wisely. For additional information about ABMS applies to business, there are a number of internet articles available.[108]

Other Science-Based Possibilities

Game theory, ABMS—the direction is right, but why aren't these techniques used more often and more successfully in many more companies? It is interesting to note that many consultants who organize many well-attended courses for managers seldom list Game Theory and ABMS among the subjects they treat. Is it because they are not useful in practical management? Or is it because they are too complex to teach in a seminar or too complex for most consultants to use effectively?

Some progress is being made that addresses these concerns. For example, IBM is offering a service which they call the "IBM Watson Engagement Advisor."[109] As IBM describes, this service combines the basics of big data handling with the Watson technologies of natural language-based processing, hypothesis generation, and evidence-based learning. The result, they claim, is that a business manager who is not a statistician or data scientist, can type in questions to probe/analyze corporate big data in meaningful ways. In their words, business professionals can quickly understand and make decisions based on Watson Analytics' data-driven visualizations. For example, one might ask and get a data-based answer to the question "What high-value customers am I most likely to close sales with during the next 30 days?"

If IBM can already do this, perhaps they will soon be able to expand their technology to include easy-to-use capabilities based on elements of Game Theory or ABMS to more accurately project business futures based on data and alternative strategies and actions. This is just one possibility. In our technologically driven world, we are confident there will be other data science developments in the not too distant future that will provide new science-based capabilities for better business management.

However, before relying entirely on computers, some caution is needed. Remember that the 2007-2008 financial crisis was due to excessive reliance on computer programs. Computers are great—when there is enough human supervision; but otherwise, managers beware.

CONCLUSIONS

To summarize, we repeat an important point: Although

science-based methodologies represent the future of business management, at the end of the day, it is humans, not mathematical theories or computers, who have to weigh the risks and rewards in making the final choice between strategies. Computerized models are only as good as the assumptions used to created them and only predict the probabilities of outcomes of different strategies.

But how we reconcile the spectacular performance of what we call Superstars with the fact that, as far as we know, Superstar leaders are not using advanced, science-based decision-making tools. So why have they succeeded where others have failed? Consider that there is another very important factor that all companies encounter today: RISK. Yes, advanced science-based tools, if properly used, allows one to balance desired performance with risk of failure, and then to choose the preferred path to follow—usually the path that minimizes risk and maximizes rewards. But there will always be leaders that defy the odds and take the path of biggest risk for the biggest rewards. These leaders are willing to take the risk of losing everything, knowing that if they succeed, they win and win big. Their companies will become Superstars. So yes, the success of management in the future will depend on the use of advanced, science-based decision- making tools; but there will always be rebels. And some of those rebels will win.

Twelve

NEW PRACTICES FOR
HIGHER PERFORMANCE

In the previous chapter we strongly advocated the increased use of science-based methodologies as the "next step" in business management. As we stated, we see this as key in transitioning business from an art (as it is often practiced today) to a science (as it must be practiced tomorrow). And this important but difficult transition must be championed and driven by the CEOs who must explain it, "preach" it, and demand it of the personnel of their companies. They are the ones who must make these and other changes happen.

However, this isn't enough. The role and key responsibilities of the CEO also need to change, as do company functions. We address what we believe are essential changes in these key areas in this chapter.

CORPORATE DIRECTION

An important, but not new responsibility of the CEO is setting the corporate financial goals and business objectives. Typical financial goals include sales, profits, cash flow, return on assets or capital employed, and earnings per share. Business objectives might include growth, market share, new products, green products, etc. In the past, it was relatively simple: establish goals and objectives, develop strategies (usually qualitative), and then implement those strategies, usually addressing one goal or one objective at a time.

However establishing goals and objectives is no longer simple in today's world where everything is becoming interconnected and more complex. Goals, objectives, strategies and external forces (e.g., competitive, economic, and political) are intertwined and interdependent. Does the company want growth in sales or profits, or can it be both? What balance of risk versus reward is acceptable, over what time period? What is the best target market, and should the focus be high volume or niche? What will be the impact of changes in the economy or political environment? And what about global competition, both direct and indirect? The list of interconnected questions to address goes on and on.

But there is one, key question: Are the **combination** of goals and objectives realistic and attainable with the chosen strategies? Well, that depends—on the business definition, business model, competition, access to products and technologies and... Bringing all of this together and optimizing the total package in a way that leads to business success is the challenge that faces today's CEOs.

This challenge is not new, but in a chaotic and rapidly changing global environment, the complexity of addressing this challenge is increasing exponentially—just like technology. So the qualitative approaches of the past are no longer adequate. However, as was discussed in the previous chapter, there is an important new development: the growing ability to quantify the outcomes and probabilities of success of combinations of alternative choices through the use of advanced computer models of the business and market in question. By adjusting the relevant parameters for each combination of choices selected, different alternative futures can be compared.

Ultimately, and in the not too distant future, with the proper, easy-to-use software, the CEO will be able to adjust the goals and determine the best strategies by having "war games" played on computers in a simulated match among competitors. Such a process will project business outcomes, answering questions such as: Which strategy (including business definition and business model) will lead to a major market share, or provide the highest profits over several years, or produce the most rapid increase in sales, etc. However, as Chapter 11 highlighted, the issue remains that to realize the full potential of new science-based methodologies, CEOs must embrace a quantitative future. In other words, a CEO must become as skilled in analyzing numbers as he or she is in using words. Or, alternatively, he or she must rely on a high level corporate expert.

STRATEGIC GOVERNANCE

The Situation Today

Much of the fate of a company is determined not only by external forces and corporate direction, but also by the management processes adopted by the company, in other words, by what we call its "Strategic Governance." By this term we mean the processes by which important strategic decisions are made and the individuals or groups of individuals who have the power to make them. In other words, "Strategic Governance" defines who makes the decisions about the future direction of the business and how those decisions are made.

Too often today CEOs "inherit" a type of Governance when they are elected to that leadership position, and they keep everything the same. However in a rapidly changing environment, a new, adaptable and more streamlined approach is often necessary for survival. Therefore in this section we discuss and critique three aspects of typical Strategic Governance of companies today: shorter term focus, risk avoidance, and decisions by committee.

We are sure that most readers are somewhat familiar with the typical organizational structures of most mid to large size companies, so we will not discuss them in detail. Suffice it to say, most companies are organized into several main Functions, commonly reporting to General Management or the President. The operational functions usually are Research and Development (R&D), Manufacturing and Engineering (where applicable), and Sales and Marketing.

The main operational focus in the business conduct of these functions, and of the company as a whole, is to reach specific objectives related to the financial performance of the company. These objectives are mostly connected with short to medium term profits and revenue growth. Company survival and success in the longer term is of course very important, but in today's economy many executives mistakenly believe that this is fairly assured if the shorter term financial objectives are achieved.

As the result of this shorter term focus, the main goal of corporate management (and thus functional management as well) in many mid-sized and large companies today is to avoid actions that can harm the profitable growth of a company in the shorter term. This leads to risk avoidance by those in charge since executives can lose their jobs if things go wrong or perceived mistakes are made (say a bad investment or an acquisition that doesn't live up to expectations). In other words, if the business takes a downturn or a particular financial objective is not met, even when the a-priori conditions appeared to be very favorable, by definition it is always a mistake.

But this low-risk approach to business has a significant

downside, as we highlighted in Chapter 10. Big rewards often involve big risks. By avoiding risks, large opportunities are likely to be lost. Just consider Superstars like Apple, Facebook, and Amazon. They have taken and continue to take big risks (e.g., new technologies, new business models, whole new businesses), and their rewards have been huge!

And risk avoidance isn't the only problem. Another, extremely common way that today's management avoids responsibility for mistakes is by diluting responsibility for decisions. This is done by the broad use of "decisions by committee" at all levels. This practice is often promoted as a way to achieve more effective teamwork and to make better decisions, but it has another attribute. If a decision has a bad outcome, the main fault becomes that of the deciding group or committee. The days of "the buck stops here" in senior management are vanishing into history.

But spreading responsibility for actions isn't the only issue with "decisions by committee." A group usually tends to adopt the view of its more conservative elements, thus further minimizing risk at the expense of potential maximum reward. Furthermore, although it is unclear whether decisions turn out to be more often "correct" when made by a committee, it is certain that they are slower. Why is this?

A typical corporate decision-making committee takes time to assemble, and frequently—due to busy schedules—only meets once a month. Often the committee does not approve a proposal right away, but wants to see revisions that take time to be made, say another month. Then, a month later, after another presentation, with luck the proposal gets approved. And often it is not clear that this proposal is improved with respect to the original one. Although in some types of organizations the time it takes for decision-making may be less critical, in a fast-paced world with aggressive competitors, rapid decisions are essential for business survival. In other words, a slow decision is always a wrong decision.

However, it is important to keep in mind that sometimes, with the increased complexity of business in our rapidly changing world, there is a need for many different types of expertise to be brought to bear on problems and decisions. The challenge is to reconcile the need for speed with the approach to handling this complexity. This will be addressed in the next section.

Strategic Governance for the Future

Today and in the near future, choosing the best types of **strategic governance** for their corporations has become one of the most important jobs of corporate leaders. This responsibility has rapidly increased in importance because of the risks of traditional strategic governance as described in the previous section. Fortunately new types of strategic governance are emerging that have shown promise in very fast-growing and successful companies.

For example, take a look at some of today's successful, high visibility companies—companies such as Apple, Facebook, Amazon, and Google. Two of the several common factors that link these companies together are the overwhelming presence and power of the head of the company and, presumably, limited **strategic** decisions by committee. The CEO decides. What are the advantages? Very fast decisions and changes of direction can result in very fast growth! And what about the disadvantages? Simply stated, the biggest disadvantage is **risk**—risks including those of poor decisions, unwise directions, and alienation of personnel. A solitary decision-maker increases such risks but also offers the possibility of huge rewards, as we described in the story of RCA. Must such risks be accepted as part of this type of strategic governance today?

Even the leaders of the current Superstars have not

always found the best combination of speed versus risk. We believe that, in the future, finding that optimum balance will require a much heavier reliance on advances in data science, and yes, even **advisory** committees. What specifically do we mean? As we said above, in a complex business environment, radically different strategies and good decisions are likely to require input from a number of different experts. How can this be reconciled with the need for speed?

One way to accomplish this is by additional **separation of responsibilities** for the collecting and analyzing of data and the developing of possible alternate decisions from the decision-making and execution of the final choices. This separation can be achieved by first assembling a diverse group of people with the needed expertise. The role of this, by nature somewhat slow moving group, is to provide and analyze data and simulate and compare different scenarios and possible alternatives using suitable computer-based technology. Such a "committee" can make useful recommendations for future possible courses of action, and do so in a reasonable, even if not fast, timeframe. Then the leader (CEO) makes the final decisions on strategies and actions based on the best data available, and can make those decisions very rapidly when needed. However, for this approach to work, it is important that the CEO anticipates when decisions need to be made, and assembles the appropriate committees well in advance of the decision "zero hour."

But there is a new twist that we also recommend. Since the committee decisions will be averaged over all members, we suggest that the CEO listen personally to the dissenting opinions. We recommend this because among the dissenters, the CEO may find a good, original idea for the forward-propulsion of the company. Such a process, similar to one used by Amazon (see Chapter 2), would encourage employees to "think outside the box" and would bring the most creative employees to the attention of the CEO. However, if the CEO decides then to take up some of these "unpopular" suggestions, that leader will have to create a separate and new team to pursue the program. Otherwise the suggestion might be torpedoed by the "less creative" employees. Harsh words, perhaps, but reality is harsh! Conflict brings innovation, as was stated in Chapter 5.

Of course this approach is not a guarantee of success. For example, if a CEO misjudges the market or picks the wrong technology, no strategy is likely to work. But, to repeat, the use of advanced computer modeling can greatly improve the probability of success with respect to where it is today. Bottom line, powerful leaders who establish strategic governance based on science-based methodologies and **keep open minds** for revolutionary dissenting opinions of a few employees are positioning their companies for future success.

THE EVOLUTION OF COMPANY FUNCTIONS

It's not good enough for just the CEO and overall business management (strategic governance) to change. It also is necessary for the different operational Functions of a company (Research and Development, Manufacturing and Engineering, Marketing and Sales) to evolve. This is extremely important because it won't help for a company to have fast general management decisions if the company Functions cannot follow equally rapidly. For example, if the CEO decides it is extremely important to install new manufacturing equipment as soon as possible, it would present a serious problem if Manufacturing could only implement that decision very slowly. Since the ways each Function needs to evolve varies, we will briefly highlight key changes for each Function separately.

Research and Development (R&D): Ideas, Technology, and Expertise from the Outside

As we have shown, in the past the evolution of ideas for business progressed at a very different pace than today. An important new idea or an "act of creation" could fuel the business of a company for many years, at times for decades. But given the new pace of business, there is an urgent need for new breakthrough ideas to be originated or obtained at a much higher rate.

This is why it is important that large companies find ways to effectively import new ideas from the outside—from startup companies, Universities, and/or Government Laboratories—places where creativity and innovation are actively encouraged. This is one specific example of the global-sourcing Agent of Change that we described in Chapter 8. And it's not just limited to ideas. Breakthrough technologies and expertise are included.

However this concept is not easy to implement. As we have mentioned, creative scientists (and their direct managers) in large companies are usually somewhat reluctant to accept new ideas and technologies from other parts of the same organization. But they are more than just reluctant to accept them from outside the company. They are often totally opposed to this way of operating. It is almost as if their ideas and technologies are "their children." And of course, no other child is as good, as smart, or as good-looking as your own. In other words, there is a type of "parental" affection and loyalty between scientists and their ideas; and other ideas and technologies are viewed as unwanted competition.

One approach to solving this dilemma is to create a new Division, reporting as directly as possible to the president or CEO of the company. This new Division would have the objective of importing breakthrough new ideas and inventions from outside the company, and developing them inside. This implies that the patents for the "breakthrough" inventions would have to be acquired from the outside, although any further "evolutionary" inventions would be credited to the inside scientists. Thus scientists in this special Division would be rewarded and receive accolades for 1) identifying breakthrough ideas and inventions from the outside world with good prospects for new business creation, 2) supporting the successful "acquisitions" of these innovations, and 3) developing products and subsequent businesses based on these breakthroughs Such an organization would involve more travel, relationship-building and **business** acumen than is customary to expect from scientists, and likely would require closer associations between scientists and marketing experts.

There is another reason why we advocate that companies look outside for new ideas. Even in companies that support innovation from within, only a very few internally generated new ideas end up being breakthroughs that revolutionize a whole business or create a major new one. Many internally generated ideas and technologies that are hailed as innovations (and indeed they are) are not really breakthroughs and end up having minimal business impact. Part of the reason for this is the limited technical horizon and culture of an internally focused company. Such a company, by extending its search for new ideas outside, broadens its technical horizon to the whole world.

An important aspect of R&D global-sourcing that needs to be drastically enhanced is the ability to spread out a company's R&D around the world, and then bring the results all together in one central location—a way of operating that we called "distributed R&D" in Chapter 8. In this way, companies can make use of the best expertise, wherever it is located. Interconnectivity enabled by digital technology has already leveled and globalized the playing field for software-based development and services and is rapidly being expanded to R&D involving new technologies. This move toward global sourcing of R&D (and everything else) is the business path to the future.

Manufacturing and Engineering: Global-Sourcing, an Example

Since the beginning of the industrial revolution, manufacturing was concentrated into factories, and mass production—needed for decreasing costs so as to make the products accessible to the masses—was the only way known to achieve the objective. The positive of this type of solution has already been stated: the ability to mass produce goods rapidly and at continually decreasing costs. BUT there is a big negative associated with it: the relative inflexibility in the type of goods being produced. In a fast developing world, while speed and low costs are essential, adaptability and flexibility are paramount. As was mentioned in Chapter 8, new technologies such as computer-aided design and manufacturing and 3D printing are enabling Manufacturing (including Engineering) to meet this challenge. In addition, a new practice is becoming pervasive in which different parts of a product are designed and produced in different areas of the world and then are assembled in one location. We called this Manufacturing global-sourcing in Chapter 8 and highlighted several examples.

A brief description of the development of Boeing's "Dreamliner" aircraft was one of these. As we summarized, Boeing's global-sourcing approach to product design and manufacturing was not without problems and delays, but it was eventually successful. And problems are always a risk one takes when exploring new avenues. Because we believe global-sourcing will be essential for complex manufacturing in the future, we summarize here the story of the

Dreamliner in more detail.[110]

As one of the world's most advanced new airplanes, the Dreamliner 787 incorporated new materials technology. It was the first airplane where the entire airframe was made from composite materials, which are lighter than aluminum, stronger than metals, require less maintenance, and are cheaper to repair. This and other new technologies incorporated in the manufacturing of the aircraft presented challenges. To address these challenges, Boeing spread out the design and manufacturing of the Dreamliner across the world, depending on where the best technology capabilities could be found. This partnership was called the Global Collaborative Environment (GCE), and included around 50 companies. Following are a few examples of specific companies and their roles. The composite material was produced by Toray Industries of Japan. The specialized tooling required for making the composite material into sections was designed and developed by Janicki Industries of the United States. Different parts of the fuselage were manufactured by four companies: Spirit AeroSystems and Vought Aircraft Industries of the United States, Kawasaki Heavy Industries of Japan, Alenia Aeronautica of Italy. The wings were manufactured by Mitsubishi Heavy Industries of Japan. And the list includes many more sub-contractors that will not be mentioned here for the sake of brevity. We have provided the above details only to give a sense of the complexity required to bring together all of these parts and produce this airplane.

In addition to the "geographical" complexity, designs were new, materials used were new for most parts, new manufacturing machines had to be designed and built, a new specially equipped aircraft had to be produced in order to transport the larger parts around the world, the amount of coordination was unprecedented, and so on. Yet this is probably the way of the future, with the possible exception of parts that will be suitable for 3-D printing in remote locations, a technique which—as mentioned above—is fast emerging.

For being so much in the lead of course a company has to pay a price. The price paid by Boeing was about a two year delay with respect to the initially scheduled market introduction, and some nagging problems that persisted for another couple of years. The most publicized problem for the Dreamliner was that of the battery, which caught fire at times of prolonged use.[111]

The National Transportation Safety Board released a report on December 1, 2014, and assigned blame to several groups:[112]

- To GS Yuasa of Japan, for battery manufacturing methods that could introduce defects not caught by inspection
- To Boeing's engineers, who failed to consider and test for worst-case battery failures
- To the Federal Aviation Administration, who failed to recognize the potential hazard and did not require proper tests as part of its certification process.

As can be seen, Boeing did learn as time passed; and fortunately, in this case there were no accidents. One side comment: We believe that in general this type of distributed manufacturing requires a new type of Quality Assurance, where quality supervisors from the "lead company" are assigned to be present at the different locations where critical parts are designed and/or manufactured. Whatever the issues and the solutions, as is the case for R&D; global sourcing of Manufacturing and Engineering is here to stay!

Marketing and Sales: Putting Data Science to Work

Many companies with global businesses made

considerable progress in creating a "distributed" Marketing and Sales capability when they decentralized operations as they created foreign subsidiaries. They quickly recognized that local Marketing and Sales personnel in foreign countries would have better contacts, could more easily develop local leads, and were more knowledgeable about local customs and preferences. Thus today, in these companies, local personnel are commonly hired and given responsibility for Marketing and Sales activities in their Countries.

Now the next challenge become adopting and effectively using the new capabilities being developed in the areas of data science and social media. For example, new approaches connected with using Social Media will undoubtedly have a rapidly increasing impact on the advertising world since they can be significantly less expensive than traditional advertising campaigns and have the capability to rapidly address a huge number of people globally. Today, social media based advertising campaigns are excellent at what we call "shot gunning" (i.e., reaching a large number of people, among which there may be some potential customers). However social media by itself is more difficult to use for identifying and targeting those individuals who are most likely to become customers— what we call "rifling." For this, developing capabilities based on advances in big data and business analytics (see Chapter 11), will be needed. This is important because we believe that in the long run, rifling using social media will prove to be the most efficient way to advertise. To explain why we are convinced of this, consider the following.

Ultimately, the efficiency and effectiveness of advertising can be measured as the specific increment in **profits** for a particular product per dollar spent in advertising that product. Keeping this in mind, first consider a company that advertises a product on TV. This is a "shotgun" approach, and a considerable amount of money is spent on such ads which are viewed not only by the target audience but also by many who are the "wrong" people. Just think about advertising campaigns for medicines, a specific example of this shotgun approach. They are expensive and effective only in so much as they address those viewers who happen to be afflicted by certain diseases.

Now compare this with TV advertising campaigns for general elections using ads based on **fear** of real or imaginary things that can happen if the other party wins. In this case TV advertising can be effective, even if it is a shotgun approach, since everyone one viewing the ads is a potential "customer." But there is another approach that ultimately may be better.

A practice has been developed and used where computer experts identify likely voters for a specific party and likely undecided neighbors. Phone calls then are made in which the first (likely party voters) are asked to visit some of their neighbors (probably undecided) and ask them to vote for their party. This approach, to be effective, requires considerable information processing, and maybe the use of big data, but certainly is an example of an excellent "rifling" technique. Is this more cost effective than conventional TV advertising? Probably, since in the shotgun example companies (or political parties) pay large sums for TV advertising, but in the rifling approach (political canvassing) unpaid volunteers do the work.

Another marketing and sales technique commonly used to attract customers is a sales promotion. The new twist to this old practice is the internet—online sales deals such as flash sales or other temporary price decreases, free shipping, two for the price of one, etc. But are such promotions really worthwhile? To answer that question, it's necessary to first model the expected effect of a proposed promotion on sales and profits both short and long term, and then monitor actual results. To do this accurately in the world of the Internet and social media requires knowledgeable use of the right big data and analytics. A challenge for Marketing and Sales of the future.

Another developing use of data science and social media for attracting customers can be effective for companies which are leaders of a fast-developing technology. Such companies, by relying on name recognition and reputation, can use a number of different advertising approaches to create high expectations for the next great new product **before** it is introduced, and have customers lining up to be the first to buy one. Contrast this with having sales people beating the bushes to create sales of products after their introduction. Apple, Inc. is a master at this "customer pull" approach to marketing and sales.

Then, of course, there is the whole field of E-commerce, brought to prominence by Amazon. The Internet (including social media) gives prospective customers the ability to see different products, compare on-line performance and price, place orders, and pay through a safe payment system, without leaving the comfort of their homes. But the Internet and social media also offer companies new ways to market and sell their products and capabilities. Those companies that develop the strongest capabilities in these areas are likely to be winners in the future.

We have provided various examples of evolutionary capabilities for Marketing and Sales, but where is the biggest area of promise over the next 10 years or so? We place our bet on big data and analytics. New capabilities in this area are being rapidly developed and becoming more cost-effective and user-friendly, thereby becoming more accessible to companies of various sizes and types. To summarize the promise of big data combined with analytics: "Big data analytics is the process of examining large data sets containing a variety of data types—i.e., big data—to uncover hidden patterns, unknown correlations, market trends, customer preferences and other useful business information. The analytical findings can lead to more effective marketing, new revenue opportunities, better customer service, improved operational efficiency, competitive advantages over rival organizations and other business benefits."[113]

FUTURE
LAUNCHING PADS

PART V

Thirteen

PREDICTING THE FUTURE
A Caution

Many predictions about the evolution of technology and future inventions have not come to pass. As examples of such wrong predictions, we take a look at an issue of *Popular Mechanics* from 1950. Admittedly this was not the most sophisticated technical publication of the time, but it was a magazine with a large readership, and some of the authors were well-known technical writers.

PREDICTIONS FROM 65 YEARS AGO: AN EXAMPLE

In the article "Miracles You'll See in the Next Fifty Years" the Science Editor of The New York Times made predictions about future developments in science and engineering.[114] Some of his predictions included: a) "Houses with 'light metal' walls only four inches thick," b) "…Wood, brick, and stone will be ruled out (in construction) because they are too expensive and will be replaced by aerated clay cut to size on the spot." c) "When (the housewife) wants to clean the house she simply turns the hose on everything," d) To build a helicopter "a punched roll is fed into a machine that virtually gives orders to all other machines in the plant," e) "The house of tomorrow will be built in a few days by pouring concrete into standard forms," f) "Flexible refrigerator bag carries fisherman's catch," g) "De-icing fluid cleans windshield," and h) "Nose doors 12 feet high in Globemaster (military plane)."

Other contributors to the article made predictions that are not listed here since we are focusing on those related to science and technology. It is interesting to note that little attention was paid to electronics by any of the writers, including the science editor, even though technology advances were already occurring in areas such as computers and television.

WHAT REALLY HAPPENED

Yes, some of the predictions listed in the previous section did come to pass: new de-icing fluids, flexible coolers, huge military cargo planes. But most others did not. And some very important advances were not predicted at all. One can rationalize many of these forecasting "mistakes" by taking into account the thinking of the times. Most predictions were based on a **linear** extrapolation of the past while the world was starting to change **exponentially**, making it very hard to predict specific advances.

However, as we alluded to above, even 65 years ago one would have expected more attention to be paid to possible breakthroughs related to electronics. Think about what actually happened. The transistor, although invented earlier, was released to the market in the early 1950's—at the same time this article was written. It revolutionized the field of electronics by eliminating the vacuum tube and enabling compact electronic designs. Then came the era of

Microelectronics, and more specifically integrated circuits, as was discussed in Chapter 4. As we have already described (and most people know) these basic inventions allowed the development and mass production of numerous new products and capabilities—from military applications such as guided missiles and drones, to the internet and social media, to a wide range of consumer electronics such as personal computers, cell phones, digital discs, digital cameras and Apple's iProducts, to space endeavors (travel to the moon, the Hubble telescope, the Mars rover and more. All in the above electronics-based list and more happened in a period of just 65 years, but nothing related to electronics was even considered by the Science Editor.

And missing the impact of electronics isn't all. In the Science Editor's predictions there was no mention of anything relating to biotechnology, an area with numerous breakthrough advances occurring and new businesses such as Genentech and Amgen emerging during the 50 years interval about which he was making predictions. What does the failure to predict any of these things mean? It does **not** mean that the science editor of The Times did not know his job. It does mean that a person with a moderate to good technical knowledge **can** predict the evolution of existing science and technology. But it is much more difficult, and probably impossible, to predict with specifics the advent of breakthrough new inventions, disruptive technologies, and what we call Launching Pads for even newer technologies. There is a clear difference between the "act of creation" of a new idea and all that it brings, and the new developments and commercialization stemming from something that already exists.

However, what is noteworthy about all of this is not the failure to predict exactly what happened. Rather, it is the enormous amount of change that occurred in a relatively short period of time. It appears that humanity is in a rapid ascent towards more complexity, like a rocket with ever increasing speed. And in such an exponentially changing future, what new science breakthroughs might have the most dramatic impacts on business, business management, and humanity in general in our future? This is the question we finally address by predicting areas from which we expect new Launching Pads to develop. Predictions about such future Launching Pads are easier to make than those about specific developments, and thus should be more accurate.

ABOUT OUR PREDICTIONS

In the remainder of this Part, we make a **leap** forward and predict the next science and technology areas where we expect inventions or discoveries, similar in impact to integrated circuits, will occur. Specifically, we identify and explore several promising research thrusts from which we believe it is very probable that breakthrough Launching Pads will develop that will propel humanity into the future, changing life and the conduct of business as we know it, as well as creating opportunities for novel businesses and whole new industries.

Why are we attempting to identify these "breeding grounds" for new Launching Pads instead of making predictions about industry-changing firms and/or business models as Clayton Christensen does in his book *Seeing What's Next?*[115] Primarily it is because our focus is creating new Superstars, and we believe it is highly probably that these "breeding grounds" will be the foundations for future Superstars. Through our easy-to-understand descriptions of efforts in these less familiar technical areas we hope to help entrepreneurs, business leaders, investors and job-seekers recognize key advances that will give them a head-start toward participating in the creation of future Superstars. In addition, as we explained above, if we tried to make more detailed and specific predictions, we would almost certainly be proven wrong as the future unfolds.

So how did we make our choices? Think about integrated circuits. It all began with a rather unassuming branch of physics (solid state physics) which at the beginning did not show much promise for useful applications. But when it developed—well, look what happened. Thus we looked for areas of science and technology that we feel might provide fertile grounds for the birth of world changing developments. The only constraints we used in making our choices were the laws of science as we know them today. These constraints differentiate our choices from science fiction.

Using this approach, we identified several possible new Launching Pads for both the near term and the future. These are described in the next two chapters. The near term ones, although still embryonic, are starting to show promise of major commercial applications. And the future possible Launching Pads? Well, give them a few more years and... Keep in mind that technology is now developing exponentially.

Fourteen

LIFE SCIENCES BREAKTHROUGHS

It is the dawning of the Life Sciences age, the successor to the Microelectronics era. At least this is what we believe. Therefore Life Sciences was our focus in the search for new Launching Pads in the near term. In this chapter are brief descriptions of our picks for Life Sciences based technology areas most likely to become Launching Pads before long.

We start with Biogenetics, the developing Launching Pad we described in Chapter 4. It is still in its infancy; with new potentially breakthrough advances being made at an ever increasing pace. At this point it is not clear if these new discoveries will just be the fuel for the current Biogenetics Launching Pad, or whether one or more will become Launching Pads in their own right. Four of these rapidly developing areas—cloning of genes and organisms, stem cell research, and the genome editing technologies of TALENs, and CRISPR—appear to us to be the most promising. So we begin our look at potential new Launching Pads with an exploration of them.

Then we turn to a rapidly advancing area of science and engineering: the field of Nanotechnology. Nanotechnology is the term used for a very broad and extremely exciting area of research encompassing many fields, but much of its promise is in the future. Therefore for our purposes, we focus on Nanomedicine, the rapidly advancing Life Science-based segment of Nanotechnology which we believe has the potential to be a new Launching Pad in the near term

Finally we address Human Brain Research. This is an embryonic area where Biogenetics, Nanomedicine, and Neuroscience intersect. As we describe, the potential for this area is great, but it will take longer for that potential to be realized.

BIOGENETICS: THE RAPID ADVANCES CONTINUE

Breakthroughs in Genome Editing

"As potential next-generation therapeutics and research tools, few life sciences technologies hold more promise than genome-editing proteins— molecules that can be programmed to alter specific genes to treat or perhaps cure genetic diseases."[116]

In simple terms, genome or gene editing refers to modifying the DNA of an organism. In other words, genome editing is a sophisticated cut-and-paste process for changing (and fixing) DNA. In more technical terms, genome editing is "a genetic engineering process in which DNA is inserted, deleted or replaced in the genome of an organism using engineered nucleases, or 'molecular scissors.' These nucleases create site-specific double-strand breaks (DSBs) at desired locations in the genome. The induced double-strand breaks are repaired …resulting in targeted mutations ('edits')."[117]

There are currently three primary families of "molecular

scissors" (engineered nucleases) being used and/or developed for genome editing: Zinc finger nucleases (ZFNs), Transcription Activator-Like Effector-based Nucleases (TALEN), and the newest—Clustered, Regularly Interspaced, Short Palindromic Repeats (CRISPR).[118] Below, we highlight the latter which is the most recent and appears to be the most promising.

CRISPR–Cas9[119]

A recent and extremely promising biogenetic technology development is the CRISPR-Cas9 system—a powerful genome editing technique that Science Magazine named as the 2015 breakthrough of the year.[120]

What is CRISPR-Cas9? CRISPR stands for "Clustered, Regularly Interspaced, Short Palindromic Repeats;" and refers to a pattern of short, repeating, palindromic DNA sequences separated by short, non-repeating, "spacer" DNA sequences that is found in bacteria. Cas9 refers to a family of proteins and specialized hybrid RNA (ribonucleic acid) molecules associated with CRISPR. The entire complex of DNA repeats, Cas proteins, and RNA molecules make up the CRISPR-Cas9 System. It was discovered in the late 1980s that acting together, CRISPR and Cas played a key role in the immune systems of bacteria. And this was the beginning of the development of CRISPR-Cas9 for genome editing.

How does CRISPR-Cas9 work as a genome editing tool? In simple terms, Cas9, carrying its modified "passenger" DNA, acts as a pair of enzymatic "scissors;" and a guide sequence of DNA (CRISPR) tells the scissors where to cut and insert the modified RNA. In other words, CRISPR-Cas9 is a tool which allows cutting and splicing material from or into DNA, thus producing a changed DNA.

Many scientists played a role in the development of CRISPR-Cas9. But the research on this breakthrough technology which started its explosive development was published in 2012 by Jinek et al.[121] Additional work from these scientists at the University of California (including J. Doudna and E. Charpentier) and others from the Broad Institute of Harvard University and MIT (including F. Zhang) rapidly developed the technology and demonstrated its potential. To summarize, over a very short period of time, these researchers showed that the newly developed CRISPR/Cas9 system could be easily programmed to identify, cut, modify, and even replace any gene sequence in multiple living organisms. The key advantages of the new CRISPR-Cas9 technology include: high efficiency of modifying targets, ease of design and use, and low cost.[122]

All of this sparked considerable enthusiasm and a rush to commercialize the CRISPR technology, including by the scientists who pioneered the technique.[123] In 2014, three startup ventures were launched. First there was Editas Medicine, located in Cambridge, MA with founders that included the original researchers Zhang and Doudna. The company was backed by $43 million of Venture Capital. Then CRISPR Therapeutics was founded by Charpentier (another key original researcher) and others, with corporate headquarters in Basel, Switzerland. This startup was backed with $23 million in Venture investments. Third was Intellia Therapeutics, cofounded by Caribou Biosciences, a technology company founded by Doudna and her colleagues to develop CRISPR. First round venture funding for this company was $15 million. And the list of new companies and laboratories working on CRISPR continues to expand rapidly.

However, this has led to an ongoing patent battle, and the battle is fierce.[124] Exactly who took the key steps to turn CRISPR into a useful genetic tool is still the subject of a huge legal controversy between the University of California, Berkeley and the Broad Institute (affiliated with

MIT and Harvard).[125] Although Charpentier and Doudna from UC Berkeley made seminal discoveries to advance the technique and filed the first patent application; it was Zhang of the Harvard/MIT Broad Institute who received the first US CRISPR patent. Perhaps controversy is inevitable when there is a technology potentially worth billions and multiple related inventions happened at different places in a relatively short time frame. But none of this may matter. CRSIPR technology is exploding, and new discoveries such as CRISPR-Cpf1 may bypass the legal problems and perform even better than CRISPR-Cas9.[126]

One last comment. There is significant ethical controversy around gene editing in general and CRISPR specifically. In the article "The Gene Genie" it was suggested that with CRISPR "...it might be possible to tweak the chromosomal abnormality associated with Down syndrome early in pregnancy, for example, or to reintroduce susceptibility to herbicides in resistant weeds, or to bring back animal species that have gone extinct."[127] This all sounds good, but in an article entitled "A Prudent Path Forward for Genetic Engineering and Germline Gene Modification" the authors, including one of the inventors of CRISPR (J. Doudna), expressed concern: "...the CRISPR Cas9 technology, as well as other genome engineering methods, can be used to change the DNA in the nuclei of reproductive cells that transmit information from one generation to the next (an organism's "germ line")."[128]

In a letter to Science, Robert Pollack from Columbia University of New York, responding to that article, states: "This is a big deal. It means that we can imagine the day when human chromosomes may be modified in the sperm and egg, to assure that one or the other aspect of a child's inheritance is designed to order," and he urges extreme caution.[129] The recommendation is excellent, but will countries like China and North Korea exercise similar caution?

The potential of CRISPR is clear. "…scientists are poised to deliver upon the promises of the genomic revolution to transform basic science and personalized medicine."[130] But the dangers are just as clear. What will the future bring? Only time will tell the outcome, but the power of genome editing cannot be questioned. Thus its emergence as a Launching Pad in the near term seems clear.

Cloning of Genes and Organisms[131]

A developing area of biogenetics is that of "cloning" of genes and organisms (including large animals). While cloning does occur naturally (e.g., identical twins), in Biogenetics the cloning is artificial. Specifically, cloning in Biogenetics refers to processes used to artificially create genetically identical copies of DNA fragments (gene or molecular cloning), of cells (therapeutic cloning), or of entire multi-cellular organisms (reproductive cloning).

Gene cloning is commonly done by researchers in order to study specific genes. However cloning genes is not only valuable for research. Today, as we highlighted in Chapter 3, a number of important pharmaceutical drugs are produced from cloned genes, including insulin and several anticancer drugs. Related to this is gene editing as discussed in the previous section.

Therapeutic cloning commonly refers to the process that produces copies of stem cells for experiments aimed at creating tissues to replace or repair injured tissues. We treat this as a separate topic and discuss it in the next section.

Reproductive cloning is aimed producing exact copies of animals. The process commonly used is called Somatic Cell Nuclear Transfer (SCNT). To explain this process, consider the first and most publicized large animal clone—Dolly, a female domestic sheep.

To make Dolly, researchers isolated a somatic cell (any cell except sperm and egg cells) from the udder of an adult female sheep. Next they removed the nucleus and all of its DNA from an egg cell. Then they transferred the nucleus from the somatic cell to the egg cell. The egg cell, with its new nucleus, was developed into an embryo which was implanted into a surrogate mother and carried to term. This resulted in the birth of the clone named Dolly in 1996. Of course it wasn't quite this simple. It took literally hundreds of tries, but eventually it was successful.[132]

Since Dolly, numerous other animals have been successfully cloned, including cats, dogs, goats, horses, and much more. One of the goals is to make copies of animals with desirable traits, such as high milk production or lean meat. Another goal is the preservation of endangered species. And of course there is the goal, made popular by science fiction movies such as "Jurassic Park," of cloning extinct creatures, thereby bringing the species back to life. And that possibility is fast becoming reality. A well-preserved Mammoth nicknamed "Buttercup" has been discovered in Siberia and a multi-national attempt to clone it is under way.

Although the success rate of reproductive cloning is still relatively low and the cost high, scientists can now design and bring to life a variety of laboratory produced animal clones. So why not clone human beings? And when that happens (not if) the question becomes where will this lead the human race? Will it be good or bad? This is an ethical/social, religious issue that is being hotly debated and has led a number of countries to ban "human cloning for reproductive purposes."[133]

Although we can't predict exactly what will happen in the broad area of cloning, we can say that advances will continue on all fronts that will have greater and greater impacts. It appears that cloning clearly has the potential to become a Launching Pad in its own right.

Stem Cell Research[134]

As we defined above, therapeutic cloning refers to the process of creating multiple clones of stem cells for research in the area of regenerative medicine. In this section, rather than focus on the process, we focus on stem cells themselves. Why is there so much interest and controversy surrounding stem cells? What are the potential benefits of stem cell treatment that are fueling research efforts?

Stem cell research is one of the most promising areas of science today. In general, stem cells can be used to increase understanding of diseases as well as to test new drugs for safety and efficacy. But there is much more. "Stem cells can be guided into becoming specific cells that can be used to regenerate and repair diseased or damaged tissues in people. People who might benefit from stem cell therapies include those with spinal cord injuries, type 1 diabetes, Parkinson's disease, Alzheimer's disease, heart disease, stroke..."[135] And the list goes on for what is being called regenerative medicine. In other words, stem cells offer the hope of treating numerous diseases and conditions. They may even offer the possibility of generating entire organs for transplant.

So what exactly are stem cells? "Stem cells are the body's raw materials—cells from which all other cells with specialized functions are generated....No other cell in the body has the natural ability to generate new cell types."[136] Stem cells that have the ability of either dividing into more stem cells or becoming any type of cell in the body are called pluripotent stem cells. Furthermore, there are basically two kinds of stem cells—adult stem cells and embryonic stem cells. Both types are described below.

Adult stem cells are found in very small numbers in tissues of adults. In general, these types of stem cells have limited ability to generate different kinds of cells, so are not particularly useful. However, scientists have been able to alter **regular** adult cells to have some of the properties of embryonic stem cells. These modified adult cells are called "induced pluripotent stem cells" (iPSCs).

More specifically, such iPSCs are adult cells that have been genetically reprogrammed to act similarly to embryonic stem cells.[137] Mouse iPSCs were first reported in 2006, and human iPSCs were first reported in late 2007. Although much additional research is needed before iPSCs can completely mimic embryonic stem cells, iPSCs are already useful tools for drug development and modeling of diseases, and scientists are investigating their use in transplantation medicine. In any case, pursuing iPSC research will help researchers learn how to reprogram "regular" cells to repair damaged tissues in the human body.

Although iPSCs appear promising, at present embryonic stem cells, which are naturally pluripotent, are much more useful for regenerative medicine and thus are the focus of much current stem cell research. The source of embryonic stem cells is just what the name indicates. They are obtained from human embryos that are 3-5 days old. Today, in spite of what is published in popular media, most embryonic stem cells are derived from embryos that develop from eggs that have been fertilized **in vitro**, and then donated for research purposes with informed consent of the donors. They are **not** derived from eggs fertilized in a woman's body. While these embryonic stem cells offer exciting promise for future therapies, significant technical hurdles remain that will only be overcome through years of intensive research.

But there is another problem associated with embryonic stem cells. Their source has given rise to intense ethical and religious controversy, similar to that associated with human cloning. As a result, in 2001, President George W. Bush restricted federal funding for research on stem cells obtained from human embryos "because the technology required the destruction of human life. At its core, this issue forces us to confront fundamental questions about the beginnings of life and the ends of science," Bush said.[138] In 2009, President Barack Obama lifted the restriction, making it possible for federally funded scientists to use excess embryos from in-vitro fertilization to obtain stem cells for study, but the ethical controversy continues.

Although some scientists claim that the eight year interruption of Government funding caused the US to lag behind other Nations in the development of this area, realizing the promise of stem cell therapy for regenerative medicine appears within reach—another biogenetics breakthrough advance that is almost ready for Launching Pad status.

NANOTECHNOLOGY: A FOCUS ON NANOMEDICINE[139]

Nanotechnology

To provide an introduction to Nanomedicine, we first take a brief look at the broader field of Nanotechnology. As described in dictionary.com:[140]

> "Nanotechnology is the science and technology of precisely manipulating the structure of matter at the molecular level. The term Nanotechnology embraces many different fields ..., but all are concerned with bringing existing technologies down to a very small scale, measured in nanometers. A nanometer—a billionth of a meter—is about the size of six carbon atoms in a row."

In quantitative terms, Nanotechnologies are commonly

defined as technologies manipulating matter smaller than 100 nanometers. This is a somewhat unfortunate definition because it covers a range of sizes governed by different laws of physics. The 100 nanometer size is in the realm where the laws of classical mechanics apply, while the 10 nanometer size is where the laws of quantum mechanics play an important role. And in between there is a gray area where elements of both are important.

To resolve this conflict, a government science advisory committee has introduced the term "Mesotechnology" to designate the size range primarily governed by classical mechanics and has narrowed the definition of Nanotechnology to designate the size range where quantum mechanics rules.[141] However, as in other fields of developing science, definitions are still evolving. Therefore, we will revert to using the term Nanotechnology as commonly defined.

A good summary of the forward thrust of Nanotechnology can be found in Physics World, where examples are given of a number of potentially high impact, ongoing projects.[142] Because of the huge variety of potential applications, governments are investing billions of dollars in Nanotechnology research. For example, the US government, through its National Nanotechnology Initiative,[143] has already invested over $20 billion.[144] However, as we stated in the beginning of this chapter, much of the potential of Nanotechnology is in the future. Therefore we focus here on Nanomedicine, the Life Sciences based segment of Nanotechnology that has the potential to be a Launching Pad in the nearer term.

Nanomedicine

"What if doctors had tiny tools that could search out and destroy the very first cancer cells of a tumor developing in the body? What if a cell's broken part could be removed and replaced with a functioning miniature biological machine? Or what if molecule-sized pumps could be implanted in sick people to deliver life-saving medicines precisely where they are needed? These scenarios may sound unbelievable, but they are the ultimate goals of Nanomedicine, a cutting-edge area of biomedical research that seeks to use Nanotechnology tools to improve human health."[145]

Simply stated, Nanomedicine is the application of Nanotechnology to medicine. It may be defined as "the monitoring, repair, construction and control of human biological systems at the molecular level, using engineered nanodevices and nanostructures."[146] It ranges from the medical applications of nanomaterials and biological devices, to nanoscale biosensors, and even to possible future applications of programmable nanomachines and nanorobots—devices that would allow medical doctors to execute procedures in the human body at the cellular and molecular levels.

However today, the majority of benefits realized from Nanomedicine involve the use of nanoparticles. Numerous products incorporating nanoparticles for targeted delivery of pharmaceutical, therapeutic, and diagnostic agents already are on the market. Such products that deliver therapeutic agents commonly target tumors, and those that deliver diagnostic agents are often part of contrast media formulations used in medical imaging.

And there are nanoparticle-based products that combine delivery of drugs and imaging agents. These are used for various purposes including: "for monitoring the biodistribution and the target site accumulation of nanomedicines, for visualizing and quantifying (triggered) drug release, and for longitudinally assessing therapeutic efficacy.[147] Dye-doped silica nanoparticles for the detection of specific molecular targets (e.g., intracellular metabolites) are an example of such a material.

How does a dual-function nanoparticle formulation work? Consider that one way treatment for serious diseases such as cancer can be administered is by injecting a drug or chemotherapy containing liquid into the body. In our example, inside the injectable liquid there are dye-doped nanoparticles engineered to slip past barriers such as blood vessel walls, latch onto cancer cells, and trick the cells into engulfing them as if they were food. These dye-doped nanoparticles mark the sick cells with their fluorescent dye and at the same time the sick cells are destroyed with an appropriate anti-cancer drug that the nanoparticle has carried with it.

The above example is just one possible scenario. Bottom line, nanoparticle based biomedical products are being increasingly used to "improve the treatments and lives of patients suffering from a range of disorders including ovarian and breast cancer, kidney disease, fungal infections, elevated cholesterol, menopausal symptoms, multiple sclerosis, chronic pain, asthma and emphysema…"[148]

But there is much more. Nanoparticles can themselves function as therapeutics. For example, thermal energy is emerging as an important means of therapy, and gold nanoparticles can convert photons into thermal energy for targeted photothermal therapy.

Magnetic nanoparticles are also attractive for their ability to mediate heat induction .And researchers are developing other kinds of functional nanoparticles that can act as ultra-sensitive detectors at the cellular level (nanodetectors) and more.

However Nanomedicine is more than nanoparticles. There are other nanomaterials under investigation for medical applications at an increasing number of universities and research institutes around the globe. One example is the ongoing research on polymeric-based nanomaterials for medical use at Cedars Sinai in Los Angeles. According to their website:

"The Ljubimova Laboratory, led by Julia Ljubimova, MD, Ph.D. and physician-scientists in the Nanomedicine Research Center in the Neurosurgery Department are joining forces to advance the field of treatment of brain, breast and lung cancers... Work in the Ljubimova Lab has led to the development of new nanodrugs and nanoimaging agents with high specificity in tumor diagnosis and treatment efficacy. These nanodrugs are synthesized on a bio-derived, biodegradable, nontoxic and nonimmunogenic polymer with unique biochemical properties, not achievable with synthetic polymers.

...Compared with conventional chemotherapy, the novel nanodrugs developed at the Cedars-Sinai Nanomedicine Research Center have been more effective in treating experimental primary and secondary tumors by increasing the concentration of the anti-cancer drug directly at the tumor site while decreasing general toxicity and immunogenicity. These nanodrugs and nanoimaging agents use an innovative delivery method allowing anti-cancer agents to accumulate directly in solid tumors and to help in fighting multi-drug-resistant cells."[149]

An article by M. Singh, et al summarizes the nanoparticle/nanomaterial focus for Nanomedicine this way:

"Nanotechnology is expected to open some new aspects to fight and prevent diseases using atomic scale tailoring of materials. The ability to uncover the structure and function of biosystems at the nanoscale stimulates research leading to improvement in biology, biotechnology, medicine and healthcare. The size of nanomaterials is similar to that of most biological molecules and structures; therefore, nanomaterials can be useful for both in vivo and in vitro biomedical research and applications. The integration of nanomaterials with biology has led to the development of diagnostic devices, contrast agents, analytical tools, physical therapy applications, and drug delivery vehicles."[150]

The future for Nanotechnology in medicine appears even more promising when one looks beyond the more "traditional" approaches. There are new ideas coming from the observation of nature. For example, there are bacteria that position themselves at the correct depth in a muddy pool to assure their survival. This is done by sensing the vertical component of the magnetic field of the earth. The bacteria has in it a chain of magnetic crystals between 30 and 120 nanometers in diameter, the correct dimension to sense the magnetic field without being subject to dividing into oppositely magnetized domains.

Following this direction, there are two groups, one in Germany and the other at the University of California, Berkeley, that "are exploring the use of magnetic nanoparticles to detect particular biological entities, such as microorganisms that cause diseases."[151]

Another promising technology utilizes the properties of light emitting diodes (LED's) to produce nanoscale-sized, so-called quantum dots.

"Quantum dots (QDs) are semiconductor nanocrystals that emit fluorescence on excitation with a light source. They have excellent optical properties, including high brightness, resistance to photobleaching and tunable wavelength. Recent developments in surface modification of QDs enable their potential application in cancer imaging. QDs with near-infrared emission could be applied to sentinel lymph-node mapping to aid biopsy and surgery. Conjugation of QDs with biomolecules, including peptides and antibodies, could be used to target tumors in vivo."[152]

In other words, QDs could have multiple applications in Nanomedicine including image-guided surgery, light-activated therapies and ultrasensitive diagnostic tests.

And then there is the "science fiction like" promise of nanodevices for Nanomedicine. For example, researchers at the University of Cambridge recently have "built" the world's smallest engine, a light-powered device small enough to enter living cells that they have named ANTs (actuating transducers).

"The prototype device is made of tiny charged particles of gold, bound together with temperature-responsive polymers in the form of a gel. When the 'nano-engine' is heated to a certain temperature with a laser, it stores large amounts of elastic energy in a fraction of a second, as the polymer coatings expel all the water from the gel and collapse. This has the effect of forcing the gold nanoparticles to bind together into tight clusters. But when the device is cooled, the polymers take on water and expand, and the gold nanoparticles are strongly and quickly pushed apart, like a spring."[153]

Nanobiosensors for measuring glucose, heart rate, blood pressure, etc. Injectable, wireless nanobots that carry out medical tasks, gather diagnostics and even deliver drugs into the bloodstream. Self-assembled, DNA based nanodevices for molecular scale diagnostics and smart drug delivery. Quantum wires for real-time sensing of biomarker proteins for cancer. Nanorobots for repairing damaged tissue, unblocking arteries, and replacing damaged organs. And the list goes on and on. The Nanomedicine technology possibilities are endless and world-changing.

Nanomedicine: An already exponentially developing, disruptive technology area that clearly fits our definition of Launching Pad.

HUMAN BRAIN RESEARCH: THE CONVERGENCE OF BIOGENETICS, NANOTECHNOLOGY, AND NEUROSCIENCE

Humans have explored much of the earth and some of the depths of the oceans, but there is something even more mysterious and powerful which is much closer to us. It is the human brain, the **most complex living structure** that we know of in the universe! But to date, the human brain has only been explored in a relatively limited fashion.

We know about the actions it inspires or controls and many of the specific, observable effects that originate from it (e.g., individual personalities, mental diseases, old-age dementia, cowardice, religious beliefs and practices, piety, cruelty, habits, fanaticism). But we have only limited knowledge about which specific structures and/or interconnections within the brain cause such effects, and more important, **how**. And we are primitive in our trial-and-error approaches to modifying those traits considered harmful with treatments such as drugs or electrical stimulation or surgical interventions.

Think about the contradictions. The brain of Hitler made him kill seven million of his citizens, mostly because they were Jewish; while the brain of Mother Theresa made her help hundreds of people who were too poor to help themselves, no matter what their race or religion. Genghis Kahn, known as the "scourge of God," is famous for his extreme acts of cruelty during his conquests in western

Europe; while Francis of Assisi practiced charity to all living beings, including (unusual for the times) animals. These are just a few examples of individuals who were led by their brains to live very different lives.

We also know that, controlled by their brains, different people react differently to unusual circumstances, such as to "silence and solitude." As we wrote in Chapter 5, this type of environment can spur creativity, but can also lead to insanity. And both insanity and creativity can coexist in the same brain as in the case of famous artists like Van Gogh. The human brain also caused specific populations to migrate all across the globe, but not all populations. Some preferred to stay where they were, even in harsh environments. Why? And the human brain allows us to transmit ideas and knowledge from one generation to the next. As J.F. Kennedy once said, referring to democracy, "A man may die. Nations rise and fall. But an idea lives on. Ideas have endurance without death."

What would advances and breakthroughs in understanding and controlling the human brain mean for humanity and the business community? As the above examples illustrate, the possibilities are vast. And progress is being made. The 2014 Nobel Prize in Physiology or Medicine was awarded to John O'Keefe, May-Britt Moser, and Edvard Moser for discovering the networks of cells that form the brain's navigational system. This fundamental work in neuroscience on a nanoscale could have applications in Alzheimer's and other diseases, but it is just the beginning. Through investment in brain research, we may find infinite new ways to harness its power and use it—for good or for bad. We do not know yet what they all are, but they will have a major impact on humanity, including human interactions and even business interactions.

Consider just one of the important actions that starts in the brain—creativity. There is creativity at every step of human-induced change and progress, but what spurs a potentially life-changing discovery? What is really happening in the brain that causes one to have a flash of insight? Whatever it is, can we create it and/or control it?

A study by N. Bekhtereva, et al. was a step toward answering those questions. These researchers used positron-emission tomography (PET) to study the location of brain activity when subjects were solving creative tasks.[154] And researchers in the Dartmouth College Department of Psychological and Brain Sciences are credited with a more recent, key breakthrough. In an article entitled "Network Structure and Dynamics of the Mental Workspace" they explain:

> "We do not know how the human brain mediates complex and creative behaviors such as artistic, scientific, and mathematical thought. Scholars theorize that these abilities require conscious experience as realized in a widespread neural network, or 'mental workspace,' that represents and manipulates images, symbols, and other mental constructs across a variety of domains...The present work takes advantage of emerging techniques in network and information analysis to provide empirical support for such a widespread and interconnected information processing network in the brain that supports the manipulation of visual imagery."[155]

In other words, this research showed that it's not just the right brain that governs creativity. It is multiple parts of the brain, interconnected by a vast network of neurons.

This Dartmouth study is a start at understanding the brain on a nanoscale. However it still doesn't answer the question as to why some people are more creative than others. But now there are many others seeking answers. The book *Neuroscience of Creativity*[156] offers an excellent summary of various approaches, viewpoints, and results. And the report issued in 2015 entitled "How Creativity Works in the Brain, Insights from a Santa Fe Institute Working Group, Cosponsored by the National Endowment for the Arts" offers food for thought from an interdisciplinary perspective.[157]

But understanding the source of creativity is only one small part of brain research. In support of broader brain research, on April 2, 2013 President Obama launched the so-called "BRAIN Initiative." It stands for: "Brain Research through Advancing Innovative Neuro-technologies." Three government agencies are involved: the National Institutes of Health (NIH), the Defense Advanced Research Projects Agency (DARPA) and the National Science Foundation (NSF). As described by the NIH, the Brain Initiative:

> "...is aimed at revolutionizing our understanding of the human brain. By accelerating the development and application of innovative technologies, researchers will be able to produce a revolutionary new dynamic picture of the brain that, for the first time, shows how individual cells and complex neural circuits interact in both time and space. Long desired by researchers seeking new ways to treat, cure, and even prevent brain disorders, this picture will fill major gaps in our current knowledge and provide unprecedented opportunities for exploring exactly how the brain enables the human body to record, process, utilize, store, and retrieve vast quantities of information, all at the speed of thought."[158]

And a report issued by NIH in 2014 states:

> "The human brain is the source of our thoughts, emotions, perceptions, actions and memories; it confers us the abilities that make us human, while

simultaneously making each of us unique. Over recent years, neuroscience has advanced to the level that we can envision a comprehensive understanding of the brain in action, spanning molecules, cells, circuits, systems and behaviors. This vision in turn inspired the BRAIN initiative... The charge from the President and from the NIH Director is bold and ambitious... The focus is not on technology *per se,* but on the development and use of tools for acquiring fundamental insight about how the nervous system works in health and disease."[159]

As a summary, here is a description of the possible long-term outcomes of the BRAIN Initiative, provided by the Whitehouse:

"The BRAIN Initiative has the potential to do for neuroscience what the Human Genome Project did for genomics by supporting the development and application of innovative technologies that can create a dynamic understanding of brain function. It aims to help researchers uncover the mysteries of brain disorders, such as Alzheimer's and Parkinson's diseases, depression, Post-Traumatic Stress Disorder (PTSD), and traumatic brain injury (TBI)."[160]

Even if only a part of the vision of the BRAIN Initiative is realized, advances from brain research will change the world. And this makes today's Brain Research the foundation of a new Launching Pad.

Fifteen

NEW SCIENCE OFFERING NEW POSSIBILITIES

In the previous chapter we described several bio-based advances and areas of technology development that we believe either already are or almost are ready to be Launching Pads. Are we right? Well, predictions about the near term future have a reasonable probability of being correct. But what about longer term? What are the areas that might give rise to future Launching Pads? In this chapter we highlight areas of science that we believe offer the possibilities of world-changing discoveries—someday. Only time will tell if we are correct in any of our choices.

COMPLEXITY SCIENCE[161]

Complexity Science can be defined as: "Any of various branches of mathematics, physics, computer science, and other fields, concerned with the emergence of order and structure in complex and apparently chaotic systems."[162] In simple terms it is an embryonic, loosely organized, academic field that is attempting to improve our understanding of complex systems—systems with a large number of independent components that continually interact with both their environments and one another to reorganize themselves into increasingly elaborate structures.

The basic mathematical principles of Complexity Science are complicated, so we will not discuss them here. We can say, however, that this area of science draws from both Chaos theory ("the study of unpredictable and complex dynamic systems that are highly sensitive to small changes in external conditions"[163]) and the evolution of Complex Adaptive Systems (systems composed of many elements, called agents, that learn or adapt in response to interactions with other agents).

Chaos theory. Complex Adaptive Systems. This is what Complexity Science is all about. For some more details we refer readers to: "Complex Adaptive Systems" by J. Stephen Lansing.[164]

As an example of what might be studied by Complexity Science, consider the second principle of thermodynamics, which is accepted by all scientists. This principle states that the entropy of a closed system is always increasing. This means that there is a constant movement towards disorder in all inanimate things in the universe, such as the expansion of a gas freed from a container. Complexity Science, on the other hand, asks: Why then are living organisms evolving towards more and more complex and ordered structures, culminating in the human brain? And some scientists further ask: "Is the cosmic compulsion for disorder (second principle) matched by an equally powerful compulsion for order, structure and organization?" In other words, is there in the universe a force that applies to living organisms and, opposite to the second principle, drives life to ever increasing complexity?

It should be noted that the concept that there is a powerful compulsion for order driving the evolution of living organisms is controversial. Many scientists believe that this evolution can be explained purely on the basis of statistics and survival of the fittest. However some proponents of complexity science argue that evolution by itself cannot account for the rapid development and changes of animal and human forms. A disagreement to say the least, with no clear answer yet.

Today, Complexity Science is being propelled forward largely by the "Santa Fe Institute" (SFI). As described in its website,[165] SFI is an independent, nonprofit, theoretical research and education center dedicated to the multidisciplinary study of the fundamental principles of complex adaptive systems. Key areas of interest are a) physics and computation of complex systems, b) human behavior, institutions, and social systems, and c) living systems: emergence, hierarchy, and dynamics. Specific projects include: Cities, Scaling and Sustainability; Evolution of Complexity on Earth; Hidden Laws in Biological and Social Systems; Emergence of Complex Societies; Neighborhoods, Slums, & Human Development.

What about the future? How will Complexity Science and understanding the dynamic equilibrium of order-disorder affect life as we know it today? And how might it affect global interactions and business transactions? We already mentioned ABMS, derived from complexity science, which is applied to markets and business (see chapter 11). And this is just one small advance. Will Complexity Science give rise to a future Launching Pad? The only prediction we can make is that eventually the impact of this developing science will be great.

SUBATOMIC PARTICLES

Subatomic particles such as electrons, neutrons, and protons have been studied for many years; providing a basic understanding of the make-up of atoms and molecules and how to manipulate them. Uses such as creating isotopes and proton therapy for cancer treatment have emerged. As our technology tools needed to discover, analyze, and measure subatomic particles have advanced, a number of new such particles have been discovered— quarks, gluons, leptons, neutrinos, and many more. Most people have heard of CERN's Large Hadron Collider (LHC), the giant particle accelerator that was built in Europe to investigate subatomic particles and to allow physicists to test the predictions of different theories of particle physics and high-energy physics. One specific goal was to prove the existence of a new subatomic particle referred to as the Higgs Boson or, as some people call it, the "God particle."

Why are subatomic particles interesting? Different subatomic particles are responsible for giving matter different properties such as mass. Some particles, like protons and neutrons, have mass. Others, like photons, do not. It has been recently discovered that the neutrino, previously thought to be without mass, does in fact have mass, a discovery that motivated the award of the 2015 Nobel Prize in Physics.[166]

And there is the "God Particle." The Higgs Boson (God particle) is believed to be the subatomic particle which gives mass to matter. And in fact, it was announced in 2013 that such a particle had been discovered in experiments on CERN's Hadron Collider.[167]

Then, in 2015, CERN scientists announced the discovery of yet another new particle called the pentaquark. It was first predicted to exist in the 1960s but, much like the Higgs boson before it, the pentaquark eluded science for decades until its detection at the LHC. Its discovery amounts to a new form of matter. CERN research leader Guy Wilkinson commented:

"The pentaquark is not just any new particle... It

represents a way to aggregate quarks, namely the fundamental constituents of ordinary protons and neutrons, in a pattern that has never been observed before in over fifty years of experimental searches. Studying its properties may allow us to understand better how ordinary matter, the protons and neutrons from which we're all made, is constituted."[168]

What are the implications of such discoveries and all those that will follow? Will scientists discover the composition of "dark matter" (see the next section)? How costly would a machine be that allows physicists to take the next step, and what practical applications would come out of these studies? Perhaps new sources of clean energy, or something not yet envisioned. Our first Launching Pad was a micro scale technology (Microelectronics). Now explosive breakthroughs are being made on the nanoscale. Why shouldn't moving to an even smaller scale bring world-changing advances? Who can say what positive (or negative) outcomes there might be if we understood how subatomic particles interacted with matter or if ways could be found to harness the power of the Higgs Boson or other sub-atomic particles?

OUTER SPACE: SEARCHING BEYOND OUR SOLAR SYSTEM

Yes, there is still much to learn about our solar system. But the mysteries of the "beyond" have always been a siren call for humankind. Today this quest ranges from reaching for the stars to understanding our universe at a more fundamental level. In this section we highlight two thrusts in this challenging exploration: the makeup of the universe and the search for life beyond Earth.

The Makeup of the Universe

As is well known, the universe contains observable bodies such as planets, moons, stars, and asteroids. However, the vast majority of the seemingly empty space consists of so-called "Dark Matter" and "Dark Energy." Based on standard cosmology models, the known universe contains 27% dark matter and 68% dark energy. That means that "the rest—everything on Earth, everything ever observed with all of our instruments, all normal matter— adds up to less than 5% of the Universe."[169] So what are these mysterious entities that make up most of our Universe?

Dark Matter

Dark Matter is a special kind of matter hypothesized in astronomy and cosmology to account for gravitational effects that appear to be the result of invisible mass. Dark Matter cannot be seen directly with telescopes, but its existence and properties are inferred from its effects on visible matter through gravity and the large-scale structure of the universe.

A number of experiments are being carried out in hopes of revealing more about the structure of dark matter. For example, data from the Chandra X-Ray Observatory, combined with that from the Hubble telescope, has set limits on how Dark Matter can interact with itself.[170] Then there is an international effort known as the Dark Energy Survey (DES) to map the location of Dark Matter. The DES involves more than 300 scientists from six countries and uses images taken by one of the best digital cameras in the world: a 570-megapixel gadget mounted on the Victor Blanco telescope at the Cerro Tololo Inter-American Observatory in the Chilean Andes. The survey started in 2013 and will continue until 2018. A preliminary map, made using data from the camera's very first test images, was released in 2015. It shows fibers of Dark Matter, among galaxies, and voids in between. The ultimate goal: "By watching how clumps of Dark Matter shift over time, scientists hope eventually to quantify Dark Energy—the even more mysterious force that is pushing the cosmos apart."[171]

Why else is Dark Matter important? Does it support some sort of life, as some astrophysicists have postulated? We don't yet know the answers, but there are science fiction-like possibilities:

> "Depending on the mass and charges of the dark fermions, they could combine to create dark atoms, with their own chemistry, dark molecules and possibly more complex structures... We could be living in such a universe without even knowing it... Until we find (answers) we must be open to myriad explanations, including the fascinating possibility that we might be living alongside a dark parallel reality."[172]

Dark Energy

At least we know something about Dark Matter. When it comes to Dark Energy, more is unknown than is known. For now, it is the most accepted hypothesis to explain the increasing rate of expansion of the universe that has been verified by multiple observations since the 1990's. Based on the change in the rate of expansion, one can calculate how much Dark Energy exists. But other than that, it is a mystery. Why should we care? The strangeness of Dark Energy:

> "...shows scientists that there is a gap in our knowledge that needs to be filled, beckoning the way toward an unexplored realm of physics. We have before us the evidence that the cosmos may be

configured vastly differently than we imagine. Dark Energy both signals that we still have a great deal to learn and shows us that we stand poised for another great leap in our understanding of the universe."[173]

Black Holes

And finally, one cannot ignore Black Holes and whatever surprises they have in store for us. A Black Hole is a region in space-time where a huge amount of mass is packed into a very small space. This results in an extreme gravitational field that prevents anything, including light, from escaping the Black Hole. Einstein's theory of general relativity predicts that a sufficiently compact mass (such as the core that is left when a massive star dies in a supernova explosion) will deform space-time to form a Black Hole. However, as is the case with Dark Matter, Black Holes cannot be directly observed. Their presence is inferred by detecting their effects on other matter nearby.

Recently:

> "...scientists have directly detected gravitational waves for the first time using the Laser Interferometer Gravitational-Wave Observatory, also known as LIGO. Gravitational waves—ripples in the fabric of space-time that Einstein predicted should radiate out from the site of any gravitational disturbance—represent an entirely new way to see the cosmos, and with enough data, they could finally confirm—or contradict—the existence of Black Holes."[174]

Summary

Dark Matter. Dark Energy. Black Holes. We don't yet understand these mysterious entities, but once we do, or if anything else surprising is discovered in the universe, the impact on our way of life, on human interactions such as business interactions as we know them today, and on our world could be immense. This is one answer to those who ask "why bother to explore the makeup of the Universe?" An even better answer is provided by D. Shukman:

> "So, I wondered, what would we have thought if Christopher Columbus or Captain Cook had spotted an unmapped coastline but turned away with a look of indifference and had not bothered to land? To them, the lure of exotic new sights and undiscovered realms proved overwhelming. And nothing has changed."[175]

Searching for Life beyond Earth

The Breakthrough Initiatives is an organization founded in 2015 by Julia and Yuri Milner. The purpose is to provide "…a program of scientific and technological exploration, probing the big questions of life in the Universe: Are we alone? Are there habitable worlds in our galactic neighborhood? Can we make the great leap to the stars? And can we think and act together—as one world in the cosmos?"[176] Breakthrough Listen, one of the initiatives, is a $100 million venture, launched in 2015. It is a 10-year effort to listen for broadcast signals from a million of the stars closest to Earth. More recently, as a part of the Breakthrough Initiatives, on April 12, 2016, the initiative "Breakthrough Starshot" was announced by Y. Milner and S. Hawking. As the Breakthrough Initiatives' website describes, the project's aims are "to demonstrate proof of concept for ultra-fast light-driven Nanocrafts, and lay the foundations for a first launch to Alpha Centauri within the next generation."[177]

But the Breakthrough Initiatives are only one set of efforts to search for life beyond Earth. Sara Seager, a tenured MIT Professor, has dedicated her research to finding exoplanets—planets orbiting a star other than our sun.[178] And, there are a number of other projects working toward the goal of understanding if life can or does exist off Earth. Here are a few of the better known examples:

- The SETI (Search for Extraterrestrial Intelligence) Institute was originally sponsored by NASA, but is now a private, nonprofit organization. Its mission is: "to explore, understand, and explain the origin and nature of life in the universe, and to apply the knowledge gained to inspire and guide present and future generations."[179] As part of carrying out this mission, SETI is pointing an array of ground-based telescopes towards space to listen for any signal from another world.

- Kepler is a NASA spacecraft, outfitted with a specially designed telescope.[180] It was launched in 2009 into an orbit around the sun with a mission to search for Earth-like planets in our part of the Milky Way. Such planets would be located in the "Goldilocks" zone of a distant solar system—not too hot and not too cold—and could potentially be habitable by life as we know it. The spacecraft provides the power, pointing, and telemetry for the specially designed telescope for its searches. Over the years, the Kepler mission has been extended and modified several times, and now includes searching a broader part of the Milky Way. Since it began its search, Kepler has identified over 1000 exoplanets, including the key discovery in 2015 of Kepler 452b, a planet which is 1,400 light-years away and orbits a sun-like star every 385 days.

- The Mars Science Laboratory, better known as Curiosity,[181] is a part of NASA's Mars Exploration Program. Curiosity is an automobile-sized robotic rover launched by NASA in 2011, landing on Mars in 2012. The original goal was to determine if Mars was ever able to support microbial life. To do this, the rover's onboard laboratory sampled and studied rocks, soils, and other geology in an effort to detect the chemical building blocks of life. Curiosity sent numerous photographs and data back to earth early on confirming that yes, once Mars would have been able to support some type of life. Today, Curiosity continues to operate and provide valuable new information, such as the existence of water and ice on Mars.

As we have described, there is renewed and extensive activity in the search for life beyond Earth. But why does it matter? As Prof. S. Hawking, the famous cosmologist, pointed out at the launch of Breakthrough Snapshot, the chance of finding life in the nearest solar system is unlikely. But he went on to say that the search is more about developing the technology to get us there. Specifically, he stated: "The rapid progress of space exploration has improved people's lives in the past. So it would not be surprising if it brought benefits (to people's lives on Earth)."[182]

And Prof. S. Hawking, at the launch of Breakthrough Listen, said something else which captures the spirit of the search for extraterrestrial life:

"Somewhere in the cosmos, perhaps, intelligent life may be watching these lights of ours, aware of what they mean. Or do our lights wander a lifeless cosmos—unseen beacons, announcing that here, on one rock, the Universe discovered its existence.

Either way, there is no bigger question. It's time to commit to finding the answer—to search for life beyond Earth. We are alive. We are intelligent. We must know."[183]

These two quotes summarize the importance of exploring the universe in the search for life far better than we could—new technologies, new worlds, and the unknown. Clearly the potential is there for multiple launching pads.

KEY FINDINGS

Although *Creating New Superstars* does address the needed revolution in business management, it is just as much about technology and science. Why? In our fast-paced, technology-rich environment, it is impossible to ignore these forces that are shaping the future for business and for humanity. Business and technology have become irreversibly intertwined. However, to emphasize the key findings discussed in our book, we do separate them in the summary of highlights that follows.

CREATING NEW SUPERSTARS

As we have described, there is a new phenomenon in the business world today—a few (very few) **large**, public companies that have sustained **exponential** growth in revenues for more than a decade. And, as we showed, these Superstars have far outperformed other public companies of comparable size.

While it is interesting to recognize this phenomenon, for this knowledge to be useful to ambitious entrepreneurs or to business leaders who want to radically change their companies or to job seekers and investors seeking exceptional opportunities, the conditions and practices which resulted in the creation and success of these

Superstars must be understood. Then, such knowledge can be used to help identify and/or create new businesses with the potential for extreme growth.

Of course factors like visionary leaders and risk-taking are important for the creation of Superstars, but they are not the only keys and may not even be the most important ones. For a new business to have the possibility of becoming a Superstar, we have identified **six fundamental requirements** which we have explored and discussed scattered throughout the book. Here, we summarize them in one place. Although they are interconnected, we highlight them separately as follows:

1. <u>Technology Launching Pads</u>. Today, to become a Superstar, a business must be **based on and/or drawing from** an exponentially advancing technology—what we have called a technology Launching Pad. In other words, exponential business growth requires exponential change in the technology on which it is based. And today, in the 21st century, for the first time in history, the explosion of advances in Microelectronics, the Internet, and Biogenetics offer this possibility. These three technology Launching Pads are changing our world and creating new high growth business opportunities today at an exponentially increasing rate.

2. <u>Acts of Creation</u>. Exponential business growth does not result from just one flash of insight. Sustained exponential growth requires a **steady stream** of disruptive innovations, one after another, building on each other. It doesn't matter whether it is one creative genius or many people making the discoveries, as long as there are technology Launching Pads available to serve as catalysts. And just as important, leaders

seeking to create Superstars **do not need to be the creative geniuses**. But if they are not, they must be able to recognize and partner with individuals who are. However, no matter what, in the beginning it all starts with the "right" disruptive idea.

3. <u>Exceptional Leadership</u>. A risk-taker who thinks "outside of the box" and embraces the unconventional—from management styles to business definitions to business models. A decisive leader able to react quickly and unafraid of making mistakes. Someone with exceptional commitment to goals who is able and willing to "reinvent" everything as circumstances dictate. An intelligent and strong-willed individual whom people will follow (but not necessarily like). These words describe the kind of leadership required to create Superstars.

4. <u>Product Focus</u>. To become a Superstar, a company must be **first** to market with **new-to-the-world** products and/or services. No fast follower has yet become a Superstar. Being a lone pioneer in an uninhabited market allows a company not only to create and shape a new market but also to "dominate" it, at least for a while. But again, doing this once is not enough. In an environment that is rapidly changing at an ever increasing rate, being the creator of one new market (or market segment) after another is an almost unbeatable advantage that allows for the possibility of exponential growth.

5. <u>Market Focus</u>. For sustained exponential business growth, the markets addressed must be huge. This almost eliminates the possibility of suppliers becoming Superstars. There just aren't

enough customer companies. Thus, to be a Superstar a company must address **end users** (consumers) on a **global** basis. It's the only way the numbers are large enough.

6. <u>Independent</u>. It is impossible (or at least very very difficult) to create a Superstar within an already existing, large, conventional company. The big company atmosphere and culture almost guarantee failure. It would be like trying to grow roses in a desert where there is nothing to nourish the tender buds. To be extremely successful, new businesses need **independence** and the ability to be **unconventional**.

Finally, while the above factors are important, they are not a recipe for creating Superstars or even for achieving exceptional business performance. Things like choosing the right technology and product concept, developing a viable business model and plan, and pursuing viable funding strategies cannot be ignored. However our six factors do serve as guidelines and provide important insights about different paths leading to extreme growth.

One final comment. Nothing lasts forever. The Superstars of today are not likely to be the Superstars of tomorrow. New ones, based on new Launching Pads will take their place. And the cycle will continue to accelerate.

NEW DIRECTIONS FOR TODAY'S BUSINESS LEADERS

Business management should not be just a single data point. It must be an evolving variable. As such, we can gauge its evolution against the backdrop of other human activities in the same time frame. However, as we have shown, there is a mismatch between the speed of evolution of business practices and approaches, on the one hand, and the speeds with which many technologies and their incorporation into the world are evolving, on the other hand. It is essential that business leaders join the age of rapidly evolving technologies to eliminate that mismatch.

Yes, good business management fundamentals are still essential; and business success is still defined in terms of basic metrics such as growth, profitability, cash flow, return on investment, etc. But today companies must do everything faster and better to survive; and that requires embracing new technology. In addition, high growth is becoming almost always technology driven and dependent on disruptive innovation. So what exactly should management do? We have championed and described several "new directions" for leaders to consider. The key ones are highlighted below.

It is very difficult, if not impossible, for an existing company to become a Superstar. But a company doesn't need to be as fast growing as a Superstar to have exceptional performance. If business management accepts the need to change and recognizes and embraces the opportunities offered by the Launching Pads, significant improvements in business results are probable. The goal for such leaders needs to be "fast and good." And it all starts with changing from management as an art to management as a science—what we called **science-based decision-making**. This includes aggressive use of new developments in big data and analytics. In addition, developing a data-based capability to rapidly identify needed changes and then implementing them effectively is also required. "Fast and good" also means changing from using teams and committees as decision making bodies to using them as resources. Yes, good data, rapid analysis of it, and the involvement of experts are essential. But they are not substitutes for a strong and knowledgeable leader as the **key decision maker**.

Science-based decision-making is essential, but there is more. Breakthrough innovations are keys for creating and sustaining exceptional growth. However it is unlikely that a large company can internally generate, nurture, and develop enough new ideas on its own to adequately fuel its growth. This means that there is a need for **nonconventional** management approaches to modify the "DNA" of the company with respect to creativity and invention. These "genetic" changes range from truly encouraging internal entrepreneurs through focused organizational changes to seeking external innovations globally (most important) to carrying out projects with a globally networked organization. In other words, leaders must seek, capture, and nurture innovation wherever it is found; and they must change the culture of their organizations to accept this as the new norm.

But there is one more "new direction" for business management to consider. To repeat, in today's technology driven environment there are three Launching Pads that so far are driving much of the extreme business growth—Microelectronics, the Internet, and Biogenetics. Even for companies not directly based on these technologies, if leaders can find ways to **incorporate elements of Launching Pads** into their businesses, the results can be exceptional. To do this will likely involve changing the way a business operates or even changing its business definition, but the results can be worth the turmoil. And longer-term, if embryonic Launching Pads can be identified and ways found to be the first to develop new businesses based on them, the results can even be close to Superstar performance.

Science not art. Faster and faster. Data-based. Technology-driven. Disruptive innovations. These words describe the world of the 21st century, but they also describe the path that business leaders must take to the future for their businesses to survive and prosper and perhaps even become Superstars.

NEW TECHNOLOGY LAUNCHING PADS: DOORS TO OUR FUTURE

As we have shown, today's fastest growing, large companies are based on or enabled by one or more of three exponentially advancing technologies (Launching Pads). First to develop were Microelectronics and the Internet. These Launching Pads have already changed the world, and there is no going back. And now there is the explosively advancing field of Biogenetics which takes changing the world and life as we know it to a whole new level. But this is just the beginning. What are the next technology Launching Pads? What do new Launching Pads hold in store for humankind?

The Next Wave of Technology Launching Pads

In the last part of our book we identify what we consider to be three developing, Life Sciences based Launching Pads for the near term: **Biogenetics** (including breakthroughs in Genome Editing, Cloning, and Stem Cell Research), **Nanomedicine**, and **Human Brain Research**. While not yet fully developed Launching Pads, all three of these technology areas are advancing extremely rapidly and are on the verge of providing useful and life-changing applications, which we highlighted. Thus it is relatively easy to predict that stemming from these three areas will be the next wave of Launching Pads.

Of course, as with all predictions about the future, we might be wrong. Nanotechnology could develop faster than anticipated, or our predictions could be supplanted by a completely unforeseen Launching Pad coming to life, originating from the ingenuity of humans. But our expectation is that it is unlikely this will occur in the near term. Why? Because, unlike Superstars which can develop in just a few years, Launching Pads need a longer incubation period to move from scientific thought and discovery to technology applications. And this takes time, even in a rapidly changing environment.

Sources for Future Technology Launching Pads

Predicting what will be sources for new Launching Pads for the longer term is much riskier. However, we took that risk and identified and described three areas of science where new discoveries are being made that might serve as possible foundations for future Launching Pads: **Complexity Science**, **Sub-Atomic Particles**, and **Outer Space**. But these are not yet even embryonic Launching Pads. No technology "rocket" that can be launched from any of these areas and be useful to humanity has yet been discovered or invented.

What do we mean? The discovery of electrons and holes still required the invention of the transistor, before it led to Microelectronics. The discovery of the God Particle does not, by itself, teach one how to create new forms of matter or energy. And so on. The path from a scientific discovery to a Launching Pad is long. But consider the exponential progress of science and technology coupled with human ingenuity. Something totally new is always possible. So we may be wrong about the sources of future Launching Pads that we have chosen. Only one thing is certain. There will be new technology Launching Pads, and they will change the world.

New Technology Launching Pads: Good or Bad for the Human Race?

Yes, much of this book is about our current and future

dependence on technology Launching Pads. So before we finish, it is important to look at Launching Pads and their impacts from a different perspective.

We, the human race, have advanced in leaps and bounds our knowledge and capabilities in the past 50 years. Such extreme change in such a short time is something new. In the past, human progress also took place in leaps, but the leaps originated from slowly advancing discoveries or technologies, so the advancement was slow. For example, in prehistoric times the discovery of fire propelled mankind to new heights. But it took many, many centuries before the Industrial Revolution opened the door to new and previously inconceivable human activities and new businesses. Progress was faster than in previous times, but significant changes still took decades.

Today, as we have repeatedly emphasized, the world is dramatically different. Changes are occurring at an ever increasing rate, thanks to the exponentially advancing technology Launching Pads. And there is another big difference from the past. Our increased knowledge and capabilities are resulting in **increased consequences** for our discoveries and actions. We now have choices to make, because we know with certainty that some new avenues of discovery are good for humankind, some are bad, and others are only good **only if handled with great discretion and wisdom**. Yet, we continue to climb exponentially on our path to new knowledge, often without trying to discriminate or manage the possible outcomes.

We have reached a room with many doors. Behind each door, there is a different future for us and our world. Should we open these doors? Do we want to? Will we? The answer is simple: Yes, because **humans always have and always will**.

Think about the time, last century, when Enrico Fermi decided to have a closer look at some "spurious" large signals he obtained when Uranium was bombarded with neutrons in his laboratory. To his surprise he found that these signals were not spurious at all, but resulted from the splitting of the atom. Earlier, Einstein had written with chalk on a blackboard (yes, that's how things were done back then) the famous formula: $E=mc^2$. These two scientists never imagined that their discoveries, when combined, would result in atom bombs dropped on Hiroshima and Nagasaki many years later. Fermi (the experimentalist) and Einstein (the theoretician) had unknowingly **opened a door**, and what was on the other side was terrifying and not fully understood or controlled.

Today we have reached a room with many doors. We know some conceal a terrifying future behind them, and some lead to great benefits for humankind. Which door is which? And once opened, **can we control what we find**?

In the last part of our book we examined several developing technology Launching Pads, where the doors are already partially open. So we have some insight into what might be good or bad.

For example, consider the genome editing breakthrough **CRISPR**. This is clearly a technology that appears to have many good uses, such as the potential to cure inherited diseases. But there are some controversial possibilities behind that slightly opened door as well. As we described in Chapter 14, the most controversial form of genome editing involves modifying the genome of a newly created embryo. Ultimately, this could create the possibility of "designer babies" and more.

These types of dangers were recognized early on. Thus initial attempts at this application of genome editing, although unsuccessful, produced an outcry about the serious consequences if it were misused. However that didn't stop research. In 2015 a group of Chinese scientists announced that they had engineered genetic changes into non-viable human embryos, and then a group of British scientists did something similar. Now take genome editing a step further. Think about the ability to not just change DNA but also to pass these changes from generation to generation—something that appears to be within our reach. Ultimately this could lead to permanent alterations to the human race.

Advances in Biogenetics keep opening that door wider and wider, and on the other side we already know there is potential for great good as well as great harm. How will we manage this growing capability? Our future depends on that answer.

We wrote about the **Brain Research**. What is behind its door? Certainly there is a lot of good, but at what price? If we can modify the human brain to cure certain diseases, can we also modify it to produce an army of robot-like creatures that will fight for a dictator to their death? Might this lead to a world of programmable living beings devoid of emotion and compassion? Again, the potential for great good and great harm lies beyond this door.

We have highlighted these areas to make our points, but this doesn't even scratch the surface. We haven't even mentioned numerous other technology advances with the potential for both great good and great harm such as robots with advanced artificial intelligence capable of learning and redesigning themselves and potentially acting independently from the humans that are supposed to be controlling them. These kinds of threats are no longer just science fiction according to experts such as Stephen Hawking and Bill Gates.[184]

To summarize, as science advances and technologies provide as yet undreamed of capabilities, behind all doors will be the potential for both great good and great harm. Only two things are certain. Which doors we open and when will determine the future of humankind and life as we know it. And once a door is opened, it can never be closed. **Everything will change forever**.

NOTES

CHAPTER 1

1. The Oxford Dictionary defines exponential growth as: "Growth whose rate becomes ever more rapid in proportion to the growing total number or size." When plotted on a linear graph, the curve starts out almost flat, and then rises ever more rapidly in the vertical direction. This can be referred to as a "hockey-stick" shape.

2. "Fortune 500," *Fortune* 173, no. 8, June 15, 2016.

CHAPTER 2

3. Information about Amazon obtained from: Brad Stone, *The everything store: Jeff Bezos and the age of amazon kindle* (New York: Little, Brown and Company, 2013), Kindle edition; John Rossman, *The Amazon way: 14 leadership principles behind the world's most disruptive company* (North Charleston: CreateSpace, 2014), Kindle edition.

4. Jodi Kantor and David Streitfeld, "Inside Amazon: Wrestling big ideas in a bruising workplace," *The New York Times* online, August 15, 2015, http://www.nytimes.com/2015/08/16/technology/inside-amazon-wrestling-big-ideas-in-a-bruising-workplace.html.

5. Information about Apple and Steve Jobs obtained from: Nikol Vega Canales, *All about Apple Inc (History)* (USA: Nicholas Vega Canales, 2014), Kindle edition; Oliver Crompt, *10 Historic Moments of Apple, Inc.* (USA: Shaharm Publications, 2015), Kindle edition; Brett T.Robinson, *Appletopia: Media technology and the religious imagination of Steve Jobs* (Waco: Baylor University Press, 2013), Kindle

edition; Brent Schlender and Rick Tetzeli, *Becoming Steve Jobs: The evolution of a reckless upstart into a visionary leader* (New York: Crown Business, 2015), Kindle edition; Walter Isaacson, *Steve Jobs*, Reissue ed. (New York: Simon & Schuster, 2015).

6. Information about Genentech obtained from: Genentech's Website, *gene.com*, accessed May 23, 2016, http://www.gene.com/; Sally S. Hughes, *Genentech: The beginnings of biotech (Synthesis)*, Reprint ed. (Chicago: The University of Chicago Press, 2011).

7. Supreme Court Case: "Diamond v. Chakrabarty 447 U.S. 303 (1980)," *justia.com*, accessed May 23, 2016, https://supreme.justia.com/cases/federal/us/447/303/case.html.

8. Originally published in the "GenenLab Notebook" produced by Genentech on its twentieth anniversary, online in "Origin of Biotechnology: A Genentech perspective," *zymergi blog*, January 22, 2013, accessed May 23, 2016, http://blog.zymergi.com/2013/01/origins-biotech-genentech.html.

9. Sally S. Hughes, *Genentech: The beginnings of biotech (Synthesis)*, Reprint ed. (Chicago: The University of Chicago Press, 2011).

10. Information about Amgen obtained from: David E. Duncan, *Amgen Story: 25 Years of Visionary Science and Powerful Medicine* (Tahabi, 2005); Gordon Binder and Philip Bashe, *Science Lessons: What the Business of Biotech Taught Me About Management.* (Cambridge, MA: Harvard Business Press, 2008).

11. Information about Gilead Sciences obtained from: Gilead's Website, accessed May 23, 2016, http://www.gilead.com/; "Gilead Sciences, Inc. History," *Funding Universe*, accessed May 23, 2016, http://www.fundinguniverse.com/company-histories/gilead-sciences-inc-history; "News about Gilead Sciences Inc. including commentary and archival articles," *The New York Times* online, accessed May 23, 2016, http://topics.nytimes.com/top/news/business/companies/gilead_sciences_inc/index.html.

12. "Gilead Sciences' CEO on creating value through innovation: An interview with John Martin," *bcg.perspectives*, November 8, 2010, https://www.bcgperspectives.com/content/videos/biopharma_medical_devices_technology_innovation_creating_value_through_innovation/.

CHAPTER 3

13. Information about Facebook obtained from: David Kirkpatrick, *The Facebook Effect: The inside story of a company that is connecting the World* (New York: Simon & Schuster, 2011); Nikol V. Canales, *All about Facebook and Mark Zuckerberg; Full Biography* (USA: Nikol Vega Canales, 2014), Kindle edition; Nicholas Carlson, "At last -- The full story of how Facebook was founded," *Business Insider* online, March 5, 2010, http://www.businessinsider.com/how-facebook-was-founded-2010-3.

14. Information about Google obtained from: David A. Vise and Mark Malseed, *The Google story: For Google's 10th birthday*, Updated edition (New York: Bantam Dell, 2008); Google's Website, *google.com*, accessed May 23, 2016, http://www.google.com/about/company/history/.

15. "2015 Best Global Brands," *interbrand.com*, accessed May 23, 2016, http://interbrand.com/best-brands/best-global-brands/2015/.

16. Richard Nieva, "Alphabet? Google? Either way, it's ready to rumble," *cnet.com*, January 29, 2016, http://www.cnet.com/news/larry-page-sergey-brin-google-alphabet/.

17. Information about Microsoft and Bill Gates obtained from: Bill Gates, *Business @ The Speed of Thought: Succeeding in the Digital Economy* (New York: Warner Books Inc., 1999); Walter Isaacson, *The Innovators: How a Group of Hackers, Geniuses, and Geeks Created the Digital Revolution* (New York: Simon and Schuster, 2014).

18. Nick Wingfield, "The Hardware Side of Microsoft Unveils a Pile of New Devices," *The New York Times* online, October 6, 2015, http://www.nytimes.com/2015/10/07/technology/the-hardware-side-of-microsoft-unveils-a-pile-of-new-devices.html?_r=0.

19. Information about Intel obtained from: Michael Malone, *The Intel Trinity: How Robert Noyce, Gordon Moore and Andy Grove built the World's most Important Company* (New York: HarperBusiness, 2014); Intel's Website, "Intel Timeline: A History of Innovation," *intel.com*, accessed June 17, 2013, http://www.intel.com/content/www/us/en/history/historic-timeline.html.

20. Erin Griffith and Dan Primack, "The Age of Unicorns," *Fortune* online, January 22, 2015, http://fortune.com/2015/01/22/the-age-of-unicorns/.

21. "The Unicorn List 2016," *Fortune* online, accessed June 17, 2016, http://fortune.com/unicorns/.

22. Daniel Thomas, "How do you turn your tech start-up into a global giant," *bbc.com*, November 6, 2015, http://www.bbc.com/news/business-34731456, Eugene Levin, "Why Europe lags behind the US in VC investment," *venturebeat.com*, March 13, 2016, http://venturebeat.com/2016/03/13/why-europe-lags-behind-the-us-in-vc-investment/.

23. Information about Uber obtained from: "Uber: From zero to seventy (billion)," *The Economist* online, September 3, 2016, http://www.economist.com/news/briefing/21706249-accelerated-life-and-times-worlds-most-valuable-startup-zero-seventy?frsc=dg%7Ca; Julian Chokkattu and Jordan Crook, "A brief History of Uber," *techcrunch.com*, August 14, 2014, http://techcrunch.com/gallery/a-brief-history-of-uber/.

24. Information about Airbnb obtained from: Leigh Gallagher, "The education of Brian Chesky," *Fortune* online, July 1, 2015, http://fortune.com/brian-chesky-airbnb/.

25. Information about Moderna and its technology obtained from: Moderna's Website, modernatx.com, accessed June 17, 2016, http://www.modernatx.com/mrna-expression-platform; Meg Tirell, "The biotech targeting personalized medicine," *cnbc.com*, May 12, 2015, http://www.cnbc.com/2015/05/12/moderna-therapeutics-is-trying-to-cure-disease-with-mrna-drugs.html.

26. Meg Tirell, "The biotech targeting personalized medicine," cnbc.com, May 12, 2015, http://www.cnbc.com/2015/05/12/moderna-therapeutics-is-trying-to-cure-disease-with-mrna-drugs.html.

CHAPTER 4

27. Christopher Saint, "Integrated Circuit (IC)," *Encyclopaedia Britannica* online, last updated May 12, 2016, accessed June 17, 2016, http://www.britannica.com/EBchecked/topic/289645/integrated-circuit-IC.

28. Information on about Noyce and Intel obtained from Intel's Website, *intel.com*, accessed June 17, 2016, http://www.intel.com/content/www/us/en/library/viewmore.results.html?prTag=rtopic:corporateinformation/history.

29. Vangie Beal, "Moore's Law," *webopedia.com*, accessed June

17, 2016,
http://www.webopedia.com/TERM/M/Moores_Law.html.

30. John Markoff, "IBM Discloses Working Version of a Much Higher-Capacity Chip," *The New York Times* online, July 9, 2015, http://www.nytimes.com/2015/07/09/technology/ibm-announces-computer-chips-more-powerful-than-any-in-existence.html?_r=0.

31. Definitions, descriptions, and information about "crossing the valley of death" obtained from: Elizabeth Clements, "Crossing the Valley of Death," *symmetrymagazine* online, February 1, 2011, http://www.symmetrymagazine.org/article/february-2011/crossing-the-valley-of-death; Martin Zwilling, "10 Ways For Startups To Survive The Valley Of Death," *Forbes* online, February 18, 2013,
http://www.forbes.com/sites/martinzwilling/2013/02/18/10-ways-for-startups-to-survive-the-valley-of-death/#31f357685e40.

32. For a brief history of DARPA see DARPA's Website, *darpa.mil*, accessed June 20, 2016, http://www.darpa.mil/about-us/darpa-history-and-timeline.

33. From "Integrated Circuit," *Wikipedia*, accessed June 20, 2016.

34. Thomas L. Friedman, "Moore's Law Turns 50," *The New York Times* online, May 13, 2015,
http://www.nytimes.com/2015/05/13/opinion/thomas-friedman-moores-law-turns-50.html?_r=0.

35. Claire Zillman, "Bill Gates Calls on the U.S. Government to Invest More in R&D," *Fortune* online, April 18, 2016, http://fortune.com/2016/04/18/bill-gates-oped-research-development/.

36. Joel Garreau, "Ch.2: Be All You Can Be," *garreau.com*, accessed June 20, 2016,
www.garreau.com/main.cfm?action=chapters&id=53.

37. "1952: Bell Labs Licenses Transistor Technology," *The Silicon Engine, Computer History Museum* online, accessed June 20, 2016,
http://www.computerhistory.org/semiconductor/timeline/1952-transistor-technology-education-and-licensing-begins.html.

38. "1952: Transistorized Consumer Products Appear," *The Silicon Engine, Computer History Museum* online, accessed June 20, 2016,

http://www.computerhistory.org/semiconductor/timeline/1952-Consumer.html.

39. From "History of Sony," *Wikipedia*, accessed June 20, 2016.

40. Ryan Advent, "The Third Great Wave," *The Economist* online, October 4, 2014, http://www.economist.com/news/special-report/21621156-first-two-industrial-revolutions-inflicted-plenty-pain-ultimately-benefited.

41. Johnny Ryan, *A History of the Internet and the Digital Future* (London: Reaktion Books Ltd., 2013), Kindle edition.

42. From "History of the Internet," *Wikipedia*, accessed June 20, 2016.

43. J. C. R. Licklider, "Man-Computer Symbiosis," *IRE Transactions on Human Factors in Electronics*, HFE-1, 4–11, March 1960, accessed online June 20, 2016, http://groups.csail.mit.edu/medg/people/psz/Licklider.html.

44. James Allen, "Engineering 'Laws' – Moore's, Rock's, Butter's and others," *SourceTech411*, December 20, 2012, http://sourcetech411.com/2012/12/engineering-laws-moores-rocks-butters-and-others/.

45. "Biotechnology," dictionary.com, accessed June 20, 2016; "What is Biotechnology? " *Biotechnology Innovation Organization* online, accessed June 20, 2016, https://www.bio.org/what-biotechnology.

46. "Timeline of Medical Biotechnology," *amgen.com*, accessed June 20, 2016, http://www.biotechnology.amgen.com/timeline.html.

47. Joseph Walker and Tom McGinty, "Biotech Labs Birth New Drugs—and New Fortunes," *The Wall Street Journal* online, June 24, 2016, http://www.wsj.com/articles/biotech-labs-birth-new-drugsand-new-fortunes-1466798095.

48. Scott DeCarlo and Jen Wieczner, "The trillion-dollar medicine cabinet," *Fortune* online, April 29, 2015, http://fortune.com/2015/04/29/biotech-fortune-500/.

CHAPTER 5

49. Arthur Koestler, *The Act of Creation – The conscious and unconscious in science and art* (New York: Dell Book, 1967), 16.

50. Felicity Mellor, "The Power of Silence," *Physics World* online, April 3, 2014, http://physicsworld.com/cws/article/indepth/2014/apr/03/the-

power-of-silence.

51. W. Heitler, "Erwin Schrodinger. 1887-1961," *Biographical Memoirs of Fellows of the Royal Society* 7(November 1961): 221-228, http://rsbm.royalsocietypublishing.org/content/roybiogmem/7/221.full.pdf; Walter J. Moore, *Schrödinger: Life and Thought* (Cambridge: Cambridge University Press, 1992).

52. Brett T. Robinson, *Appletopia, Media Technology and the Religious Imagination of Steve Jobs* (Waco: Baylor University Press, 2013), Kindle edition.

CHAPTER 6

CHAPTER 7

53. Information about the Industrial Revolution obtained from: "Industrial Revolution," *history.com*, accessed June 22, 2016, http://www.history.com/topics/industrial-revolution; "Industrial Revolution," *Encyclopaedia Britannica* online, last updated January 20, 2016, accessed June 22, 2016, http://www.britannica.com/event/Industrial-Revolution.

54. Information about the beginning of the automobile industry obtained from: John Bell Rae, "Automotive industry," *Encyclopaedia Britannica* online, accessed June 22, 2016, http://www.britannica.com/topic/automotive-industry; "Automobiles," *history.com*, accessed June 22, 2016, http://www.history.com/topics/automobiles.

55. Information on about McDonald's obtained from: Eric Schlosser, *Fast Food Nation: The Dark Side of the All-American Meal* Reprint ed. (New York: Mariner Books 2001); "McDonald's Corporation," *Encyclopaedia Britannica* online, last updated January 21, 2016, accessed June 22, 2016, http://www.britannica.com/topic/McDonalds-Corporation; Tracy V. Wilson, "How Fast Food Works," *HowStuffWorks.com*, August 22, 2006, http://science.howstuffworks.com/innovation/edible-innovations/fast-food.htm.

56. Margaret B. W. Graham, *The Business of Research: RCA and the Video Disc* (Cambridge: Cambridge University Press, 1980).

57. Information on the history of FedEx obtained from:

Eugene Linden, "Frederick W. Smith of Federal Express: He Didn't Get There Overnight," *inc.com*, April 1, 1984, http://www.inc.com/magazine/19840401/8479.html; Roger Frock, *Changing How the World Does Business: Fedex's Incredible Journey to Success - The Inside Story* (San Francisco: Berrett-Koehler, 2006).

CHAPTER 8

58 Philip Kotler and John A. Caslione, *Chaotics: The Business of Managing and Marketing in the Age of Turbulence*, (New York: AMACOM, 2009).

59. Antonio Regalado, "Technology Is Wiping out Companies Faster than Ever," *MIT Technology Review* online, September 10, 2013, https://www.technologyreview.com/s/519226/technology-is-wiping-out-companies-faster-than-ever/.

60. Sam Gustin, "BlackBerry Crushed: RIM's failure to keep up with Apple has turned it into a tech basket case," *Time* online, July 16, 2012, http://content.time.com/time/magazine/article/0,9171,2118523,00.html; "Smartphone Vendor Market Share, 2015, Q2," *IDC* online, accessed June 22, 2016, http://www.idc.com/prodserv/smartphone-market-share.jsp; "BlackBerry is a Value Investment Looking to 2016,"*gurufocus.com*, April 17, 2015, http://www.gurufocus.com/news/331029/; "Thin harvest: Blackberry's future," *The Economist Espresso* online, June 23, 2016, https://espresso.economist.com/b3848d61bbbc6207c6668a8a9e2730ed.

61. Thomas H. Davenport, Jeanne G. Harris and Robert Morison, *Analytics at Work – Smarter Decisions, Better Results* (Boston: Harvard Business Review Press, 2010).

62. Richard D'Aveni, "The 3-D Printing Revolution," *Harvard Business Review* online, May 2015, https://hbr.org/2015/05/the-3-d-printing-revolution; Dan Simmons, "Airbus had 1,000 parts 3D printed to meet deadline," *BBC News* online, May 6, 2015, http://www.bbc.com/news/technology-32597809.

63. Ron Jones, "Social Media Marketing 101, Part 1," *searchenginewatch.com*, February 16, 2009, http://searchenginewatch.com/article/2064413/Social-Media-Marketing-101-Part-1.

64. Pierre Omidyar, "Social Media: Enemy of the State or Power to the People?" *TheWorldPost* online, February 27, 2014, updated December 1, 2014, http://www.huffingtonpost.com/pierre-omidyar/social-media-enemy-of-the_b_4867421.html.

65. Joe Coscarelli, "Hurricane Sandy: A Perfect Social Media Storm," *nymag.com*, October 30, 2012, http://nymag.com/daily/intelligencer/2012/10/hurricane-sandy-perfect-social-media-storm.html.

66. Kelly Moffitt, "How social media is playing a role in Ferguson," *St. Louis Business Journal* online, updated August 14, 2014, http://www.bizjournals.com/stlouis/blog/2014/08/how-social-media-is-playing-a-role-in-ferguson.html?page=all.

67. Thom Poole, "Turkey coup: How mobiles beat tanks and saved Erdogan," *BBC News* online, July 18, 2016, http://www.bbc.com/news/world-europe-36822858.

68. "The New Conversation: Taking Social Media from Talk to Action," *A Report by Harvard Business Review Analytical Services*, August 1, 2010, http://www.sas.com/events/pbls/2010/las-vegas/documents/TheNewConversation.pdf.

69. Ryan Holmes, "5 Trends That Will Change How Companies Use Social Media in 2016," *FastCompany* online, December 9, 2015, http://www.fastcompany.com/3054347/the-future-of-work/5-trends-that-will-change-how-companies-use-social-media-in-2016.

70. "Moving on Up: Is the Recession Heralding a Return to Henry Ford's Model?" *The Economist* online, March 27, 2009, http://www.economist.com/node/13173671.

71. Shelly Banjo, "Inside Nike's Struggle to Balance Cost and Worker Safety in Bangladesh" *The Wall Street Journal* online, April 21, 2014, http://www.wsj.com/articles/SB10001424052702303873604579493502231397942?cb=logged0.6063367940951139.

72. Thompson Reuters, "Dell's Outsourcing Plan Could Be Rough Going," *PCmag.com*, September 8, 2008, http://www.pcmag.com/article2/0,2817,2329649,00.asp.

73. Benjamin Kabin, "Apple's iPhone: Designed in California but Manufactured Fast All around the World," *Entrepreneur* online, September 11, 2013, https://www.entrepreneur.com/article/228315.

74. Bruce Einhorn and Matthew Philips, "Construction Outsourcing: A Philippine Builder Delivers," *Bloomberg.com*, September 5, 2013, http://www.bloomberg.com/news/articles/2013-09-05/construction-outsourcing-a-philippine-builder-delivers.

75. Greg Botelho, "FAA finds Boeing Dreamliner could lose all power, issues maintenance mandate," *CNN.com*, May 5, 2015, http://www.cnn.com/2015/05/02/us/boeing-787-dreamliner-faa-directive/index.html; Christopher Harress, "Boeing 787: A Complete Timeline of the Dreamliner's Legacy of Failure, After Cracks Discovered in Wings," *International Business Times* online, March 10, 2014, http://www.ibtimes.com/boeing-787-complete-timeline-dreamliners-legacy-failure-after-cracks-discovered-wings-1560491.

76. Ted Reed, "Boeing's 787 Dreamliner Has a Nice Problem - Demand Exceeds Supply," *TheStreet* online, March 29, 2015, http://www.thestreet.com/story/13129411/1/.

77. Thomas L. Friedman, *The World is Flat: A Brief History of the Twenty-First Century* Release 3.0 (New York: Picador, 2007), 6-7.

78. John K. Borchardt, "The Globalization of R&D," *Lab Manager* online, July 13, 2011, http://www.labmanager.com/business-management/2011/07/the-globalization-of-r-d?fw1pk=2#.V2xV3LnNGfY; Steven D. Eppinger and Anil R. Chitkara, "The Practice of Global Product Development," *MITSloan Management Review*, Summer 2009, updated November 21, 2009, Reprint #: 50437.

79. Helen Fields, "Invasion of the Snakeheads," *Smithsonian*, February 2005, accessed online June 24, 2016, http://www.smithsonianmag.com/science-nature/invasion-of-the-snakeheads-85051261/?no-ist.

80. Information about Toyota's history obtained from: "Toyota history: corporate and automotive," *toyoland.com*, accessed June 24, 2016, http://www.toyoland.com/history.html; "History of Toyota," *toyota-global.com*, accessed June 24, 2016, http://www.toyota-global.com/company/history_of_toyota/.

81. Information about "dumping" obtained from: Brian Winfield, "U.S. Sets Anti-Dumping Duties on China Solar Imports," *Bloomberg* online, October 10, 2012, http://www.bloomberg.com/news/articles/2012-10-10/u-s-sets-anti-dumping-duties-on-china-solar-imports; Bloomberg News,

"U.S. Revises Tariffs and Duties on Chinese Solar Imports," *Bloomberg* online, July 9, 2015, http://www.bloomberg.com/news/articles/2015-07-09/u-s-imposes-dumping-duties-on-imports-of-chinese-solar-goods; Biman Mukherji, John W. Miller, and Chuin-Wei Yap, "Why Chinese Steel Exports Are Stirring Protests," *The Wall Street Journal* online, March 15, 2015, http://www.wsj.com/articles/why-chinese-steel-exports-are-stirring-protests-1426466068; Sonja Elmquist, "U.S. Steel Says South Korean Companies Are Dumping Pipes," *Bloomberg* online, March 25, 2014, http://www.bloomberg.com/news/articles/2014-03-25/u-s-steel-says-south-korean-companies-are-dumping-pipes; James R. Hagerty, "The Next Trade Fight: Office Paper," *The Wall Street Journal* online, January 21, 2015, http://www.wsj.com/articles/the-next-trade-fight-office-paper-1421816462.

82. S. Pellegrino Company Website, accessed June 24, 2016, https://www.sanpellegrino.com/us/en/company-intl-41.

83. Rick Newman, "Four Lessons from Kodak's Comedown," *U.S. News* online, January 19, 2012, http://www.usnews.com/news/blogs/rick-newman/2012/01/19/4-lessons-from-kodaks-comedown; "The last Kodak moment?," *The Economist*, January 13, 2012, accessed online June 24, 2016, http://www.economist.com/node/21542796.

84. Evelyn M. Rusli, "Quest for Patents Brings New Focus in Tech Deals," *The New York Times* online, August 16, 2011, http://dealbook.nytimes.com/2011/08/16/quest-for-patents-brings-new-focus-in-tech-deals/?_r=0.

CHAPTER 9

85. Information about RCA obtained from: Margaret B. W. Graham, *The Business of Research: RCA and the Video Disc* (Cambridge: Cambridge University Press, 1980); Alfred D. Chandler Jr., *Inventing the Electronic Century: The Epic Story of the Consumer Electronics and Computer Industries* (Cambridge, MA: Harvard University Press, 2005).

86. One of the authors (EF) worked for both RCA and its British parent, Marconi Co. As an "insider" (although he was not present when all of the episodes narrated in this chapter took place), he was exposed to some of the detailed history of the events

described here and presents a different perspective than may be found elsewhere.

87. Details about RCA's VideoDisc can be found at "Capacitance Electronic Disc," *Wikipedia*, accessed June 24, 2016.

88. P. Ranganath Nayak and John M. Ketteringham, *Breakthroughs! How the Vision and Drive of Innovators in Sixteen Companies Created Commercial Breakthroughs that Swept the World* (New York: Rawson Associates, 1986), 23-49.

89. Gadget_Gizmo, "Beta vs VHS," *cnet.com*, March 13, 2007, http://www.cnet.com/forums/discussions/beta-vs-vhs-238194/.

90. Alfred D. Chandler Jr., *Inventing the Electronic Century: The Epic Story of the Consumer Electronics and Computer Industries*, (Cambridge, MA: Harvard University Press, 2005), 48-49.

CHAPTER 10

91. Betsy Morris, "Sorry, Jack (Welch)! Welch's rules for winning don't work anymore (But we've got 7 new ones that do)," *Fortune*, July 10, 2006, accessed online June 24, 2016, http://archive.fortune.com/2006/07/10/magazines/fortune/rules.fortune/index.htm.

92. Maurice Ramsey, "Three Cultures," *Physics World* (August 1994): 72.

93. Carly Fiorina, *Tough Choices: A Memoir* (New York: Penguin Group, 2007).

94. Bryan Williams, "Elite Universities Are Turning Our Kids into Corporate Stooges," *New Republic* online, April 26, 2015, https://newrepublic.com/article/121644/elite-universities-are-turning-our-kids-corporate-stooges.

CHAPTER 11

95. Carol L. Fatuzzo and Ennio Fatuzzo, *Survival in the Sea of Economic Chaos* (USA: CreateSpace, 2011).

96. Thomas H. Davenport and Jeanne G. Harris, *Competing on Analytics: The New Science of Winning* (Boston: Harvard Business School Press, 2007), 7.

97. "Data, data everywhere," *The Economist*, Feb 25th 2010, accessed online June 27, 2016, http://www.economist.com/node/15557443.

98. Michael Schroeck, Rebecca Shockley, Dr. Janet Smart, Professor Dolores Romero-Morales, and Professor Peter Tufano, "Analytics: The real-world use of big data," *IBM Global Business Services Executive Report*, IBM Institute for Business Value (2012), accessed June 27, 2016, http://www-935.ibm.com/services/us/gbs/thoughtleadership/ibv-big-data-at-work.html.

99. Foster Provost and Tom Fawcett, "Data Science and its Relationship to Big Data and Data-Driven Decision Making," *Big Data*, 1, no. 1 (March 2013), 51-59, http://online.liebertpub.com/doi/pdfplus/10.1089/big.2013.1508.

100. For detailed information about Game Theory see: Adam M. Brandenburger and Barry J. Nalebuff, *Co-opetition: A revolutionary mindset that combines competition and cooperation* (New York: Doubleday, 1996); James Miller, *Game Theory at Work: How to use Game Theory to outthink and outmaneuver your competition* (New York: McGraw-Hill 2003); John McMillan, *Games, Strategies, & Managers: How Managers can use Game Theory to make better business decisions* (New York: Oxford University Press,1996); Pankaj Ghemawat, *Games Businesses Play: Cases and Models* third printing (Cambridge, MA: the MIT Press, 2000); Shaun Hargreaves-Heap and Yanis Varoufakis, *Game Theory: A Critical Introduction* 2nd edition (New York: Routledge, 2004).

101. Roger B. Myerson, Game Theory: Analysis of Conflict (Cambridge, MA: Harvard University Press, 1997), 1.

102. James Miller, *Game Theory at Work: How to use Game Theory to outthink and outmaneuver your competition* (New York: McGraw-Hill 2003). This is a somewhat technical description of the basics of Game Theory for the non-expert and provides easy-to-understand examples of different business "games."

103. Raymond Smith, "Business as a War Game: A Report from the Battlefront," *Fortune*, September 30, 1996, 190-2, accessed online June 27, 2016, http://archive.fortune.com/magazines/fortune/fortune_archive/1996/09/30/217445/index.htm?iid=sr-link2.

104. One of the sites, accessed June 26, 2016, you may find useful for identifying consultants is: http://www.gametheory.net/links/consulting.html. This Web site lists a number of consulting firms specialize in Game Theory. Note: The authors do NOT have knowledge of any of these firms, and hence this reference should in no way be considered a

recommendation.

105. Nancy A. Nichols, "Scientific Management at Merck," *Harvard Business Review*, January-February 1994, https://hbr.org/1994/01/scientific-management-at-merck-an-interview-with-cfo-judy-lewent/ar/3.

106. "Game theory in practice: Computing: Software that models human behaviour can make forecasts, outfox rivals and transform negotiations," *The Economist*, September 3, 2011, http://www.economist.com/node/21527025/.

107. The following references all provide good, but different, introductions to ABMS: Robert Axelrod, *The Complexity of Cooperation: Agent-Based Models of Competition and Collaboration* (Princeton: Princeton University Press, 1997); Nigel Gilbert, *Agent-Based Models: Quantitative Applications in the Social Sciences* annotated edition (Thousand Oaks, CA: Sage Publications, 2008); Michael J. North and Charles M. Macal, *Managing Business Complexity: Discovering Strategic Solutions with Agent-Based Modeling and Simulation* (New York: Oxford University Press, 2007).

108. Following are examples of articles about ABMS applied to business: Eric Bonabeau, "Agent-based modeling: Methods and techniques for simulating human systems," *Proceedings of the National Academy of Sciences* 99, suppl. 3 (May 14, 2002), http://www.pnas.org/content/99/suppl.3/7280.full; Eric Bonabeau, "Predicting the Unpredictable – Can You Predict the Unpredictable?," *Harvard Business School Working Knowledge* online, May 13, 2002, http://hbswk.hbs.edu/archive/2934.html; William Niedringhaus, "An Agent-Based Model of the Airline Industry," *The MITRE Corporation* (2002), accessed online June 27, 2016, http://www.caasd.org/library/papers/ACSEM.pdf; David Buxton, Richard Farr, Bart MacCarthy, "The Aero-Engine Value Chain Under Future Business Environments: Using Agent-Based Simulation to Understand Dynamic Behavior," *MITIP2006* (September 11-12, 2006), accessed June 27, 2016, http://www.anylogic.com/upload/iblock/cf1/cf1fa4baac81b4caa46d81f980b879fd.pdf; Takao Terano and Kenichi Naitoh, "Agent-based modeling for competing firms: from balanced-scorecards to multiobjective strategies," *Proceedings of the 37th Hawaii International Conference on Systems Sciences* (2004), accessed online June 27, 2016, https://www.computer.org/web/csdl/index/-/csdl/proceedings/hicss/2004/2056/03/205630090.pdf.

109. "IBM Watson Engagement Advisor," *IBM Watson Solutions,* May 2013, accessed online June 26, 2016, http://www-05.ibm.com/de/watson/pdf/ibm_watson_engagement_brochure.pdf; Dylan Love, "Remember When That Watson Supercomputer Won Jeopardy? Here's What's Going on with It Lately," *Business Insider,* December 7, 2013, http://www.businessinsider.com/ibm-watson-future-2013-12.

CHAPTER 12

110. Claude G. Luisada and Steven D. Kimmell, *The Boeing 787 Dreamliner* (Atglen, PA: Schiffer Publishing Ltd, 2014).
111. Greg Botelho, "FAA finds Boeing Dreamliner could lose all power, issues maintenance mandate," *CNN.com,* May 5, 2015, http://www.cnn.com/2015/05/02/us/boeing-787-dreamliner-faa-directive/index.html.
112. Christopher A. Hart, "Safety Recommendation," *National Transportation Safety Board,* December 1, 2014, accessed online June 28, 2016, https://app.ntsb.gov/doclib/recletters/2014/A-14-113-127.pdf.
113. "Big data analytics," *WhatIs.com,* accessed June 28, 2016, http://searchbusinessanalytics.techtarget.com/definition/big-data-analytics.

CHAPTER 13

114. Waldemar Kaempffert, "Miracles You'll See in the Next Fifty Years," *Popular Mechanics* (February 1950): 112-121, accessed online June 28, 2016, http://www.amusingplanet.com/2010/11/miracles-youll-see-in-next-fifty-years.html.
115. Clayton M. Christensen, Scott D. Anthony, and Erik A. Roth, *Seeing What's Next: Using the Theories of Innovation to Predict Industry Change* (Boston: Harvard Business School Press, 2004).

CHAPTER 14

116. Peter Reuell, "Toward genetic editing," *Harvardgazette,* November 3, 2014, http://news.harvard.edu/gazette/story/2014/11/toward-genetic-

editing/.

117. "Genome editing," *Wikipedia*, accessed June 28, 2016, https://en.wikipedia.org/wiki/Genome_editing.

118. Thomas Gaj, Charles A. Gersbach, and Carlos F. Barbas, "ZFN, TALEN, and CRISPR/Cas-based methods for genome engineering," *Trends in Biotechnology* 31, no. 7 (July 2013): 399-405, accessed online June 28, 2016, http://www.cell.com/trends/biotechnology/pdf/S0167-7799(13)00087-5.pdf.

119. Information about CRISPR technology obtained from: Andrew Pollack, "A Powerful New Way to Edit DNA," *New York Times* online, March 3, 2014, http://www.nytimes.com/2014/03/04/health/a-powerful-new-way-to-edit-dna.html?_r=0; Alice Park, "Life, the Remix: A New Technique That Lets Scientists Edit DNA is Transforming Science—and Raising Difficult Questions," *Time* (July 4, 2016), accessed online June 29, 2016; http://time.com/4379503/crispr-scientists-edit-dna/; "CRISPR: What's All the Excitement About?," *about.com*, updated February 23, 2016, http://biotech.about.com/od/technicaltheory/a/Crispr-Whats-All-The-Excitement-About.htm.

120. John Travis, "Making the Cut: CRISPR genome-editing technology shows its power," *Science* 350, no. 6267 (December 17, 2015): 1456-1457, accessed online June 29, 2016, http://science.sciencemag.org/content/sci/350/6267/1456.full.pdf

121. Martin Jinek, Krzysztof Chylinski, Ines Fonfara, Michael Hauer, Jennifer A. Doudna, and Emmanuelle Charpentier, "A programmable dual-RNA-guided DNA endonuclease in adaptive bacterial immunity," *Science* 337, no. 6096 (August 17, 2012): 816-821, accessed online June 29, 2016, http://science.sciencemag.org/content/early/2012/06/27/science.1225829.full.

122. Ed Davis, "Genome Editing: Which Should I Choose, TALEN or CRISPR?," *Genecopoeia.com*, 2014, accessed June 39, 2016, http://www.genecopoeia.com/resource/genome-editing-talen-or-crispr/.

123. Jenny Rood, "Who Owns CRISPR?," *TheScientist*, April 3, 2015, http://www.the-scientist.com/?articles.view/articleNo/42595/title/Who-Owns-CRISPR-/; Christopher VanLang, "Who Invented CRISPR?,"

quora.com, October 1, 2015, https://www.quora.com/Who-invented-CRISPR.

124. Farai Chideya, "The Battle Over CRISPR Could Make Or Break Some Biotech Companies," *FiveThirtyEight.com*, January 25, 2016, http://fivethirtyeight.com/features/the-battle-over-crispr-could-make-or-break-some-biotech-companies/.

125. Joe Stanganelli, "The State Of CRISPR/Cas9: Patents And Possibilities," *Bio ITWorld*, October 25, 2017, http://www.bio-itworld.com/2017/10/25/the-state-of-crispr/cas9-patents-and-possibilities.aspx

126. "Even CRISPR: A new way to edit DNA may speed the advance of genetic engineering," *The Economist*, October 3, 2015, http://www.economist.com/node/21668031; Max-Planck-Gesellschaft; "Cpf1: CRISPR-enzyme scissors cutting both RNA and DNA," *ScienceDaily*, April 22, 2016, https://www.sciencedaily.com/releases/2016/04/160422115327.htm.

127. Margaret Knox, "The Gene Genie," *Scientific American* 311, no.6 (December 2014): 42 – 46, accessed online June 29, 2016, http://nickrath.weebly.com/uploads/6/5/4/1/6541061/the_gene_genie.pdf.

128. David Baltimore, Paul Berg, Michael Botchan, et al., "A Prudent Path Forward for Genetic Engineering and Germline Gene Modification," *Science* 348, no. 6230 (April 3, 2015): 36-38, accessed online June 29, 2016, http://reviverestore.org/wp-content/uploads/2015/04/15Science.pdf.

129. Robert Pollack, "Eugenics lurk in the shadow of CRISPR," *Science* 348, no. 6237 (May 22, 2015): 871, accessed online June 29, 2016, https://www.researchgate.net/publication/277080659_Eugenics_lurk_in_the_shadow_of_CRISPR.

130. Thomas Gaj, Charles A. Gersbach, and Carlos F. Barbas, "ZFN, TALEN, and CRISPR/Cas-based methods for genome engineering," *Trends in Biotechnology* 31, no. 7 (July 2013): 397, accessed online June 28, 2016, http://www.cell.com/trends/biotechnology/pdf/S0167-7799(13)00087-5.pdf.

131. Information about cloning obtained from: "Cloning," *National Human Genome Research Institute*, NIH, accessed June 30, 2016, https://www.genome.gov/25020028; Genetic Science

Learning Center, "What is Cloning?," *Learn.Genetics*, June 22, 2014, accessed June 30, 2016, http://learn.genetics.utah.edu/content/cloning/whatiscloning/.

132. "Cloning Dolly the sheep," *AnimalResearch.Info*, accessed June 30, 2016, http://www.animalresearch.info/en/medical-advances/timeline/cloning-dolly-the-sheep/.

133. "Cloning: Frequently Asked Questions," *npr.org*, accessed June 30, 2016, http://www.npr.org/news/specials/cloning/faq_blanknav.html.

134. Information about stem cells and their potential benefits obtained from: National Institutes of Health, "Stem Cell Basics," *stemcells.nih.gov*, last modified April 8, 2015, http://stemcells.nih.gov/staticresources/info/basics/SCprimer2009.pdf; Engineering, and Public Policy Committee on Science, "How is Reproductive Cloning Done?," *Scientific and Medical Aspects of Human Reproductive Cloning* (Washington DC: National Academies Press, 2002), 25, accessed online June 30, 2016, http://www.nap.edu/read/10285/chapter/4#25.

135. Mayo Clinic Staff, "Stem cells: What they are and what they do," *mayoclinic.org*, accessed June 30, 2016, http://www.mayoclinic.org/tests-procedures/stem-cell-transplant/in-depth/stem-cells/ART-20048117.

136. David Baltimore, Paul Berg, Michael Botchan, et al., "A Prudent Path Forward for Genetic Engineering and Germline Gene Modification," *Science* 348, no. 6230 (April 3, 2015): 36, accessed online June 29, 2016, http://reviverestore.org/wp-content/uploads/2015/04/15Science.pdf.

137. "What are induced pluripotent stem cells?," *stemcells.nih.gov*, accessed June 30, 2016, http://stemcells.nih.gov/info/basics/pages/basics10.aspx.

138. Alice Park, "George W. Bush and the Stem Cell Research Funding Ban," *Time* online, August 20, 2012, http://healthland.time.com/2012/08/21/legitimate-rape-todd-akin-and-other-politicians-who-confuse-science/slide/bush-bans-stem-cell-research/.

139. Syed Abeer, "Future Medicine: Nanomedicine," *JIMSA* 25, no. 3 (July-September 2012): 187-192, accessed online July 1, 2016, http://swisstronix.com/nbic/PDF/nanomedicine.pdf; S. Moein Moghimi, A. Christy Hunter, and J. Clifford Murray, "Nanomedicine: current status and future prospects," *The FASEB*

Journal 19, no. 3 (March 2005): 311-330, accessed online July 1, 2016, http://www.cpe.vt.edu/globaltechseminars/downloads/nanomedicine_applications.pdf.

140. "Nanotechnology," *dictionary.com*, accessed July 1, 2016, http://www.dictionary.com/browse/nanotechnology.

141. Mesoscale Science Subcommittee, "From Quanta to continuum: Opportunities for mesoscale science," *Department of Energy Basic Research Needs Report* (September 2012), accessed online July 1, 2016, http://science.energy.gov/~/media/bes/pdf/reports/files/OFMS_rpt.pdf.

142. "Focus on Nanotechnology: Reaping the Benefits of Nanomaterials," *Physics World Focus Issue* (June 2014), accessed online July 1, 2016, http://mag.digitalpc.co.uk/fvx/iop/physworld/nano14/.

143. "Nanotechnology Investments by Governments," *nanotechnologyInvesting.us*, accessed July 1, 2016, http://www.nanotechnologyinvesting.us/government.htm.

144. NSTC/CoT/NSET, "NNI Supplement to the President's 2015 Budget," *nano.gov*, March 25, 2014, http://www.nano.gov/node/1128.

145. "Nanomedicine Overview," *genome.gov*, archived page, accessed July 1, 2016, https://www.genome.gov/11508736/nanomedicine-fact-sheet/.

146. Robert A. Freitas Jr., "Nanomedicine: Welcome to the Nanomedicine Page," *Foresight Institute*, accessed July 1, 2016, https://www.foresight.org/Nanomedicine/.

147. Larissa Y. Rizzo, Benjamin Theek, Gert Storm, Fabian Kiessling, and Twan Lammers, "Recent Progress in Nanomedicine: Therapeutic, Diagnostic and Theranostic Applications," *Current Opinion in Biotechnology* 24, no. 6 (December 2013): 1159-1166, accessed online July 1, 2016, http://www.ncbi.nlm.nih.gov/pmc/articles/PMC3833836/.

148. "What is nanotechnology and what is nanomedicine?," *British Society for Nanomedicine Explore* (2012), accessed July 1, 2016, http://www.britishsocietynanomedicine.org/what-is-nanomedicine.html.

149. "Ljubimova Laboratory," *cedar-sinai.edu*, accessed July 1, 2016, http://www.cedars-sinai.edu/Research/Research-Labs/Ljubimova-Lab/Ljubimova-Laboratory.aspx.

150. Mritunjai Singh, Shinjini Singh, S. Prasada, and I. S. Gambhir, "Nanotechnology in Medicine and Antibacterial Effect of Silver Nanoparticles," *Digest Journal of Nanomaterials and Biostructures* 3, no. 3 (September 2008): 115, accessed online July1, 2016, https://www.researchgate.net/publication/256463087_Nanotechnology_in_medicine_and_antibacterial_effect_of_silver_nanoparticles.

151. A. Paul Alivisatos, "Less is more in Medicine," *Nanotechnology, from the Editors of the Scientific American* (New York: Warner Books, 2002) 56, accessed online July1 2016, http://www.scientificamerican.com/article/less-is-more-in-medicine-2007-09/.

152. Hua Zhang, Douglas Yee, and Chun Wang, "Quantum dots for cancer diagnosis and therapy: biological and clinical perspectives," *Nanomedicine* 3, no. 1 (February 2008): 83-91, accessed online July1, 2016, http://www.medscape.com/viewarticle/574914.

153. "Little ANTs: Researchers build the world's tiniest engine," *physics.org*, May 7, 2016, http://phys.org/news/2016-05-ants-world-tiniest.html.

154. M. G. Starchenko, N. P. Bekhtereva, S. V. Pakhomov, and S. V. Medvedev, "Study of the Brain Organization of Creative Thinking," *Human Physiology* 29, no. 5 (2003): 652-653, accessed online July 2, 2016, http://academic.research.microsoft.com/Publication/48571128/study-of-the-brain-organization-of-creative-thinking.

155. Alexander Schlegel, Peter J. Kohler, Sergey V. Fogelson, Prescott Alexander, Dedeepya Konuthula, and Peter UlricTse, "Network structure and dynamics of the mental workspace," *PNAS* 110, no. 40 (2013):16277–16282, http://www.pnas.org/content/110/40/16277.full.

156. Oshin Vartanian, Adam S. Bristol, and James C. Kaufman, eds., *Neuroscience of Creativity* (Cambridge, MA: MIT Press, 2013).

157. Santa Fe Institute Working Group, "How Creativity Works in the Brain," *National Endowment for the Arts*, July 2015, https://www.arts.gov/sites/default/files/how-creativity-works-in-the-brain-report.pdf.

158. "What Is The BRAIN Initiative?," *National Institutes of Health*, last updated February 23, 2016, http://www.braininitiative.nih.gov/.

159. Brain Research through Advancing Innovative Neurotechnologies (BRAIN) Working Group, "Brain 2025: a

Scientific Vision," *National Institutes of Health*, June 25,2014, http://www.braininitiative.nih.gov/pdf/BRAIN2025_508C.pdf.

160. "BRAIN Initiative," The White House, September 30, 2014, accessed July 2, 2016, https://www.whitehouse.gov/share/brain-initiative.

CHAPTER 15

161. M. Mitchell Waldrop, *Complexity: The Emerging Science at the Edge of Order and Chaos* First Touchstone Edition (New York: Simon and Schuster, 1993); Ilya Prigogine and Isabelle Stengers, *Order out of Chaos* (New York: Bantam Books, 1984); Stuart A. Kauffman, *The Origins of Order: Self-Organization and Selection in Evolution* (New York: Oxford University Press, 1993); Jamshid Gharajedaghi, *Systems Thinking: Managing Chaos and Complexity* third edition (Burlington, MA: Morgan Kaufmann, 2011); Thomas Homer-Dixon, "Complexity Science," *Oxford Leadership Journal* 2, no. 1 (January 2011): 1-15, http://www.homerdixon.com/wp-content/uploads/2015/08/Homer-Dixon-Oxford-Leadership-Journal-Manion-lecture.pdf.

162. complexity theory definition, Dictionary.com, *The American Heritage® Science Dictionary*, Houghton Mifflin Company, http://www.dictionary.com/browse/complexity-theory (accessed: December 13, 2017).

163. chaos theory definition, Dictionary.com, *Dictionary.com's 21st Century Lexicon*, Dictionary.com, LLC, http://www.dictionary.com/browse/chaos-theory (accessed: December 13, 2017).

164. J. Stephen Lansing, "Complex Adaptive Systems," *Annual Review of Anthropology* 32 (October 2003): 183-204, http://othello.alma.edu/~cartrite/abm/Lansing%20-%20Complex%20Adaptive%20Systems.pdf.

165. Santa Fe Institute, *santafe.edu*, accessed July 4, 2016, http://www.santafe.edu/.

166. Jonathon Webb, "Neutrino 'flip' wins physics Nobel Prize," *BBC News*, October 6, 2015, http://www.bbc.com/news/science-environment-34443695.

167. John Heilprin, "'God particle' discovered, physicists say," *USA Today*, March 14, 2013, http://www.usatoday.com/story/tech/sciencefair/2013/03/14/hig

gs-boson-science-universe/1987039/.

168. Matthew Chalmers, "Forsaken pentaquark particle spotted at CERN," *Nature* 523 (July 16, 2015): 267-268, accessed online July 4, 2016, http://www.nature.com/news/forsaken-pentaquark-particle-spotted-at-cern-1.17968.

169. "Dark Energy, Dark Matter," *nasa.gov*, accessed July 4, 2016, http://science.nasa.gov/astrophysics/focus-areas/what-is-dark-energy/.

170. "Six Galaxy Clusters: Dark Matter is Darker Than Once Thought," *Chandra X-ray Observatory*, accessed July 4, 2016, http://chandra.harvard.edu/photo/2015/dark/

171. Jonathon Webb, "Dark matter map unveils first results" *BBC News*, April 13, 2015, http://www.bbc.com/news/science-environment-32284995.

172. Bogdan A. Dobrescu and Don Lincoln, "A Hidden World of Complex Dark Matter Could Be Uncovered," *Scientific American* 313, no. 1 (July 2015).

173. "What is Dark Energy?," *hubblesite*, accessed July 4, 2016, http://hubblesite.org/hubble_discoveries/dark_energy/de-what_is_dark_energy.php.

174. Kate Becker, "Are Black Holes Real?," *NOVA NEXT*, March 10, 2016, http://www.pbs.org/wgbh/nova/next/physics/are-black-holes-real/.

175. David Shukman, "New Horizons: Why bother exploring the Solar System?," *BBC News*, July 18, 2015, http://www.bbc.com/news/science-environment-33569565.

176. *Breakthrough Initiatives*, accessed July 4, 2016, http://breakthroughinitiatives.org/.

177. *Breakthrough Starshot*, accessed July 4, 2016, http://breakthroughinitiatives.org/Initiative/3.

178. "Research," *Sara Seager*, accessed July 4, 2016, http://seagerexoplanets.mit.edu/research.htm.

179. "Our Mission," *SETI Institute*, accessed July 4, 2016, http://www.seti.org/about-us.

180. *Kepler*, accessed July 4, 2016, http://kepler.nasa.gov/.

181. "Curiosity Rover," *NASA Jet Propulsion Laboratory*, accessed July 4, 2015, http://mars.jpl.nasa.gov/msl/.

182. Alissa Walker, "Hawking: An Interstellar Space Mission will bring Benefits to People's Lives on Earth," Gizmodo, April 12,

2016, http://gizmodo.com/hawking-an-interstellar-space-mission-will-bring-benef-1770607490.

183. Pallab Gosh, "Prof Stephen Hawking backs venture to listen for aliens," *BBC News*, July 20, 2015, http://www.bbc.com/news/science-environment-33596271.

184. James Barrat, "Why Stephen Hawking and Bill Gates are Terrified of Artificial Intelligence," *huffingtonpost.com*, April 9, 2015, http://www.huffingtonpost.com/james-barrat/hawking-gates-artificial-intelligence_b_7008706.html; Eric Mack, "Bill Gates Says You Should Worry About Artificial Intelligence," *Forbes* online, January 28, 2015, http://www.forbes.com/sites/ericmack/2015/01/28/bill-gates-also-worries-artificial-intelligence-is-a-threat/#684260ef3d10.

AUTHORS' BIOGRAPHIES

As stated in the "About the Authors" section, Dr. Ennio Fatuzzo and Dr. Carol L. Fatuzzo are husband and wife, both of whom have held leadership positions in multinational corporations and founded and now run successful consulting businesses. They began their professional careers as scientists, then became corporate leaders, and now are business entrepreneurs.

Drawing on their business experiences and interactions with academia, the Fatuzzos have co-authored and/or published several books (available from amazon.com), including: *Survival in the Sea of Economic Chaos (Perspectives on Leadership Actions for Businesses in Crisis)* and *Dynamic Business Planning Basics (An Adaptable Planning Process for Disruptive Times)*.

Information about these books and the Fatuzzos' other publications can be found on their Amazon author's pages and on their joint Web site: fatuzzobooks.com.

Following are brief biographies of the Fatuzzos. Additional information may be found on their respective companies' Web sites: efmainc.com and nhbvinc.com, and on their joint Web site fatuzzobooks.com.

ENNIO FATUZZO

Dr. Ennio Fatuzzo is the President and CEO of EF Management Associates, Inc., an enterprise he founded in 2004 providing guidance to companies for business survival and turnaround in a disruptive business environment. Previously Dr. Fatuzzo founded and managed AIM, Inc., an international business consulting company. Prior to AIM, he held business executive positions in 3M Company, where his responsibilities ranged from global business management to leading a New Business Ventures organization to heading the Strategic Planning Committee for the company's largest Sector. In addition, Fatuzzo has held management positions in Radio Corporation of America (RCA) in Switzerland and the English Electric Group in the UK.

During his career, Dr. Fatuzzo has given many invited seminars and lectures, and developed and taught courses on various aspects of business management both in the U.S. and abroad. In these he often made the connection between science and business leadership. To summarize, for most of his management career, Dr. Fatuzzo has specialized in helping businesses regain momentum under intense competitive pressure and/or difficult economic conditions.

Dr. Fatuzzo has an Italian Doctorate in Physics, holds 15 U.S. patents, has published over 40 papers, and is the co-author of a technical book entitled "Ferroelectricity" published by North-Holland Publishing Company.

CAROL L. FATUZZO

 Dr. Carol L. Fatuzzo is the founder and President/CEO of New Horizons Business Ventures, Inc., a company providing management assistance for R&D Turnaround and growth. Prior to founding NHBV in late 2004, Dr. Fatuzzo served as a Technical Director of a number of different business and technology laboratories in 3M, one of the 100 largest U.S. Manufacturing Corporations.

Dr. Fatuzzo's professional career at 3M included over 30 years of technical leadership positions. During this time she had responsibilities for providing business/organization strategic direction; identifying and developing new businesses; and forming, restructuring, and rebuilding technical organizations. Organizations she led were responsible for inventing, developing, and commercializing over 100 new products for which she and her people won numerous internal and external awards. She also held leadership positions for assessing new business opportunities, acquisitions and joint ventures. In addition, she developed several different multi-phase New Product Commercialization Systems that were successfully used by 3M.

Dr. Fatuzzo has a Ph.D. in Physical Chemistry from the University of Illinois and is trained in the Six Sigma Process. She is the holder of two patents and has 15 published papers.

www.ingramcontent.com/pod-product-compliance
Lightning Source LLC
Chambersburg PA
CBHW021403170526
45164CB00002B/479